PRAISE FOR
Stress-Free Producti

"Yes! You can be productive and creative without sacrificing your emotional health. In this groundbreaking book, Boyes has created an exciting new paradigm for productivity that is based on your unique self and your psychological well-being."

—Guy Winch, TED speaker, author of
Emotional First Aid, and cohost of the *Dear Therapists* podcast

"A brilliant, practical handbook to manage the wide-ranging psychological barriers to producing exceptional work. It is an entire master class in creating productive habits, healthy decision-making, anxiety management, curiosity, self-compassion, and creativity."

—Dr. Todd B. Kashdan, Professor of Psychology, Director of the Well-Being Laboratory at George Mason University, and author of *The Art of Insubordination: How to Dissent and Defy Effectively*

"Using the latest research on topics like habits, creativity, resilience, and emotional health, Boyes has created a guide to productivity that's nurturing, approachable, and packed with practical strategies for how you can do your most innovative work and survive your workweek."

—Scott Barry Kaufman, author of
Transcend and host of *The Psychology Podcast*

"Boyes challenges the unhealthy—and simply false—notion that there's a necessary trade-off between productivity and mental well-being. On the contrary, she shows us how to use evidence-based tools to get things done without overworking, pulling our hair out, and wearing ourselves down. I've already used several of these tips in my own life and plan to return to them again and again."

—Amy Gallo, workplace expert,
cohost of HBR's *Women at Work* podcast,
and author of the *HBR Guide to Dealing with Conflict*

"Boyes will show you how to find creative ways to be productive. She goes into detail on how to cultivate a compassionate inner voice and is working with self-compassion in interesting new ways."

—Christopher Germer, clinical psychologist, co-creator of the Mindful Self-Compassion program, and author of *The Mindful Path to Self-Compassion*

"The productivity paradigm is shifting, and Alice Boyes is leading the way. In her signature style she integrates practical tools and inspirational wisdom to offer a truly refreshing perspective on what it means to be a productive human being."

—Seth Gillihan, clinical psychologist and author of *Retrain your Brain: Cognitive Behavioral Therapy in 7 Weeks*

"Boyes shows you how to use self-awareness to advance your career with a practical plan that's tailor-made to your unique situation. Anyone who is fed up with one-size-fits-all guides to productivity should read this book. You'll learn how to be productive in a self-compassionate, creative way that incorporates the best elements of you."

—Emma Seppälä, Science Director of Stanford University's Center for Compassion and Altruism Research and Education

STRESS-FREE
PRODUCTIVITY

STRESS-FREE PRODUCTIVITY

A Personalized Toolkit to Become
Your Most Efficient and Creative Self

ALICE BOYES, PhD

A TarcherPerigee Book

An imprint of Penguin Random House LLC
penguinrandomhouse.com

Most TarcherPerigee books are available at special quantity discounts for bulk purchase for sales promotions, premiums, fund-raising, and educational needs. Special books or book excerpts also can be created to fit specific needs. For details, write: SpecialMarkets@penguinrandomhouse.com.

Trade paperback ISBN: 9780593191330
Ebook ISBN: 9780593191347

Printed in the United States of America
1st Printing

To my mother

CONTENTS

PART 1

Self-Observation

CHAPTER 1

....

You Are the Solution,
Not the Problem

B y now you may have heard the story of how Lin-Manuel Miranda came up with the idea for *Hamilton*, his groundbreaking smash-hit musical. Struggling for inspiration, he took a much-needed break. While on the beach, he read a book about Alexander Hamilton, and voilà, the idea for the musical was born.

Usually, this story is cited to show how important time off is for creativity. It is a great exemplar of that. Our brains are adept at solving problems and generating great insights and ideas when we're not laser-focused.[1]

But there's more to learn from this story than "take your vacation." Psychologically, much is going on beneath the surface.

Productivity advice emphasizes being focused and undistracted. But focus isn't the full story of how great things get done. Outstanding work comes about through alternating between focusing and letting your mind wander. It happens through switching between being disciplined and going off on a tangent, like devouring a book about a founding father if what you're trying to do is write a blockbuster musical. To do our best work, we have to allow ourselves to go off-topic sometimes.

When experts explain how important the unfocused mind is in productivity, what they often gloss over is how much courage it takes to harness its potential. Modern productivity culture gives us the message that focus and rigid habits are safe goals. But to be your most productive, you'll need to devote time to being unfocused. What makes this harder than it might seem? To do it, you have to trust yourself. You need to trust that some of the time, your mind will wander someplace interesting and insightful. You'll need psychological tools for tolerating uncertainty about when, how, and if good ideas will show up. And you'll need to override guilt and the accompanying mental chatter that what you're doing is wasting time, and time-wasting = bad. These are some of the cognitive-emotional skills you'll learn in this book.

When people aren't accustomed to trying to be innovative or creative, they often fear that if they let their mind wander or go off on tangents, it won't go anywhere interesting. If you're anything like me, you're not reading an 800-page biography on your vacation like Lin-Manuel was. And you may be wondering if that romance novel or crime podcast is really going to spark innovation or creativity. Well, what would be wrong with that? It's not just lofty interests that spark the creativity that produces wonderful work. Allowing yourself to be influenced by pop culture can do it too. Someone like Shonda Rhimes is a phenomenal example of how powerful that can be. Take the story about how the Featherington family on her very popular Netflix series *Bridgerton* was influenced by the Kardashians (and not just the books that the show is based on).[2] Inspiration can happen in both big and small ways.

In case you're wondering, you don't have to be a creative genius and envied for your productivity, like Lin-Manuel or Shonda, to benefit from all this. And you don't need to be in a traditionally creative field. The same basic mental processes apply universally to everyone, including you.

People often see productivity and creativity as separate, but that's not always helpful. It's not as simple as thinking we need creativity for idea generation and then need perseverance, focus, and habits for execution. In reality, it's more iterative and cyclical than that. Creativity and productivity aren't separate or opposing goals. They're intertwined.

Almost anything worth doing will require creativity. Productivity comes from creativity, but not solely. Creativity doesn't always mean you need to connect ideas no one has ever connected. Personal creativity, when it's the first time you've connected ideas yourself, will help you solve your productivity stumbling blocks.

Lin-Manuel had the instinct for when he needed a beach vacation and a book, and that's self-knowledge you can develop too. I'll help you gain skills for being efficient and focused, and skills for unlocking your creative potential. And I'll help you learn about your productivity patterns so that you can flit successfully between these skill sets and have the confidence to do so. (If you're hoping for tips for how to procrastinate less, yes, those are included.)

You are your greatest productivity tool, even if you don't know it yet. Great work rarely comes from connecting several areas in which we have little knowledge. Your most innovative work will come from seeing the unfamiliar through a lens of the familiar, or vice versa. Lin-Manuel's lens was that he had already written a successful hip-hop musical, *In the Heights*. With *Hamilton*, he brought himself, his preexisting experience and expertise, and his culture into it, but paired that with an area in which he had interest but less expertise—the Founding Fathers.

Magic doesn't always happen when we're forcing it. But it also doesn't happen if you're not open to it or when you don't set an intention to do innovative work. There's an art to how to let your mind wander productively, and a science, both of which I'll guide you through. There's a messiness to the idea that your most productive course of action might not be taking twenty books to the beach to attempt to force a lightbulb moment or getting together with a team to generate ideas at a whiteboard. There's an untidiness that you need skills for stickability and efficiency, but also to tolerate inefficiency and the frustration of "unproductive" time. Sometimes people struggle with this. Humans like certainty. But none of this has an exact formula. What I'll help you do is learn all these skills and combine them into your own array, one that will evolve and grow when you do and when your projects change. This is how you'll achieve stress-free productivity.

Your Weaknesses Are Part of the Solution, Not the Problem

As a kid in the eighties and nineties, I remember watching makeovers on talk shows. The participants got haircuts, makeup, and new clothing. The goal was to bring the mostly female guests closer to the stereotypical beauty norms of the day.

This book is not the productivity version of that. It's not my intention to give you tools to inch you closer to the stereotype of how an elite performer acts and thinks. It's not my aim to help you be more like Elon Musk, Jeff Bezos, or other productivity idols. Nor will I guide you to emulate any of the long-dead white dudes eternally cited as the poster boys for how to be visionary (Isaac Newton, Thomas Edison, etc. You know who I mean).

Other books may promise that—if you follow their "simple" steps—you will become like titans of industry. But more often than not, people have trouble following those steps, however simple they may seem. If you fail to comply with standard productivity advice, you might conclude there's something wrong with your personality or your willpower. However, I'm here to tell you that you're not the problem. You—with all your quirks and "flaws"—are the solution. The most creative solutions are often those that arise from constraints. Here, your personality, skills, weaknesses, and circumstances are the constraints.

When you learn to work with these, self-improvement can be a relaxed, artistic endeavor. It can feel like self-discovery and self-expression, and less like an exhausting never-ending project aimed at stamping out all your imperfections.

Instead of trying to fit yourself into someone else's productivity framework, we'll try a different way. How? I'll help you harness your inner expert to learn what helps you create, produce, and flourish.

Who Am I to Give You This Advice?

I have a PhD in psychology. Early in my career, I worked as a clinical psychologist. My job was to help people with problems like anxiety and depression. This work involved teaching people how to overcome patterns of procrastination, avoidance, perfectionism, worry, and rumination. These client groups have some of the most severe stuckness in getting things done. But those with depression or anxiety are much more than their diagnosis. They're individuals, each with their own dreams, goals, unique personality, strengths, weaknesses, preferences, and responsibilities. Therefore, any treatment is tailored to the particular individual.

Alongside my work as a therapist, I started blogging and writing for magazines about how techniques and tools used in clinical settings could be used for solving everyday problems. I made a career switch to writing once I had success and it became clear that my reach would be far greater as a writer than working with individuals one-on-one.

Most productivity books target either your behavior (e.g., habits) or your thinking. They tend to focus on one or the other. When those books are based on psychology research, they usually take knowledge from one small area of psychology and extrapolate that to techniques people can use to be more disciplined.

That's not what I'm going to do here. I'll draw from many areas of psychological research to help you understand how your thoughts, behaviors, and emotions interact. Many books on productivity seem to treat emotions as an inconvenience and attempt to help you learn to ignore them. I'll show you how all emotions can be helpful for productivity in their own ways. Your humanness, like your moods or your distractibility, isn't a threat to your productivity. All these aspects of being human can be assets to your productivity, if you understand them. I'll help you do that so you can do productivity your way.

The Approach We'll Take Together

Your solutions to your productivity problems can be some of your most original thinking. With some pointers, you'll invent solutions that are much more effective than any advice I could spoon-feed you (and that you've likely heard before anyway).

Copying a model for high performance isn't our goal. You will create your own model for high performance. You're the one who best understands what you're willing to do and what you're not. You know the productivity goals that matter to you. We'll harness that self-knowledge and create your own personal model for productivity.

Our end game is to uncover how you can be the most (a) growth-oriented, (b) effective and efficient, and (c) creative and visionary version of yourself. (By creative, I mean original and resourceful, not limited to the arts.) When you combine these powers, you'll achieve more success. You'll gain the freedom to use your time and energy on what's most meaningful to you.

The reason for this triple focus is:

1. Without being growth-oriented, you'll be too easily put off by anything hard.
2. You won't get to a place of freedom in your working life if you're creative but don't find successful, efficient processes you can exploit through repetition.
3. On the other hand, your achievements will be limited if you're good at executing and you're well organized, but you stay on a narrow path. To perform optimally, you need to focus deliberately on being creative and innovative.

How I Define Productivity

While this book is about productivity, I mean that in a broad sense. I'm referring to doing your most impactful, meaningful work, not merely getting things done.

Here's the definition of productivity I like most, which I will repeat a few times. Personal productivity is about doing your most meaningful work by utilizing who you are, what you know, and whom you know.[3]

Increased productivity commonly gets defined as producing more with the same inputs (whereas efficiency is achieving the same with less).[4] My definition of productivity is a variation on this classic one. Who you are, what you know, and whom you know are the inputs.

Success Is Not Purely About Being More Focused

No matter how resistant to distraction you are and how infrequently you check your email, if you're not doing work that matters, that's not being productive. What you focus on matters. You can never guarantee your work will have a seismic impact, but you can at least do work that has that potential. Conceive of impact broadly. Your work can matter if it impacts your life, field, or community. For example, creating an automated income stream might be incredibly meaningful to you, even if it changes nothing but *your* world.

Working more productively could involve steady effort on a long-term project. Alternately, it could be trying something new, such as restructuring your approach to a core task, learning a small skill, testing an assumption, or exploring a novel partnership. Superficially, working in a way that will create more impact might not look different from what you do now, but something about it is bolder than usual.

What I say next will probably shock you: Time management and habits are a small part of being more productive. Let me explain.

Why Consistent Daily Habits Are Overrated

People presume that stacking their day with strong, productive habits will automatically turbocharge their success. But you might not want to build your productivity strategy entirely around habits. Let's look at the benefits and costs of nurturing strong habits.

The benefits: Productivity relies on conditioning yourself to focus on the most valuable work you can do and to persist with solving challenging problems. Making hard work a habit that you do at the same time and place and in the same way makes sticking to it less effortful. You need less self-control to stick to actions you do consistently. This point isn't up for debate—there's excellent research evidence for it.[5] Habits can also help reduce unnecessary decision fatigue. The impact of minor habits compounds, eventually paying dividends down the road.[6] And consistent behavioral habits (work, exercise, socializing) provide structure to our days and help us regulate our biology (sleep, eating, and mood). These plusses can make habits an incredible tool for getting difficult things done.

The costs: Being too habit-bound will reduce how often you have the novel experiences essential for creativity. What's more, attempting to maintain too many rigid time-consuming habits will stress you out. It doesn't make for effective prioritizing, and it can feel as if your life is passing in a blur. This monotonous approach is a recipe for burning out and not enjoying what you're doing.

When you're being productive, you'll experience astounding growth. What this means is that consistent daily habits that work swimmingly for a time (or the length of a project) are likely to be outgrown at some point. They'll no longer be the best use of your time. When you think of it this way, aspiring to keep up many long-term habits makes less sense.

And here's the kicker: The extent to which people prefer consistent daily routines as opposed to more spontaneity is part of temperament.[7] It's part of your wiring, like whether you're a morning person, a night owl, or somewhere in between. Some people thrive on regularity. Everyone does to an extent, but some people need and want it less.

It's not that habits aren't important. They are, but they're not everything. It's tempting to conclude if something is good, more of it will be better. That's not the case. If we spend around 40 to 50 percent of our days behaving habitually,[8] that's about the right number.

If you have no desire to be a flawlessly self-disciplined robot, that's healthy. Feeling compelled to enact habits with extreme consistency is not associated with robust psychological well-being. In fact, the opposite is true. Feeling distressed if you ever skip a routine or if you're prevented from enacting a habit is a hallmark of disorders with obsessional elements, like anorexia or obsessive-compulsive disorder. An enjoyable path to greater productivity is being more human, not more robotic or habit-bound.

Why "Wasting Time" Is Fine

Now that I've explained some downsides of habit stacking, here's why I discourage rigid time management. Contrary to popular belief, you'll encounter some nasty surprises if you obsessively focus on maximizing all of your time.

First off, it's important to know that success isn't about taking an efficient approach to everything. Big successes often arise from behaviors that feel like an inefficient use of time in the beginning. When you learn a new skill or craft or make another investment of time in something, there can be little immediate payoff. It's often not until much later that you experience large rewards. Creative and visionary insights and inventions often come from wandering off whatever appears to be the most efficient path.

Second, being tightly focused on optimizing all of your time can make you miserable. Reduced happiness is not an acceptable side effect of efficiency. When you're accounting for every second, you'll resent diversions and get upset about any lost time. Events you can't control will stress you out. You'll get excessively frustrated by two hours spent correcting someone else's mistake or by your kid's being sick.

This leads to my third point. Being obsessively time-focused isn't good for relationships. Other people won't fall neatly in line with your priorities and schedule, and this will inevitably lead to more frustration.

Fourth, having the time to be inefficient, when it matches your other priorities, is one of life's great luxuries. You might prefer not to outsource all your childcare or meal prep, or to learn to repair something yourself, even though it could be replaced cheaply. It's soothing to have the time for this when you want it, even when it might be inefficient.

Fifth, there is often a trade-off between being efficient and being resilient (able to respond nimbly to changing circumstances). For example, working with the same collaborator might be efficient, but it's also not resilient to rely on one relationship.[9] A quest for efficiency can lead you to put all your eggs in one basket, which isn't resilient.

Sixth, people who constantly plow forward in a traditionally efficient sense can develop large blind spots about their ideas. Smart folks need to retreat and see their ideas from a broad vantage point. When they don't, they can overlook when those ideas could inadvertently alienate or harm people or produce other unintended consequences.

Last, those intolerant of wasting time can get stuck in a mode of continuous iterative improvements, trying to be a smidge better or faster.

If you do this, you might miss opportunities to achieve your goals by taking an unusual approach.

Time management strategies, like timeboxing (scheduling what you'll do for each hour of your day), can be useful. Taking them too far and trying to apply them perfectly is counterproductive.

I Want to Be an Elite Performer. Does This Book Have Anything to Offer Me?

This book aims to deliver a kinder, gentler approach to productivity. It assumes that doing impactful work matters to you. Nothing in it is inconsistent with the goals an elite performer would have. Neither is there an expectation that you approach your work like Olympic athletes approach their careers. Not everyone wants to be the founder of a unicorn company or join the .001 percent. But if you do, there is plenty in this book for you. And if that's not your speed, there's plenty for you too.

How This Book Is Structured

This book is divided into three parts, each one offering an essential set of tools to enhance your productivity.

Part 1. Self-Observation

The first third of the book is about being a self-scientist. It's about becoming a better observer of yourself. Self-observation is the most important productivity tool you're underutilizing.

You can learn as much from observing yourself as you can from experts, from gurus, and even from research studies. I'll give you many tips from behavioral science, but these are best combined with your self-observations. When you become an expert at self-observation, you'll undoubtedly experience insights science hasn't gotten to yet!

Science-based behavioral advice is always developing. For example, some ideas treated with skepticism during my training years now enjoy better scientific support. One tectonic change we've seen in recent years has been that modern psychology is becoming more open to the benefits of diverse mental or physical states. Unpleasant emotions aren't pointless. There's good evidence some of our thinking processes improve when we are tired, sad, or angry.[10]

Because psychological science isn't perfect, it's critical to learn to observe and think for yourself. Doing this, you'll learn to recognize the ways conventional wisdom is true for you and the ways it's not. For example, the idea that stellar work comes only from laser focus doesn't completely fit my experience. Having skills for staying focused matters. However, I find a "distraction break" useful for giving myself a mental refresh. When my concentration is fading while I'm writing, I'll often self-interrupt. I'll read a blog article or check my email. When I return to what I'm doing, I can see my work from a big-picture perspective. With fresh eyes, I find it easier to move around sections in my writing for better flow or to cut repetitive information.

While I was doing the research for this book, I found a study showing that task switching can benefit creativity.[11] This flies in the face of conventional wisdom. The zeitgeist is to stress the harm of task switching. If you study yourself closely, you'll detect much more nuance than prevailing notions suggest.

The idea you can do remarkable work only when undistracted also feels exclusionary. Certain psychological concepts carry a whiff of being for people with a high level of privilege. Spending hours in an undistracted state of flow isn't possible when your child needs a sandwich or your coworker needs a meeting.

It's tempting to believe that if you could follow conventional wisdom and stick to it consistently, you'd succeed in all the ways you want to. This is convenient. It makes perfect productivity seem within our control. Whenever we're ready to flip that switch, we'll thrive. Yet that's not accurate. Conventional wisdom has enough flaws, limitations, and contradictions that this is not likely to be true. This includes the latest and broadly accepted science. This is why it's so important that you do the work to understand yourself—and to put what you learn into practice.

Part 2. Efficiency

The second section of the book is about being effective and efficient.

If you are currently in survival mode in your life and work, you may want to read part 2 of this book first. Part 2 is chock-full of practical tips that require less self-reflection and mental space than the rest of the book. If you don't have the mental space for self-reflection or big-picture thinking, start with part 2. To me, part 2 of this book is the lowest step on the ladder, but it's also the section that will provide the most instant gratification. If that's what you need right now (or it's all you can do), there's no shame in that.

I hope that by the end of this book, you'll ultimately be motivated to be more creative and visionary than to be more efficient. However, the potential links between the two are sometimes underappreciated. Try this—aim to be efficient if this supports your creativity and innovation, rather than for the purposes of doing a greater volume of work. You will learn how to do this in part 2.

If you create successful processes you repeatedly exploit (based on the tools you learn from part 2), your reward will be freedom from pressures related to your basic needs, like earning money or accomplishing your baseline deliverables. People who automate or outsource aspects of their workflow aren't heroes or deities to be worshipped. That said, there are strategies you can use to keep you from feeling as if you're fighting to keep your head above water.

Meandering exploration of ideas is essential for creativity. If you're attending to many urgent tasks, you won't muster the energy for that. But if you create streamlined systems for prioritizing and making other choices, you will reduce decision fatigue so that you retain the mental energy to be creative.

Establishing effective, efficient, repeatable processes is itself a creative endeavor. Creative problem-solving sharpens the mind. You can train yourself to see multiple potential routes. Solving simple problems can give you analogies to draw on when solving more complex conundrums.

Being effective and efficient can confer social benefits too. Being well-organized and easy to deal with makes other smart people want to work with you. When you accumulate solid but medium-sized wins, this can elevate your credibility. It can give you access to a higher tier of collaborators. Working with smarter, more experienced folks can lift you to become more creative and visionary.

Finally, no one can do novel, creative, and visionary thinking all the time. Even for the most talented people, their brilliance ebbs and flows. No one functions at their personal peak constantly. It's grounding to maintain some straightforward, familiar to-dos you can execute simply. Outsourcing everything repetitive in your life is not that fun or productive. Why? There's a sweet spot between having too many familiar tasks and too few. If you've got too many, you won't have time or energy for seeking novel challenges. But this counterpoint is overlooked: Simple tasks can help you maintain forward momentum. Familiar, undemanding tasks can make you more resilient during times you're struggling creatively. They can help stop you from plunging into depression or anxiety when the part of you that's brilliant has taken the day off.

As in part 1, the focus in this section won't be on generic concepts. Instead, we'll concentrate on how you can develop your self-expertise. We'll tap into your innate capacity to be insightful and grow. You'll find realistic ways to become more efficient and effective. These will utilize your strengths. They will feel meaningful and be positive expressions of your unique self.

Everyone needs some skills for being efficient, but if you think efficiency and discipline alone are the solutions to being more productive, you're on the wrong track. Think of these as relatively minor tools in your arsenal. Being innovative is much more important and distinguishing. Overfocusing on efficiency (and discipline) can interfere with that. It can also be a sign you're trying to compensate for doing work that's not especially innovative by doing a huge volume of it. Aiming to do a crushing volume of medium-quality work might be one path to greater productivity, but it's not a very rewarding one. Part 3 of the book offers an alternative.

Part 3. Creativity

Part 3 is what we've been building toward in the two earlier sections. It includes specific strategies to improve your creative thinking.

What has creativity got to do with productivity? Creativity provides the building blocks for innovation. Sure, you could focus on making a horse and buggy go faster. Or you could invent the car. Which is more productive? In reality, you don't need to do anything nearly that impressive to be innovative. There are plenty of opportunities even for those with average creativity to be more innovative, but you have to prioritize innovation ahead of volume or speed of working (at least some of the time).

Most folks stay within their lane and don't consider whether they're doing the most meaningful, creative work they could be. For example, observant cops who have been patrolling the same neighborhoods for years might harbor phenomenal ideas about how to help their communities. If they limit themselves to their role of handing out tickets and summonses, those ideas are lost.

If you don't see yourself as being creative or visionary, trust me when

I say that you have it in you. To be the most innovative version of yourself, you need a diversity of ideas to connect, pockets of deep knowledge, appreciation of your strengths, and enough mindfulness, openness, and bravery to let your best ideas surface.

There are a variety of reasons to become more creative and visionary. They're mostly obvious, but let's do a quick rundown.

Creative/visionary thinking is harder and more distinguishing than executing established processes. You'll be more valuable in any workplace if you're a creative and insightful problem solver. This applies whether you're an employee, an entrepreneur, or an activist; whether you're homeschooling your kids or volunteering at your church.

Being creative will give you opportunities to do what's most meaningful to you. If you're creative and visionary, you won't need to follow the herd. When you're creative, you can personalize your life more. You can do the work you want to, in the way you like to do it. This applies not just on a day-to-day basis but also in terms of your career trajectory. You won't need to follow the traditional path. You won't be limited to "Success in my field looks like this." You won't be restricted to "This is the training/degree/experience I have, so this is the only work I can do."

Creative and visionary thinking has stress and anxiety management benefits. When you can think creatively, you can withstand setbacks and frustration more easily. If you feel overwhelmed with your workload, creative thinking skills can help with that. When you trust in your creativity, you can be less fearful. You'll tolerate uncertain situations better. You'll know you can trust yourself to generate creative solutions to novel problems whenever they arise.

Productivity writers will often say that lack of discipline is what causes stagnation, and this is what's stopping you from achieving your potential.

But let's look at this another way. Most people diligently and conscientiously show up to their workplace, right? They do their jobs, regardless of whether they feel like it. You attend work for half your waking hours. You return emails, pay bills, file taxes. You feed, clothe, and hug those who depend on you. If you do these things, your self-discipline is already impressive.

Even tiny kids are skilled at delayed gratification. In the early 2000s, scientists replicated the famous marshmallow experiment. This is where kids can eat one marshmallow immediately or wait to get two. Almost 60 percent of four-year-olds could resist a marshmallow sitting in front of them for ten minutes. Even parents underestimate their kids' capacity to delay gratification. How did these results compare to the past? In the 1960s, only about thirty percent of the little kids in the original research could hold out.[12] This is not exactly consistent with the idea that the use of technology is rotting our willpower.

In recent years, researchers uncovered a fascinating twist to the marshmallow experiment. If kids grow up in a home with adults who deliver on their promises, they typically "pass" the marshmallow test. Kids who gobble the single marshmallow are more likely to have parents who don't follow through on what they say. Seen in this light, those kids' decision to grab what they can now is adaptive.

Compared to all this impressive self-discipline, vast numbers of people report spending little or no time attempting to be creative and innovative in their work. Arguably, this is what we're doing worse at, not self-discipline. (At least for the 60 percent of us who would've passed the marshmallow test as four-year-olds.) Because many people devote so little effort to being creative and innovative (in how they live their lives and in the broader sense), doing this has the potential to produce massive gains and will help you do work you feel proud of and enjoy a better quality of life.

When you're creatively exploring, it can often feel like an inefficient use of your time. We often feel tension when choosing between executing a familiar process with a known payoff and exploring a new process with an uncertain one. People sometimes even classify behaviors that support their creativity as time-wasting. For instance, I enjoy watching

YouTube creators. This is fun. But I don't watch just for fun. Experiencing other people's creativity inspires me. However, productivity experts usually put videos (and anything to do with the internet) high on their "what not to do" lists. Again, my experience differs from conventional wisdom. It's difficult to trust your experience over dominant cultural messages, even if you've done your self-observation and know that the dominant ideas will not necessarily work for you.

As you read, think about what balance of focusing on discipline and efficiency versus attempting creativity and innovation is right for you. The latter shouldn't be 0 percent! But if you're like a lot of readers who are immersed in hustle culture, with its emphasis on being undistracted and efficient, the effort you put into creativity and innovation might currently be close to zero.

Experiments

Each chapter in this book contains thought experiments. You don't need to do every experiment, only what most interests you. View them as what you could do, not things you have to do, or even necessarily should do. A good ballpark is to do one experiment per chapter. As you **read**, keep some Post-it flags on hand to mark any experiments you want to do later.

The exception to this is chapter 2, which contains only one in-depth experiment. Please do that one. The other chapters contain many small experiments you can pick from.

Here's a research-backed tip about how to excel at the experiments. Many types of creative problem-solving benefit from an incubation period between when you hear a problem and when you try to solve it.[13]

You'll do better if you read an experiment and then go do something else for five minutes before you come back and attempt it yourself. Fold a few pieces of laundry or take your trash out. Pick an activity that gets you out of your seat. Then come back to it.

Why does this help creativity? One reason: If you work on a creative exercise straight after reading examples, the examples will anchor your thinking too much and limit your creativity.[14] Doing an unrelated activity for five minutes in between will help you produce creative ideas that aren't merely variations on the examples.

Quizzes and Other Resources

As you read further, you'll come across quizzes. If you're reading a paperback, circle your answers on your book. If you're reading an ebook or don't want to write in your book, you'll find links to web versions of the quizzes and other resources mentioned on a dedicated resources page. Go here—http://www.aliceboyes.com/StressFreeResources. Anytime you're directed to the book's resource page, that's where you'll find it.

Be Prepared: Reading About Productivity Can Trigger Productivity Shame

As you read, you might notice productivity shame crop up. Stories of other people's successes can trigger anxiety. Culturally, we're told we should all do more, more, more. We should always be disciplined. We should all hack our coding so we run like super-efficient robots, not like humans.

This is tinged with the opposing message that we should also practice more self-care. We should sleep more and exercise more. Cruelly, this creates inner tension and stress. You might sense you can't win no matter what you do.

Chapter 4 has strategies for reducing productivity shame. In the meantime, treat those thoughts and feelings lightly. Don't personalize them. They're more a product of confusing cultural messages than anything wrong with you.

When we've been subjected to certain messaging for a long time, we'll read those messages into anything we come across. For example, even if I say you should aim to do one experiment per chapter, you might still feel that if you don't do all of them, you've failed. You might hear a message of "Do more, do more," even if that's not what is written on the page. This happens whenever people develop a sensitivity. It's like how, when people have been criticized too much in their life, they then detect criticism and feel criticized even when it's not occurring. Keep an eye out for times the material you read here causes you to sense extra pressure. It's not intended, but you might be hypersensitized to react like that (from your prior experiences of twenty-first-century living). Let those feelings go as best as you can.

CHAPTER 2

. . . .

Your Success
Story So Far

From here, each chapter in this book will begin with a short, fun quiz. These will orient you to the themes of the chapter, and they'll help you assess which chapters will be most relevant to you.

Each quiz has five questions. The answers are labeled A through D. Pick whichever answer most closely reflects you. Don't overthink your answers. Go with your instinct and choose fast. If no answer is a perfect fit, choose the closest.

Each quiz has the same scoring system. If your answers are mostly As and Bs, you're already doing well with the concepts the chapter covers. Skim the chapter to pick out small points you haven't previously considered. If you're getting more Cs and Ds, give the chapter a more thorough read.

Because the quiz questions preview the chapter content, occasionally a concept in a quiz question might be unfamiliar to you and the question may feel confusing. In this case, move on and read the chapter.

Try your first quiz now.

Quiz

. . . .

1. How stressed out do you feel if you're not productive for a few days?

   (A) Not at all. Sometimes I need to recover or decompress. Breaks stimulate some of my best work and ideas.

   (B) I get niggling anxiety, but my workload is manageable enough that I can coast sometimes.

   (C) My workload is so heavy I can't ever pause. Catching up afterward is so brutal, the pause is not worth it.

   (D) I expect myself to be productive at all times and feel guilty when I'm not.

2. How many diverse factors have contributed to your major successes? These factors could include periods of intense work, chance encounters, capitalizing on unexpected observations, or new interests that took you in a different direction.

   (A) All these and more!

   (B) One or two serendipitous factors have influenced the directions I've taken, but my success has predominantly been due to traditional elements like training and mentors.

(C) Specific people have been important in my success journey, but aside from that, I attribute my accomplishments only to hard work and training.

(D) I see my success as a function of only my innate intellect and talent, my grit, job-specific training, and on-the-job experience.

3. How many twists and turns has your success journey taken to date?

(A) Many. I have developed new interests and have had new or revised ideas, and collaborations have caused pivots in my journey.

(B) A few, mostly related to changing jobs.

(C) Maybe one.

(D) None. I've followed a conventional path. I rarely change my thinking, explore new ideas, learn new skills, or work with different collaborators.

4. Has your work changed who you are as a person? For example, have you become more open or trusting due to experiences with mentors? Have you developed unexpected interests or skills?

(A) My work has changed me in exciting, profound, and unexpected ways. I have a much broader range of skills, interests, ideas, and relationships due to my work.

(B) I've gained confidence or maturity through my work. However, my work seems like it reflects my preexisting talents and interests. I can't see how it has led to my developing new strengths or passions.

(C) I've made friends through my work, but I can't see how it has impacted me in any other ways.

(D) The only impact my work has had on my nature is that it has made me tired, cranky, and cynical.

5. Are you working on a multi-year project that, if it succeeds, will impact your life, field, or community? (Parents, if you're raising a child make sure you count that!)

(A) Of course!

(B) A few people might recognize my work, but it's not likely to have a broad impact.

(C) No, but I've done so in the past and would like to in the future.

(D) I'm not working on any long-term projects. They're all short-term.

The goal of this chapter is to prompt you to take a long-game view of your success. This should help you worry less about being perfectly disciplined every minute.

Relax, You Don't Need to Be Productive Every Day

The first and most important point to make regarding productivity is that you should never feel pressured to be at peak production every day.

Having some unproductive days or even weeks is inconsequential for your success. Why? The trajectory of someone's success is largely determined by a few pivotal moves each year. You can succeed if you have periods of bravery, prescience, and intense work. It's not realistic to be in these states constantly. Nor is it needed. You don't need to be always on task, never getting distracted and never procrastinating. Hence my argument against rigid time management.

Aiming for steady productivity can be bad. If you overvalue steady productivity, it crowds out everything else. Most productivity advice overvalues consistency. Not only is this an unachievable dream that's not in line with the natural ups and downs of human psychology, but it's not a useful goal. People ask themselves, "How can I be consistently productive?" without asking themselves, "Do I *need* to be consistently productive?" In fact, you don't, and trying to do that can have a detrimental effect. If you overvalue consistent productivity, this can cause you to be less likely to try behaviors now and again that have the potential to create big wins, like becoming obsessively interested in a topic that's tangential to your core work or doing something much braver than you typically feel able to do.

You won't seize these moments if you are trying to produce them on top of maintaining a level of steady productivity that already feels like it's crushing you. It doesn't work like that. You can't expect to have more mental space without creating room for it. Something has to give. And that something is likely to be consistent production. Mustering bravery can require you to work up to and recover from it.

You may have read books about productive people who seem like they are very brave. They make bold moves and charge ahead, no matter how scary and anxiety-provoking those actions might seem. You might be left with the sense you'd need a personality transplant to be like them. However, you don't need to feel capable of that all the time, only some of the time. And all of us have moments in which we feel braver and more capable of being bold.

Even consistent hard work can result in underperforming if it's not accompanied by at least occasional calculated leaps of faith. Sure, you need to do focused, challenging, deep work. But skipping that some days isn't an existential threat to your success.

An intense focus on maintaining consistent output can lead to myopic vision and the production of medium-quality, minimally im-pactful work. When you're too focused on consistency, you'll miss opportunities to develop new strengths, interests, and relationships. These are what often propel you to opportunities to do visionary work.

Big leaps in success often come from trying things that are new to you and/or undertaking challenging long-term projects. Pivotal moments can arise from brief flashes of courage. This courage is often interpersonal. Perhaps you reach out to new collaborators. Or you hatch a plan for a shared dream with your spouse.

Pivotal moments often happen when you're in an exploring mindset, not in a mindset of exploiting your existing resources and methods. People who are in an exploring mindset experiment with new ideas, skills, behaviors, and relationships. They expect that some of these investments will pay off in the future and build their resilience. As mentioned earlier, there's sometimes a trade-off between resilience and strict efficiency. For example, a business might be more efficient when it uses one supplier for a key part, but also less resilient. Resilience comes from having a broad base of knowledge, skills, experiences, curiosity, relationships, and tools, including the tools to manage yourself.

There's another misconception I hope to challenge in this chapter.

Maximum productivity does not come from conceiving a plan for yourself at the outset and then executing it without wavering. Productive paths have lots of changes of direction. This might not seem efficient, but it is often optimal.

We know from research that your interests are not innate, pre-baked aspects of yourself. You will develop new interests, passions, and strengths through novel experiences.[1]

Being productive, in the sense of getting meaningful things done, involves following your nose. Unexpected experiences in your work can lead you down new paths:

- A piece of work you do is surprisingly impactful.
- A frustrating setback spurs you not to have a repeat experience.
- You revise your opinion of your strengths.
- Or your instinct tells you to grab an unexpected opportunity, even if it wasn't part of your original plan.

The Pivotal Moves of Your Life

In some cases, you'll know when you're experiencing a pivotal move. Other times you won't. You'll walk through life opening some doors and closing others. You'll be guided by your intuition and instincts as well as logic. This will form your path. When you make intuitive decisions, you might not know what your life will end up looking like or what your contribution to the world will be. You *will* know what you're drawn to and repelled by.

Stanford professor, health psychologist, and bestselling author Dr. Kelly McGonigal has focused her career on teaching, even though this is traditionally viewed as less prestigious than a research career for folks with a PhD. But far from impeding her success, the courses she has taught at Stanford have led to her writing bestselling books on topics like willpower and stress, and giving a massively popular TED talk.[2] That talk has now been watched by more than 26 million people. She was prepared to give an outstanding TED talk because, through her teaching, she already had years of experience attempting to inspire people through science. Several of her books combine her health science training and author skills with her other passions—yoga and group exercise. One of those books is on yoga for pain relief and another is on the science behind the joy of movement.

Your knowledge about what you can contribute to the world will evolve as you do. Your twenty-year-old self does not yet know your thirty-year-old self, who doesn't yet know your forty-year-old self. It doesn't make sense for you to develop and follow a strict master plan for someone you don't even know yet.[3] The most productive, impactful work you have an opportunity to do will change with greater exploration and experiences.

There are lots of people who diligently do their jobs. They keep up the skills relevant to their career, but never explore nontraditional ways to use their knowledge, skills, and connections. They never consider whether they could do work that's more important than whatever they're doing now, that's also more aligned with their values. That person (who might be you!) misses out on an opportunity to feel uniquely valuable, and the world misses out on those skills and ideas.

My Story

Sometimes people head in interesting directions when a traditional path feels too difficult, which is what happened to me. Soon I'm going to ask you to tell your story, but I'll start you off with mine.

In 2007, I graduated with my PhD. After many years of study, I was desperate for an adventure. I moved from my home country of New Zealand to the UK and landed a job at a university near London. My then-partner, now-spouse and I agreed to a long-distance relationship while I tried it out. She didn't want to leave a job she loved in New Zealand.

I felt iffy about whether I wanted to be an academic. I also wasn't good at it. I had taken an unusual training route. I did a research PhD in social psychology, studying couples. Concurrently, I completed training in clinical psychology to treat mental health disorders, like anxiety and depression.

Because I had taken this dual path, I was green with research and teaching compared to peers who had devoted their entire training to that. Ultimately, I also couldn't cope with the British weather. Truth be told, this was the major reason I left that job. I didn't enjoy living in chilly, gray England enough to persuade my partner to follow me. So I returned home to New Zealand and started a clinical psychology practice.

Launching my own practice instead of taking a job at a hospital was out of necessity. I'm an extreme night owl who gets up late and stays up late, and I take an afternoon nap almost every day. Traditional nine-to-five jobs don't work for me. I'm also a sensitive introvert who can't cope with being around people all day.

As marketing for my new practice, I started blogging. I also reached out to some magazines to say I was available for comment on stories. I have no idea what gave me the confidence to do this. After blogging on my website for a few years, I emailed an editor at *Psychology Today* to inquire if I could write for them. They turned me down. Darn!

Sometime later, I tried again. They accepted me. After I had written for *Psychology Today* for a year, more or less, with my articles frequently appearing on their "most popular" list, two literary agents contacted me the same week to ask if I had a book idea. I didn't, but my instincts screamed, "Grab this opportunity!" so I came up with one. Writing a proposal and selling that book, *The Anxiety Toolkit*, happened quickly. Anxiety hadn't been the focus of my PhD, but I had experimented with a lot of approaches to manage my own anxiety and to help my clients. My anxiety articles resonated most with readers, so this ended up being my first book topic. The book you're reading is my third book. And I've since expanded my writing to include outlets like the *Harvard Business Review*, *The Washington Post*, and *Forbes*.

In addition to my writing, I'm also a real estate investor. Here's how that unfolded. Back in 2013, after years of applying, my spouse won the U.S. green card lottery. There's nothing more serendipitous than winning a lottery, but our success was also due to consistently applying every year. The win gave us the chance to move to the United States. We planned to live in New York City, a city I love when the weather is warm. What transpired? I didn't even make it through one full winter. Weather wimpiness again!

We lived in a subletted apartment, and that agreement ended in the middle of our first January there. My spouse went to Cambodia to do medical volunteering. I decided to head west temporarily for warmer weather. I spent most of that winter near Palm Springs. I negotiated to live at a hotel Sunday through Thursdays, when the area is quiet, for about the same as what rent cost in New York. I'd go to L.A. on weekends when hotel rates in Palm Springs doubled or tripled. For something to do in Palm Springs, I started going to open houses. I wasn't in the market to buy. I was simply interested in mid-century modern architecture.

On another whim, I went to Las Vegas for a week instead of making another weekend trip to L.A. Since I'd been perusing open houses, I went to some in Vegas too. Five years after the 2009 financial crisis, homes there were still incredibly cheap. I was curious to see how inexpensively we could buy a house with a pool.

After that week, I convinced my spouse to join me and look for a house to buy in Vegas. Our 1,100-square-foot house, with that pool, albeit in a low-income neighborhood, cost $90,000. At the time we made the purchase, we'd spent only a few weeks in Nevada. I'm anxious by nature and overthink many minor decisions, but for some major ones, I act quickly.

This purchase kicked off a real estate investing bug. We'd kept our New Zealand home as a rental, so we had fallen into owning rental property already. I had an open mind about where we would invest, and I started reading the real estate investing forum BiggerPockets. Through the forum, I found a Midwest-based investor. He'd been an accountant before making a career switch to rehabbing houses after the financial crisis. He was not soliciting investors, but I reached out to him anyway after reading his forum posts. We've since developed a deep level of trust. With his help, I've purchased four distressed houses in Indiana, a state I have still never visited! One we flipped, and the other three are now renovated and rented. Alongside my income from writing, this provides me with a base of income for my family.

Written out like this, my story might sound like I'm brave. I am, but only occasionally. I read Tim Ferriss's book *The 4-Hour Workweek* in 2007. I've never had a four-hour workweek. However, my mix of income streams means I don't have to worry where the money for this month's bills will come from. I don't mind periods of hard work. I enjoy thinking about work when I'm relaxing rather than resenting it. And many hours of my days are spent caring for my five-year-old.

Sometimes I work efficiently, but often I work meanderingly. That working style is why I've accumulated a unique knowledge base. When I was a recent graduate, starting my career was tougher because I'd split my attention across different fields within psychology. Now the diversity of my knowledge across many areas of psychology is an asset. It gives me a unique perspective and more interesting ideas than someone who has followed a narrower, more focused path.

Now that I've told you my story, it's your turn.

Your Successes So Far

The rest of this chapter is about your story. The end product will be a timeline of your major successes to date and the factors that have led to them. Depending on where you are in your life, what's a major success for you might not be for someone else. Everyone's peaks will be different. The reason for a timeline approach is to get you thinking about a long-game, big-picture view of your productivity.

I want to challenge any expectation you might have that a book about productivity should be a makeover book packed with suggestions for morning routines and other life hacks. Any impactful project you do is likely to be the culmination of years of work. Therefore, our focus will be on your future accomplishments over years and decades, and how you will achieve them.

A Guide to Constructing Your Timeline

To get started making your timeline, think about what natural phases your adult life has had. Use the eras of your life as markers to give your timeline architecture. I think of my adult life as having these phases: college, when I lived in England, when I had my psychology practice in New Zealand, when I lived in the United States before becoming a parent, and after becoming a parent.

Within the eras you picked, start adding anything significant you've accomplished personally or professionally. Some examples could be: learning a valuable skill; starting a business; buying a house; finding your life partner (the person you partner with in your personal life will affect your productivity!); beginning to contribute to retirement accounts; developing fruitful professional relationships or a repeatable formula or model for your success (like flipping houses in a particular neighborhood and price range). Other examples are accidental successes (like an accidental discovery, or a favor you did for a friend that turned into a side hustle), far-reaching ideas, and pivots from less impactful to more impactful work.

If sketching a timeline intimidates you, do it in another way. Write out your story narratively. Or film it as a video or record it as audio.

While I was researching this book, I interviewed my friend Tam. He earns $100 to $200 a day of side income through reselling. Over time, he has developed a network of colleagues. They give one another a heads-up whenever they find something that can be resold for a profit.

I asked him about the first time he ever resold anything. As a college freshman he bought many units of a particular pair of headphones in the United States. He then resold them in Hong Kong with the help of his sister, who lived there. That opportunity dried up. He needed to move on to something else. I kept asking him, "And then what happened?" or "What did you do next?" This way, I drew out the full story of how he got from those headphones to where he is today. At the end, we went back and fleshed out how his nature and upbringing led him to that first headphones deal, creating a personal timeline.

What Are the Mechanisms of Your Success?

Once you've put your major successes in your timeline, add in what contributed to those. Following on the next page are elements I suggest including. This is a long list. Skip any that don't seem interesting to you. Or answer some of these now and come back to the rest later. Aim for one example for each question. Once you have your examples, then assign them to the era of your timeline they belong to.

If you struggle to answer, ask someone who knows you well to answer the question for you. Other people sometimes remember examples we've forgotten or minimized.

- How have periods of hard work contributed to your success? (I've provided a few examples for this first one to get you started.)
  - My spouse got through medical school. She now has a great deal of job flexibility because it's an in-demand and high-paying career.
  - A friend built a tiny house on his property, rented the main house, and lived in the tiny house with his wife. Later he built a house on a small farm, again mostly by himself.
- How has a strength you developed in another arena helped your work productivity?
- What have you improved on? What was something you tried that had mediocre or inconsequential results, but it ended up being a springboard to something else you tried that did work for you?
- What are the novel (new to you) things you've tried that might've gone nowhere, but had a significant impact on your success?
- What's a skill that felt challenging when you first tried it? Now it feels routine, or at least well within your capacity. Broadly, what are the skills that are essential to performing your job well, and how did you acquire them?
- What are the personal strengths and talents you've always had and recognized? In contrast, what have you learned about yourself that was surprising to you?
- What role has instinct played in your pivotal decisions? (Quite a few of my best life decisions might've been considered harebrained.) Were some of your best decisions well researched and thought out? Were others made more quickly or with less exhaustive research?
- How has revising your ideas contributed to your success? This could be revising your ideas about yourself—e.g., what your strengths are. Or modifying your ideas more generally—that is, exhibiting intellectual humility.
- When have you had a consistent daily schedule of focused and challenging work? How has this been important to you?

- What are the other habits that serve you well? What habits work well for you that don't fit conventional wisdom, such as habits you pick up and drop?
- How has practicing skills played into your development?
- What have been your big financial moves? How did those come about? In particular, think about how taking small actions has helped you, perhaps before you felt completely certain or ready. For instance, if you've bought a house, perhaps you contacted a real estate agent or started looking online before you were sure that was something you were going to do. The act of moving in a direction sometimes comes before a firm decision.
- How does your career path reflect a particular interest or value you have that might not be common to most people in your field?
- When have you taken a nugget of success and run with it?
- How have unconventional routes you've taken played a role in your success? What drove you to take these unconventional routes? Perhaps a traditional path felt too difficult or meaningless to you.
- How have your career and successes influenced who you are? Have you discovered interests or strengths through your work?
- How have other people been critical to your achievements? Who has prompted you to improve your skills? Who has helped you see strengths and talents in yourself you didn't recognize? Who has propelled you to see the world differently? Who have you partnered with who has different strengths than you do?
- What form do role models take for you? Role models aren't necessarily people you know well. They could be an author, a podcaster, or a person in your field whose career path or thinking style you admire. It could be an extended-family member. It could be someone you encountered briefly whose influence has stuck with you. How have books or sources of information impacted your success journey?

Define Your Takeaways

I write my books to be reference books. There will be more ideas in each chapter than you can absorb in one reading. Don't attempt that! At the end of each chapter, define one or two takeaways. The rest of the info isn't going anywhere. When you're facing new challenges, you can dip back in and get new ideas.

To help you not feel inundated, at the end of each chapter, there will be one or two review questions. These will help you identify what you want to retain now. Don't overthink what you choose. Whatever first comes to mind will be just as good an answer as one you spend ten minutes waffling over.

Write your answers somewhere portable (that you can access anywhere) and easily searchable. Good options are Google Doc or emails to yourself with a consistent subject line like "Productivity Book." This way, it'll be easier to add to your answers systematically and help you keep them all in the same place in case you want to look back at them in the future.

Your takeaways should connect the material with how it relates to you. When you choose a takeaway, note why you want to remember it. In what ways do you expect that insight to influence you? If you've gained a fresh perspective, spell out how you want that to flow into a change in your behavior.

Here's the takeaway question for this chapter.

1. How has outlining your success story made you think differently about your productivity?

Example answer: When I wrote out my story to put it in this chapter, it emphasized how critical partnering has been to my achievements. It sometimes seems like I need to accomplish success all on my own. This feels like a weighty pressure. But that pressure isn't based in reality. I've had great partnerships. My spouse has been a stable base for my exploration. I've had nurturing relationships with collaborators and editors. The partnerships I have with bigger brands, like the *Harvard Business Review* and *Psychology Today*, have been critical to my success. *The real-world implication of this insight is that I should devote more time to exploring new partnerships.*

Write a similar answer about an insight you've gotten from reading this chapter or from creating your timeline. There will be no spoon-feeding you a precise system to follow in this book! My aim is to draw out your inner expert. Don't doubt your capacity to think for yourself. You've got this!

CHAPTER 3

. . . .

How to Lift Yourself
Above Your Daily Grind

To recap, for all these quizzes, scoring mostly As and Bs means you can probably skim the chapter. If you score mostly Cs and Ds, read in more detail. Choose the best answer. If no answer is a perfect fit, choose the closest.

Quiz

. . . .

1. Do you step back from your daily grind to look at the big picture of your life?

    (A) Yes. I often step out of my usual routines to do this.

    (B) I have strategies for how I like to do this, but I don't do it as much as I could.

    (C) This happens once a year or less.

    (D) No, and I wouldn't know where to start.

2. How well are your day-to-day efforts and to-dos aligned with your overarching drives? Your drives could be, for example, making discoveries, improving the public good, working with people who sharpen you, lowering the stress in your life, or achieving financial stability.

    (A) A close match.

    (B) A moderate match.

    (C) I get too bogged down on urgent tasks to advance my overarching drives.

    (D) I'm supposed to know what my overarching drives are?!

3. Do you capitalize on life changes and transitions (like moving, changing jobs, or becoming a parent) as a time to align your actions with your goals? For example, when you changed jobs, you used it as an opportunity to start automatically diverting more of your salary to retirement savings.

    (A) Yes. I can identify several examples of this, including some recent ones.

    (B) I can identify at least one example of this from the last five years.

    (C) I can identify some examples of this, but from a long time ago.

    (D) No. I can't identify a time when a life change or transition has brought anything other than negative stress.

4. How much of your focus is on survival (short-term focus, like how you can meet this week's deadlines)?

   (A) Not much. My focus is long-term, on strengthening my capacities to do meaningful work.

   (B) Survival becomes my focus a couple of days a week.

   (C) Almost all. I only occasionally think about building my skills and relationships or improving my strategies.

   (D) Can people really work any other way? When are we going to get to the part of this book that's about managing email? Achieving inbox zero is all I care about.

5. Do you have a clear sense of your mission—that is, the broad aim you are trying to achieve through your work?

   (A) Yes, I could sum this up in a sentence.

   (B) I do, but fatigue makes me feel disconnected from it.

   (C) I do, but it seems far removed from what I spend most time on.

   (D) I don't have a sense I'm doing anything important.

   Many of us feel a nagging sense that the work we're doing isn't important. The demands, bustle, and distractions of modern life pull us into survival mode. They drag us toward behaviors that give us an immediate sense of getting something done. We ignore alternative choices for what we could do that might yield a bigger but more uncertain payoff in the future.

When the work people do isn't as meaningful as it could be, they often feel like they're giving up life for work. Their life is on pause while they're at the office, only to resume when they get to go home. There's no perfect way to use your time. However, some pieces of work have more potential than others to change your life or your field, or to have a social impact.

Doing work that matters may not always take immense effort. Perhaps you need no more than a day to write up a proposal with ideas you've been percolating for months. Perhaps you need only two days to write a draft of a TED talk. To connect with an amazing collaborator, maybe you just need twenty minutes to craft a thoughtful email. What leads to you putting that twenty minutes or that couple of days aside? What makes you do it when there have been many hours or days when you haven't?

Finding the time and energy might seem like a simple matter of prioritizing and self-discipline. It's not. Don't fall for that self-critical explanation.

It's hard to drag yourself away from the urgent and familiar. It's hard to find space to do things that are creative, visionary, or novel. People often feel temporarily soothed by checking items off their list, even when they're minor, and this can give a false sense of productivity.

Luckily, psychological research tells us a lot about what helps people get around to doing big things.

NOTE

This chapter will feel overwhelming if you see it as a to-do list. Don't do that. Mostly it involves asking yourself questions that you need to let percolate. You don't need to act immediately. You don't need to do everything. Absorb one or two points. Leave the rest for another time, or another person!

Remember that you should focus on what will change the trajectory of your success, what will matter a year from now, but you can't expect yourself to make those moves every day.

How to Think About the Big Picture

Just Focus on It

People who are more innovative spend more time trying to be innovative.[1] Big-picture thinking works the same way. The more you attempt to focus on the big picture, the more you'll successfully do it.

This broad principle applies on lots of levels. At the lowest level, it applies to your work processes. For instance, for writers, snappy titles are crucial. Despite knowing this, authors might still treat titles as an afterthought when writing blog posts or articles. In this context, big-picture thinking means paying attention to what makes titles appealing. It means having a workflow so titles aren't an afterthought.

Or let's say you're a therapist. You know rapport is mission-critical. The last time you thought about how to make your office inviting was when you moved in six years ago. So you spend ten minutes today asking yourself the question *How could I make visiting my office feel less stressful and more nurturing?*

What are creative solutions?

- You might make the experience more spa-like—for example, set up an additional room as a tranquility zone with calming lighting for clients to decompress after their sessions.
- Perhaps you provide a bowl of fruit in case people need a snack while they're waiting. You stock a fridge with free cold waters.
- You offer to make clients a "cuppa" when they arrive, as you'd do for a visitor to your home.

When you do focused creative problem-solving like this, solutions will emerge. The problem is that people don't step back to do it. They fail to optimize impactful aspects of their work that could easily be improved.

On a larger level, big-picture thinking might be reevaluating the projects you're working on or the methods you use.

- You may have outgrown one of your activities. A line of work you're engaged in might've been your best idea when you started it. Now you have better ideas.
- You own a business you don't want to work in forever, but you have no exit plan.
- You and your romantic partner need to discuss how to make a life goal happen, but you never get around to it.

Sometimes making your dreams happen is solely a matter of getting around to it.

My spouse had a long-held dream of doing medical volunteering overseas. She's anxiety-prone, like I am. She didn't want to make a lengthy service commitment or work in a remote or dangerous area. Once we'd clarified what she was hoping to do, she started talking to colleagues about it.

Shockingly, she heard about a doctor who lived only a few miles from us in New Zealand but ran an organization in Cambodia. My spouse ended up volunteering in Cambodia, using three to four weeks of annual leave each year over the next five years. Getting this dream off the ground required nothing more than spreading the word about what she wanted to do. Honestly, neither of us expected such a simple strategy to work, but it did. It may not be as simple for you, but you'll never know until you try. The point is, achieving a dream will sometimes turn out to be much easier than you expect!

EXPERIMENT

1.   What is the most influential aspect of your workflow you spend little time on now?
2.   What are the significant projects you want to get done? Pick one of these. What do you most need to do next? Think, talk, research, or crunch numbers? Pick one route forward.

Define Your Core Mission

Identifying your driving force matters. Here's what the research tells us. People who succeed at self-control set goals that feel authentic to them. They endorse statements like "Having this goal makes me feel in touch with the real me."[2] Being values-driven helps people regulate themselves well.[3]

How easy is it for you to sum up what your core mission is? Take a minute now to try. Here are a few examples:

*   My spouse says her core mission is to ensure her patients have the maximum number of years in good health.
*   If you're a teacher, your driving force might be to help your students love learning. Or to teach them to think critically.
*   If you're an accountant, your driving force might be to take away the stress and distraction of taxes for your clients so they can focus on their core work. Or it might be to help your clients build their wealth and grow their businesses by keeping more of their money.

Try thinking beyond excelling in your current role. If your mission seems too tied to it, go bolder. For example, try "help my students learn to love learning" rather than "help my students pass their grade."

EXPERIMENT

Do your best to identify your core mission now. Define it in a sentence. Pick the framing you're most attracted to rather than what seems socially desirable. Write this in the same portable, easily searchable place you're writing your other answers. Perhaps also print it out and stick this on your wall or inside a cupboard you open often.

Will your core mission be fixed forever? No. Your sense of your mission might change as your strengths, skills, and resources grow. Why? When these grow, the opportunities available to you change. Knowing what your core mission is can help you focus. Allowing your core mission to change as you evolve can help you stay maximally productive across your career.

Consider Alternative Ways to Use Your Knowledge, Skills, and Connections

A narrow view of productivity is to think about only one way to use your skills, knowledge, and connections. There isn't just one way.

If you're an editor, you could edit a piece of work. Or you could make a cheat sheet for your writers of strategies to eliminate excessively long sentences or ways to punch up their writing with stronger, more emotive word choices. Or you could write a mini-course on how to self-edit.

If you're a fourth-grade teacher, standing in front of your class delivering curriculum each day is one use of your skills. Another might be to create games to teach science or art concepts. Or you teach parents how to help their children learn conceptually or how to engage their kids' curiosity. Or you create a video course using an innovative teaching method you've developed. For every one you sell, you donate one download to a low-income family.

Take a broad view of the most impactful ways to use your time within your current role. Don't limit yourself to choosing among your habitual behaviors.

Try on fresh ideas, such as

- "Can I experiment with approaches that might produce better results than business as usual?"
- "Should I do more or teach others to do what I can do?"
- "Can I innovate to change processes or how decisions are made?"
- "Should I work with my current partners or do I need to branch out?"

At first glance, those questions might not seem like they apply to your work. Take a broad view to imagine how they might. Think creatively about who your potential business or community partners are.

What if you're not looking to make any big changes in your life? Keep your ideas in the back of your mind. Explore them if you get the impetus to.

What I say next might surprise you. Thought leaders often stress that productivity is about creating specific action plans. But improved productivity can come also from valuing your incomplete ideas more. What are incomplete ideas? They're ideas you don't fully understand or see the relevance of yet.[4] Innovative ideas rarely come fully baked. They don't need to be relevant to your life straightaway. Revisit your incomplete ideas. See if new relevance or clarity emerges.

Align More of Your Day-to-Day Tasks with Your Core Mission

Your daily tasks need to line up with your driving force, the core mission you wrote down earlier. But doing this on an ad hoc basis would be exhausting. How do you make this happen? In practice, it will happen gradually as you create systems and habits.

If you're a teacher who wants to encourage students' love of learning, how does that manifest in your classroom routine? How does your mission infect each part of the day? Perhaps your students start each day by googling something they're interested in. Then pairs of classmates swap knowledge. Or to engage your kids, you teach one subject through another subject, such as teaching science through art (dioramas of discoveries like Newton and the apple) or history through music.

Figuring out the most productive work to do is foundational to this book. There's no urgency to have fully formed answers right now. Part 3 of the book, in particular, will show you how to come up with creative ideas to utilize your knowledge, skills, and relationships.

EXPERIMENT

How do elements of your routine reflect your mission? How can you inject more of your mission into a required task? You won't achieve perfect alignment immediately, but you can gradually move toward that.

Do Long-Term Projects

Long-term projects have lots of advantages. If you devote a few hours or days to a project, how impactful it is might not seem to matter much. If you devote several years to working on a project for a few hours every day, you'll be much pickier about whether the work is important. Long-term projects are more likely to focus on harder problems and bigger ideas. Ultimately, they have a higher likelihood of having a real impact.

There's another, subtle reason that long-term projects have high creative potential. When you're focused on a topic over a long period, there's more surface area. Diverse ideas you encounter from other realms and everyday life have more chance to collide with the topic you're working on. You'll likely be thinking about the project outside work, over a longer period. This means that you'll be more likely to make connections between disparate observations from the wider world and your topic than when you're working on a project for only a few days or weeks. These diverse connections will form your most creative ideas.

Finally, when you commit to a long-term project, you need to tolerate not knowing what the eventual outcome will be. That's anxiety provoking. But this can be productive anxiety. If you have a healthy level of anxiety and intellectual humility, you'll be constantly asking yourself: *In what ways might I be wrong about this? What blind spots might I have?* This mindset can encourage big-picture thinking.

EXPERIMENT

If you don't have a three-to-ten-year project, as you read the rest of this book, think about what you might choose.

Use Estimation to Gauge the Potential Impact of Work and Compare Choices

This chapter is about doing work with a larger potential impact ahead of work with less potential. How do you judge that? Doing some quick back-of-the-napkin calculations using estimation can help you judge the value of potential strategies or compare between choices.

Two-minute calculations can shift your perspective, help you spot false assumptions, and allow you to evaluate claims for yourself.

Numbers provide objective units for making judgments and comparisons. You don't need to be precise with your estimations—ballparking is usually enough.[5]

EXPERIMENT

Pick one of these questions and come up with a strategy for how you could quickly estimate an answer. (If you feel stuck, come back to this experiment after you've read the rest of this section. The concepts should be clearer after I've unpacked them more.)

- Is increasing youth turnout a viable strategy for winning an election?
- Is that pricier accounting firm worth it?
- How likely is it that you'll regret it if you don't have a prenup?
- How likely is it that a more expensive health insurance policy with higher premiums but lower copays and deductibles will end up being a good deal?
- How likely is it that violin lessons will be more valuable to your child than swim lessons?
- Do you save time ordering takeout, or does it take just as much time as cooking?

Simple math can help you see when something does not compute early on. Sometimes I get the urge to do more real estate investing on my own rather than partnering with people for whom it's their full-time work. When I calculate how much time that would take away from writing and family, it makes no sense.

Quick calculations can help you see if tweaks might improve a situation or whether a more radical shift is required. Is it even possible to juggle all your projects and leave work on time?

Estimation can help you see if you have a workable model. If you're considering a side hustle, how much would you need to scale it for it to be worthwhile? How hard would that be? If you want to be at a certain place in ten years, where do you need to be in five years, three years, and one year? Is that workable? What growth would you need to achieve?

You can use quick calculations to identify your return on an investment. Then compare your investment choices.

- Should you devote time today to a potentially high-impact task that might lead nowhere or to a moderately productive activity?

- If you spend time and money to change your business structure now, how many years will it take to recoup that in lower taxes? How does that compare to alternative investments you could make?
- If you need to write a 3,000-word essay for class, should you read twenty-five papers or thirty? What's the added benefit of reading those extra papers?
- How much more productive would your team be if everyone felt comfortable speaking up, instead of only the 30 percent of people who do now? What's it worth investing to make that change happen?
- If I put ten hours into helping my child be independent with managing herself now, how much will it free up my time going forward? What's my payback time? The same math could apply to training employees.

EXPERIMENT

What in your life might benefit from doing some quick estimations? It could be the broad brushstrokes of how you spend your hours each week. It could be related to your finances or growth you'd like to achieve. If nothing comes to mind now, don't sweat it. As you go about your life over the next week, look out for a candidate.

Change Your Routine

Here's a curious paradox for people who rely on strict daily routines to stay on track. Changing your routines makes you more creative.[6]

When our routines change, it unmoors us from our habits. Changes in our routines often happen because of transitions, like changing jobs, moving, or forming/breaking up relationships.

These events don't happen every day. Instead, you can deliberately change your routine. You can go small. If you eat your lunch sitting under a tree in a park near your office, try a different tree. (If you don't believe me when I say that this could have an impact, later in the book, in chapter 9, I'll give an intriguing example of an even smaller change that has been studied.)

Or think bigger. You can also create conditions that stop you from getting stuck in a rut. Back in 2013 and 2014, I bounced around between New York City, Hawaii, Mexico, the Palm Springs area, L.A., and Las Vegas. Our one- to two-month apartment stays meant that every month or two we needed to evaluate where we wanted to live next. Creatively, that was a kick-ass period. It's when I wrote my first book, *The Anxiety Toolkit*.

Personal projects that change your routines can work especially well. A friend's family did a yearlong experiment in reducing their waste. They almost entirely stopped shopping at the regular grocery store. They got a weekly delivery of seasonal fruits and vegetables. They brought meat at a butcher and did the rest of their shopping at a store that sold ingredients in bulk bins. They did a lot more baking and yogurt making. Their family project disrupted many aspects of their prior routines.

Personal projects promote an attitude of exploration and experimentation. Projects cause people to experience themselves in different ways. They help people recognize strengths and a capacity for change they didn't know they were capable of. You might discover a new passion for an activity you never thought you'd like. This change in your sense of self has the potential to permeate your core work roles too.

Personal projects that are outside your comfort zone may also result in gaining more connections with people who think differently from you. Exposure to different thinking styles can help you see your work from novel angles. You gain people you can go to for input on work or life problems.

EXPERIMENT

What change or project are you interested in? How might it unmoor you from your habits? How might that help you see the big picture more clearly?

Utilize Crises, Negative Life Events, and Struggles

This might surprise you. Negative emotions can help productivity, under some circumstances. All emotional states are associated with different thinking patterns. For example, grief spurs autobiographical thinking. People experience grief after an event like losing a job or losing a loved one. As psychologist Dr. Art Markman puts it, "The purpose of grief is to help you reweave the story of your life together."[7] Grief can propel people to want to seek meaning. It can propel people to reevaluate their beliefs about the world and their place in it.

Different emotional states help you think from different vantage points. Mortality salience, or awareness of aging, can prompt big-picture thinking. It can give meaningful work a sense of urgency and encourage you to go bigger and bolder.

Like other big life changes, crises disrupt routines. They separate us from all our habit cues and help take us off autopilot. If your marriage breaks up, your routine will change. Negative life events give a sense of a fresh start or of one chapter closing and another one starting.

Crises often align the urgent and the important. During the pandemic, people thought creatively about how their skills and resources might help people. People asked what capacities they had that could be repurposed to help with the crisis. In normal times, we feel barriers to putting ourselves and our skills out there. In a crisis, it can feel like these barriers dissolve.

Personal crises, like burnout, that cause people to consider leaving their jobs, making a radical career shift, or leaving the workplace altogether are painful and traumatic. But these can also force big-picture thinking once the person realizes the status quo is untenable. When it becomes clear that iterative changes won't solve a problem, that can spark radical creativity.

EXPERIMENT

How can you better utilize struggles and hard times to help you focus on the big picture? Think back to your timeline from chapter 2 to find examples of when you've done this before.

If you find it difficult to function when you're experiencing powerful emotions, I got you. We'll work on this in depth in the next chapter.

Your Takeaways

1. What single point from this chapter was the most helpful to you? In practical terms, how could it help you be more productive? Write a sentence or two. If you wrote your takeaway for the last chapter in a Google doc or email to yourself, add to that, or write yourself another email with the same subject line (for easy search later).

2. Which single point from this chapter seemed least interesting or applicable? To stretch your brain, come up with an idea of how that principle could apply to you. How could you use it? This question will get you to think in ways out of your norm. You're not committing to doing anything. It's a thought experiment. Small or big ideas are fine.

CHAPTER 4

· ·

How to Sustain Growth-Oriented Thinking

To recap, for all these quizzes, scoring mostly As and Bs means you can probably skim the chapter. If you score mostly Cs and Ds, read in more detail. Choose the best answer. If no answer is a perfect fit, choose the closest.

Quiz

· ·

1. Do you believe that to achieve greater productivity you need to improve your self-control?

   (A) Being productive is about far more than self-control.

   (B) It seems like self-control is about 25 to 50 percent of the issue.

   (C) My self-control is decent, but making it even better seems like the number one way to be more productive.

(D) I agree 100 percent. My problem is that I need to pro-crastinate less, require less downtime, and turn myself into a productivity machine.

2. How much does productivity shame bother you?

(A) Rarely. I'm okay with not being a robot.

(B) I'm not perfect and I wish I were, but logically I'm sat-isfied with what I get done.

(C) I'm not Elon Musk and it grates on me.

(D) It really gets me down. I don't feel good about myself.

3. Do you feel like better strategies, practice, and developing fruit-ful relationships will help you achieve your most important goals?

(A) Sure, why wouldn't they?

(B) I think those things would help me succeed more, but I still can't see myself succeeding as much as others, even if I did all that.

(C) I doubt my capacity to do any of that. My flaws and lack of self-discipline get in the way.

(D) No. Even if I did a lot of the right things, I'd still find a way to sabotage my success.

4. How skilled are you at utilizing difficult emotions to help you stay focused?

   (A) This is already a strong habit for me. If I feel worried, frustrated, guilty, angry, and so on, I can channel that into being more focused on doing exceptional work.

   (B) I've never thought about this, but there are probably times when I use negative emotions to fuel my dedication to what's meaningful to me.

   (C) I struggle to concentrate when I feel negative emotions. I can manage that, but I can't think of a positive benefit to negative emotions.

   (D) My difficult emotions cause me to procrastinate or give up. They never positively benefit my focus.

5. When a piece of productivity advice isn't right for you, how easily can you ignore it?

   (A) It's easy for me.

   (B) I can ignore it, but I have some lingering anxiety about what other people successfully do that I can't.

   (C) I usually feel angry toward the author and misunderstood, but I still feel bad that I can't take the advice.

   (D) I'm disappointed with myself that I can't do all the things productive people apparently do.

You've Probably Heard of the Concept of a Growth Mindset

Here's a common misunderstanding people have about this concept. A growth mindset is a belief you can improve through effort, better strategies, and input from others. It's the opposite of believing your capacities are fixed. People often, wrongly, focus solely on improving through practice, which is just one part of the growth mindset equation. Better strategies and learning from others are equally central to the concept.[1] A growth mindset is not merely a thinly veiled argument for practice and discipline.

A growth mindset is a necessary fuel for ambition. Why? It helps people withstand setbacks and negative emotions. The problem is this: It's often treated as a prerequisite to self-improvement. It's seen as a skill people should already have mastered or a switch they should flip. How to get and sustain a growth mindset is often glossed over. Left to figure it out on their own, people often draw their own conclusions about how to hone a growth mindset—and they're not always the right ones.

Growth Is Not About Controlling the Frustrating Parts of Yourself

If you've read much productivity advice, you might've noticed it can take one of two directions.

1. How can I marshal my no-good, lazy self into working hard when my "true" self always wants to goof off?

   Or,

2. How can I hack my life/work/the system so I can get lots of rewards for little effort?

In both scenarios, people are selling themselves short. It's surprisingly hard to convince people that their productivity imperfections aren't all caused by poor self-discipline (or the presence of Twitter and Slack in our lives).

In the introductory chapter, I mentioned the radical perspective that most of us are reasonably good at self-discipline. I'll expand on that idea here. Self-control and self-discipline are evolutionary advantages. Those who excelled at those skills were more likely to survive. They were more likely to pass those qualities on to their offspring. This pattern was repeated and compounded over many generations. It would make absolutely no sense to think you haven't inherited those qualities from your industrious ancestors. It makes no sense they'd be qualities only an elite few have.

Since effort is adaptive, humans have evolved in such a way that it feels good to work hard and try new things. You're a whole person. We all have innate desires to work sometimes, rest sometimes, and play sometimes. You have all these different desires because they're adaptive. Your biological wiring is set up so you have the drive to be productive. You don't need to overcome some inbuilt maladaptive laziness. That's not how humans are wired. Just because we desire to be productive only some of the time, that doesn't mean we're failures. Everyone has other desires mixed in. It's how we've evolved.

Throughout this chapter, we'll dispute the idea that your "caveperson" self (innate, evolved self) is a threat to your productivity. Your caveperson self gets angry, jealous, and anxious, and worries about social acceptance. Far from being a pain in the butt, all these tendencies are useful, as you'll see.

When we have external support, like the risk of a fine for not wearing a seat belt and the preinstallation of seat belts in every car, we mostly succeed at sticking to disciplined behaviors. Most people complete the tasks required of them, like showing up to work and filing their taxes. We struggle if sloth-like habits are engineered that way. We battle if unhealthy foods are engineered with fat, salt, and sugar all in one bite to encourage overconsumption. We struggle if the next episode of a TV series auto-rolls at the end of the last one. We struggle if structures and systems encourage laziness, like cities that are not walkable.

I once read a research study about habits that quoted Gwyneth Paltrow. She said she'd made exercising a habit by doing it every weekday at ten A.M. and religiously sticking to this routine.[2] Here's the thing. Almost all of us could stick to a daily activity at ten A.M. For most people, ten A.M. is peak willpower time. As you might've heard, surgeries go better in the mornings.[3] Judges make fairer decisions earlier in the day.[4] Apparently, Jeff Bezos has a high-level ten A.M. meeting every day for this reason.[5]

Anyone who has control over their day can slot an activity that requires discipline into their peak willpower zone and stick to it. This is especially true if you have the power to ensure external support for your habit. If you can afford a trainer who knocks on your door every morning at 9:45 A.M., you'll keep up your 10:00 A.M. exercise habit. Not everyone can assign their peak willpower hour to the gym. If you could do that, you'd probably have no problem sticking to it, either.

Hacks to become more self-disciplined aren't the primary way you can increase your productivity. If you look at Google Trends data (see the resources page on AliceBoyes.com for a link), you will see that interest in life hacks has been declining since its peak in around 2014. Why? I think people have realized that the promise of life hacks mostly doesn't pay off. To be productive, time management techniques and hacks for working faster aren't enough. You need to be creative, curious, and brave. Without those, time management is shuffling the deck chairs on the *Titanic*.

Let Go of Your Productivity Shame

....

Not everyone who reads this book will have productivity shame,[6] but if you do, it's important to address it.

Shame is a powerful emotion. It's different from guilt. Guilt is about specific actions you wish you had done or hadn't done, or you're ambivalent about because you enjoyed them but then felt guilty afterward. Shame, on other hand, is more fundamental. It's when you sense that you don't have it in you to conform to the mold that you think is essential for achieving your dreams. You won't have a growth mindset when you feel this sort of shame, because it will seem like strategies, practice, or advice can't overcome your innate flaws and limitations.

When people feel productivity shame, they're reactive. They usually react by avoiding challenging, innovative work altogether. Some people will try to outrun their shame by doing or achieving more and more. But when you can let go of productivity shame, it'll become easier to see how a growth mindset will help you achieve your goals. It will seem like strategies, practice, advice, and support will work for you, just as they'd work for anyone else.

Perfectionists in particular often feel anxious that they don't fit the definition of a productive person. But this is because many of us have a warped idea of what a productive person does. We imagine our productivity heroes (and competitors) are always focused, never too anxious to start a task, never moody. But that's not realistic. Productive people are unproductive for some of the time, they procrastinate, and they tie themselves in knots.

What's your notion of a productive person? Someone who works all day at their day job, then goes home to work on their side hustle? Who builds an empire? Who wants a job that comes with great responsibility?

Perhaps you don't want those things. You might have a challenge that you're working with, like a predisposition to depression or anxiety. Or you don't want to hustle 24/7. Perhaps you're not a genius. You might've read about innovators who were incontrovertibly gifted their entire lives. What if that's not you? You're "regular" smart. You're in the 75th, 80th, or 90th percentile. But there were always bright people who outpaced you. You don't think of yourself as creative.

Whatever your hang-up might be about what you're missing, let that go. Whatever you think you lack—a fundamental drive, a level of intelligence, a personality characteristic, or emotional bulletproofness—let that go. Trust that you have what it takes to contribute to your field or community.

Don't let your self-critic choose your goals.[7] Don't choose your goals based on what you think a productive person does, because you think acting the role will help you escape productivity shame. You don't need to act the role of a productive person, or whatever socially prescribed vision you have of that.

Productivity shame and anxiety get entrenched the way wine stains do. We internalize cultural messages and messages from our families and subcultures (like the subculture of whatever your field is—for example, engineers or teachers). For people who were smart kids, the pressure can be worse. Early in life, smart kids are praised for their smartness.[8] They can come to believe it's their most worthy quality above all others. When this happens, people develop self-protective strategies like perfectionism. They use achievement to validate their worth and bolster their sense of self. When they're imperfect, they attempt to use self-criticism as a motivator to do better.

Experiment 1

If you feel productivity shame, where has that come from? Where have you developed your ideas about what it means to be productive? How have your expectations of yourself formed? Consider the broader culture. Also, consider microcosms such as your particular family or the places you've worked. Consider which role models you're seeking to emulate.

What's the point of doing this experiment? When you see where ideas have come from, you'll see they're not truisms. You can drop messages you've internalized from our frenetic rat-on-a-wheel work culture. Being productive doesn't need to look one particular way.

Experiment 2

This experiment will help you process your emotions more deeply and work through them.[9] It will help painful memories become less intrusive and distracting. Bring to mind a specific memory in which you felt productivity shame. It could be from the recent or distant past. It can be an event that was a big deal, or a minor situation that had a disproportionate effect on you, like an offhand comment you ruminate about. Write out the memory. Then write some compassionate words to yourself. Spend at least ten minutes doing this. Repeat for four to five days with the same memory. This will help you remove that wine stain you've been walking around with from the past and give you a clean slate to define your own measures of success. If you'd prefer, you can video yourself recalling your memory and talking to yourself compassionately. Do this selfie-style so you are looking at yourself speaking, for more resonance. As you write (or speak) about your memory, you will likely feel more emotional initially, and then your emotions should cool off as you continue to process the memory.

Your self-compassionate talk should include three components: (1) acknowledging all your specific emotions (which might also include anger, worry, anxiety, hopelessness, etc.), (2) acknowledging that those emotions and similar experiences are universal, and (3) speaking some kind words to yourself.[10] For an article with tips for how to talk to yourself kindly, visit the resources page on AliceBoyes.com.[11]

Tip: You can use this same technique for any other emotional memory that is distracting you from being productive. Write out your memory in detail (or video yourself talking about it), plus respond with compassionate self-talk. An example would be if tackling a new task is making you remember a time you did poorly on a similar task in the past. Repeat the process of writing or videoing yourself for four or five days in a row. This is an excellent technique for weakening emotional pain that can cause procrastination and inefficiency.

Don't Internalize Advice That Isn't Right for You

There are many problems with traditional productivity advice. To start with, fairly typical advice works less well or even backfires for certain groups. For example, research suggests that advice to network more may not help women progress much in their careers (because men get more help from their networks than women do).[12] Women who ask for higher salaries may be penalized for asking. For men, "fake it till you make it" may not be the best advice, given that men are more likely to have a problem with overconfidence. Advice to write shorter emails may work for some people but may lead to others being perceived as unfriendly or curt. Advice like "the laundry can wait while you go do some self-care" can leave people feeling more stressed out when there is real catch-up to do afterward.

Off-target productivity suggestions can leave people demoralized, angry, or overwhelmed. If you read anything that makes you feel bad, consider not making a self-critical evaluation of that experience. Notice if the shadow of productivity shame creeps over you. Don't automatically buy into that. The advice might be bad, not right for you, or not right for you right now. Empower yourself to identify what's not helpful or important to you.

There are so many tropes in the productivity literature. It's easy to get sucked into these.

For example, celebrities and other successful people are asked incessantly about their morning routines. The person dutifully answers the questions. They might fudge a little for brand management purposes. They might not even give/write their answers themselves. What ends up coming across to readers? It sounds like these people think their morning routine is critical to their success, while in reality they were simply replying to a PR request.

Even when I know better, I find it extraordinarily challenging not to get lured into regurgitating typical productivity advice. After interviews, sometimes journalists follow up with questions like "My editor wants me to write something about how meditation is helpful for this. What do you think?" I want to be easy to work with. I give the journalist a quote about meditation. It's accurate. But there's a good chance I didn't think encouragement to meditate was the most useful advice their readers could get on the topic.

Another issue is that in work-related writing, self-help and policy articles are siloed into separate categories. This can leave readers with the impression that people in the self-help field think all problems and solutions lie within individuals. As previously mentioned, the sheer volume of articles on hustle or discipline and the corresponding glut on self-care can leave you sensing there is no way to win. You end up constantly oscillating between these perspectives, debating which you should focus on, without doing either.

If you react negatively to anything you read about productivity, allow yourself that reaction. This includes anything you read in this book! It's okay to conclude, "It's not me, it's them," when advice leaves you feeling worse.

If you think you should follow all the standard productivity advice, you'll have endless open loops of shoulds. Close those loops. Label specific suggestions as not helpful. Cross them off your list. It's hard to have a growth mindset if you have an endless list of shoulds.

See the Nuances of Tips That Help Sometimes but Not Always

To feel less internal pressure, acknowledge that contradictory tips can help on different days. There will be some days in which you need to focus on doing the work that's in front of you,[13] not focus on the big picture. Other days, the reverse will be true. There will be occasional days when focusing on surviving, not thriving, will be the better choice. Accepting this can help you feel okay if you don't consistently apply the same advice every day.

Get to know yourself well enough that you know which advice to apply when. For example, the advice to "keep a tidy house" mostly isn't necessary for my productivity. I'm still productive even when my house is messy. However, when I'm struggling to focus, I sometimes start by dismantling my bed (lifting the mattress and base off the frame) to vacuum under it. This is a tip I learned as a therapist working with kids with attention difficulties. I learned that lifting heavy things (engaging your big muscles) can help with focus. I do this only every few months, but it works really well and usually kicks off a good few days of focused effort on my most important work.

It's easier to maintain a growth mindset if you're curious and enjoy the nuances of learning about yourself and human psychology. Don't expect your questions about how you work best to have black-and-white answers. To an extent, having a growth mindset about your productivity involves learning to accept that your questions about how you can be your most productive will have messy answers. Author Gretchen Rubin has a great quote. As she says, "The opposite of a great truth is also true."[14]

If there is a self-imposed rule that helps you be productive most of the time (like never work on the weekends), it's likely the exact opposite will be true at least occasionally.

EXPERIMENT

What are three pieces of common productivity advice that aren't helpful to you? What advice can you cross off your to-do list?

Drilling down further, what's a piece of advice that's helpful to you sometimes but feels like excessive pressure at other times?

Use Your Difficult Emotions to Focus

When researchers measure people's ability to use negative emotions to focus, they ask them how true statements like these[15] are for them:

- When I am faced with obstacles related to my goal, my frustration serves to energize me.
- I find worrying helpful to solving goal-related problems.
- When people distract me from my goal, I use any anger that arises to stay focused.
- I get motivated by guilt when I fail to meet my own expectations pursuing my goal.

An individual's capacity to harness difficult emotions for goal pursuit is part of a broader three-element skill termed *psychological flexibility*. The other two parts are (1) whether you avoid goals that are difficult or stressful, and (2) if you accept that stress and unpleasant feelings are part of the pursuit of a goal. (People who are more innovative are more stress tolerant.)[16] I'll link to a quiz for this on the resource page on AliceBoyes.com so you can assess yourself more fully.

Psychological flexibility yields all sorts of positive outcomes.[17] People with more of it perform better at work. They are more goal-oriented. They have a superior quality of life and greater psychological and physical health. There's no trade-off between performance and well-being. The more psychological flexibility you have, the more likely you are to lead a productive and healthier life. And modern psychology has evolved an epic distance from the oversimplified idea that you need to be happy to be productive. The times you're least happy are also fertile periods for exceptional work.[18]

Need more reasons not to be scared of strong emotions when it comes to your productivity? Strong emotions have been linked to creativity.[19] People who report frequently feeling intense emotions (positive or negative) score higher on tests of creative capacity.[20] And when we feel ambivalent emotions (positive and negative emotions together), it puts us on the lookout for unusual associations, potentially enhancing our creativity.[21] It's likely that doing hard but meaningful work stimulates ambivalent emotions quite a bit. Being open to your full range of emotions is associated with creativity.[22]

EXPERIMENT

Can you recall any recent situations in which you've recruited difficult thoughts or emotions to help you focus? Have you used challenging emotions (like feeling anxious, competitive, angry, or dejected) to improve your dedication or concentration? You're unlikely to have been aware of doing this, but looking back, you may see you've done it unconsciously.

A quick example: During the early days of the pandemic, I used reading Twitter as a way of increasing my fear. It felt unpleasant, but it helped me stick to staying home and taking precautions whenever I left the house.

Create Habits for How You'll Respond to Difficult Emotions

The stereotypical habit is a daily routine, like brushing your teeth. But habits are much more than this.

Habits can be triggered by external factors like time or place. Or they can be cued by a preceding activity (like, after you've brushed your teeth, you take your medication).

Not everyone wants rigid time-based habits or daily routines. While some people thrive on that, others don't.

There's another critical type of habit that virtually no one thinks about.

You can create habits for how you respond to particular thoughts and emotions. Habits triggered by your internal states have the same properties and benefits as other types. The more consistently you respond to the same thoughts and feelings, the more automatic and effortless it will become. The way to make the management of emotions easier is to use internally cued habits.

Use if-then plans to do this. For example:

- "*If* I experience worry that my work isn't any good while I am working, *then* I will implement something I know improves my writing, like shorter sentences, clearer writing, more funny moments, or more compelling storytelling. I will do this in up to five places within the work."
- "*If* someone mistreats me, *then* I will work hard to put myself in a position of enough power and authority that I won't need to tolerate that."
- "*If* I feel bored with my work and I'd rather be at the beach, *then* I will remind myself about why my work matters, and I will make what I am working on matter more through being brave."

- *"If* I don't like the ways things are done and I feel angry, *then* I will create my own model for my success."
- *"If* I genuinely don't have the skills to execute a vision I have for myself, *then* I will find someone who can teach me how."

EXPERIMENT

When do you experience frustration, guilt, sadness, anxiety, or anger at work? Construct an if-then plan for each scenario that's common for you. Choose how you will use those emotions to help you stay focused and on-mission.

Whatever you come up with, try it out and see if it helps. Expect to improve on your initial ideas to find what works. These if-then rules are like mini-habits. The more you use them, the more they will become automatic. When you create mini-habits for how you'll respond to difficult emotions, it's like you are baking in a growth mindset for exactly the moments when you need it the most.

How to Handle Social Comparison

When you see others succeeding, you might ruminate on "Why can't I be like so-and-so?" You may fret about why you don't have their charisma, quick wit, discipline, decisiveness, capacity to see into the future, social engineering skills, depth or breadth of knowledge, or whatever it is.

Social comparison can be energizing. However, that energy can sometimes leave you running in circles trying to copy the path or skills of someone else. You need to find your path to success with your own skills, strengths, interests, and personality.

EXPERIMENT

Construct an if-then statement for how you'll handle negative social comparison. How can you transform social comparison into laser focus?

Examples:

- *"If* I am thinking, *Why can't I be more like so-and-so?* I will remind myself I know nothing about what work that person puts in to get their results. *Then* I will refocus on what I can offer because of who I am, what I know, and the skills I have. I will focus on what impactful perspective I can offer that the person I'm comparing myself to does not have."
- *"If* another person has a skill I admire, *then* I will inject that into my work in one specific way. I will do this once today. For example, if I want to be more charming, I could be more encouraging of my colleagues at the meeting I am about to attend."

What's the Difference Between Using Mini-Habits and Being Tough on Yourself?

People who try to be perfectly disciplined by being self-critical want to eliminate strong "negative" emotions. They get frustrated with themselves for feeling frustrated. They are anxious when they're afraid. They get angry about being angry.

When you use your negative emotions to propel you, you won't feel so resentful of having them. When I'm upset or anxious, I often use familiar work (like writing a blog post) to settle myself. This doesn't feel like disciplining myself. It feels a lot more like self-care. I allow myself to get back to a predictable form of work. I reassure myself that whatever worries or ruminations I'm having, I don't need to solve those problems right now. When you hit on effective ways to channel difficult emotions, you'll feel this way too. The emotions won't feel inconvenient, and you won't need to wrangle them. Your routines for channeling your strong emotions to help you focus can become a safe harbor to dock in when the sea is rough.

Pushing yourself to work isn't always the best response to feeling crummy. Everyone should take some mental health days off of work to recover emotionally from stress, but work also can help you bounce back from feeling upset. As writer Anne Lamott says, "Almost everything will work again if you unplug it for a few minutes, including you." Doing that is one way of channeling difficult thoughts in service of your broader goal. Sometimes the more disciplined behavior (of stepping back) looks like the less disciplined behavior.[23] Sometimes you'll need days off to get the mental space you need to solve challenging problems.

Your Takeaways

1. What did you learn from this chapter about how to maintain a growth mindset? How do you expect that to help you?
2. What's one way you can use a difficult emotion to help you focus? Pick the emotion first (e.g., worry, anger, guilt, frustration), then outline how you can use that to be more productive.

Note that if these questions feel challenging, it's because they are. Even if you're a smart person and you've read carefully, you may need to rescan the chapter or mull over the ideas to be able to answer.

CHAPTER 5

. . . .

How to Become a
Self-Scientist

To recap, for all these quizzes, scoring mostly As and Bs means you can probably skim the chapter. If you score mostly Cs and Ds, read in more detail. Choose the best answer. If no answer is a perfect fit, choose the closest.

Quiz

. . . .

1. Consider your typical workweek. Do you know how many hours you spend on which tasks?

    (A) I've tracked this, so I know accurately.

    (B) I have a rough idea.

    (C) I could estimate, but I expect my estimates would be substantially off.

    (D) I fear what I'd see if I were ever to track this.

2. Do you notice when you're more creative than usual?

(A) Yes, I notice when I see unusual solutions to problems or when I'm more receptive to diverse perspectives. I engineer my working life to create these conditions.

(B) I know when I'm more creative (e.g., when I'm trying new things, working with new people, or feeling vulnerable), but I don't deliberately create these conditions.

(C) If I have a creative idea, I get a buzz from that, but it seems random.

(D) I haven't seen creativity as relevant to my role, so I pay no attention to it.

3. Do any of your productivity patterns surprise you?

(A) Certainly they do. How I work best doesn't always fit conventional wisdom. I adjust my expectations based on my self-knowledge.

(B) I know my patterns, but if they differ from conventional wisdom, I have a hard time trusting that.

(C) I look only for patterns I've heard about. I don't notice patterns that might differ from common productivity philosophies.

(D) I would have a hard time even describing what my productivity patterns are.

4. Do you understand how your behaviors are connected? For example, doing creative work may make you want to exercise more (because you need the balance).

    (A) Yes, I've even noticed some connections that might surprise other people. I use these connections to my advantage.

    (B) I'm aware of them, but I'm not sure what's a cause and what's a consequence.

    (C) I'm either in productive mode in all areas of my life or in sloth mode everywhere.

    (D) I've never thought about it.

5. Do you learn about yourself from natural experiments? For example, when a forced or accidental change in your routine, or an adverse event, leads to surprising productivity.

    (A) Sure, often.

    (B) Perhaps once or twice a year.

    (C) I might fleetingly notice this, but I don't translate it into changes in my systems and routines.

    (D) No.

In this chapter, you'll learn how to use self-science to understand the mix of routines that help you be the most productive.

As you read, keep in mind the difference between focused work and work with the potential to have an impact. As previously mentioned, focused work in and of itself is unimportant. Focused work on its own— without a specific direction—could lead you to become hell-bent on increasing the time you spend being focused and undistracted. But if you have no larger goal in mind, all that effort would be put into work with low potential to impact your life, your field, or your community. What you're focusing on is what matters! Concentrate on what helps you do work that has the potential to matter one year from now.

Okay, now that you have your end goal in mind, it's time to turn inward. Most of your useful insights into yourself will come from being an astute observer. I call this *naked observation*. This is the most potent productivity tool you're underutilizing. It involves observing your thoughts, feelings, and behaviors to learn how to bring out the best in yourself.

You'll also need some tools for understanding what your naked eye misses. We'll augment your naked self-observations (the core method we'll use) with a small sampling of automated self-tracking. This will help you see how aspects of your life fit together and observe your behavior from different vantage points.

Self-science might not be something you're enthusiastic about. If we were to take a traditional approach to it, your preconceptions would be well founded. Most self-science involves a lot of tracking and data mining. You might be fed up with our metrics-driven culture. Or you hate treating yourself like a robot. That's understandable, which is why my version is much more chill than what you're probably imagining. I won't suggest you manually track anything, since who has the motivation for that? I also won't suggest you look at your data on a daily or even weekly basis.

The Dangers of Bad Self-Science

Research on fitness trackers shows that many people give up on daily tracking after six months.[1] Over-monitoring and overfocusing on specific metrics creates problems. People can become too driven by a metric. They lose sight of how the metric is an imperfect proxy for their broader, more meaningful goals. People start behaving in ways that will improve their metrics and not their goal.

Funny story: Once I started counting how many times a week I went to the gym. Because I was counting only the days I went, I started rocking in there at 8:40 P.M. when it closed at 9:00 P.M. If you're ever a slave to your metrics, you'll know when you're overoptimizing for the metric and have lost perspective on the broader goal.

When self-tracking is done wrong, you gain few if any useful insights that contribute to your positive evolution as a person. And doing it will make you miserable. Doing it right means doing it sparsely and personalizing which metrics you track. Regrettably, folks who constantly track self-data often struggle to get enough nonobvious insights from the activity to justify the effort. You shouldn't check your stock portfolio every day or every week. Neither should you constantly check your productivity data.

Done right, automated self-tracking can quickly generate helpful insights. The point isn't that it will answer every great mystery about you, but that you'll get a smattering of useful insights quickly. When you use self-tracking along with other observations and reflection, you'll get a fuller, more accurate picture of yourself.

Science always provides plenty of surprises, and self-science is no exception. You'll learn things about yourself you don't expect. Be open to those insights, including when a pattern you expected isn't reflected in your data. For example, maybe traditional time management advice like spending less time on email doesn't affect how much impactful work you do.

All that said, if self-measurement or anything else in this book doesn't appeal to you, skip it. It's not my intention that anything should feel like homework. Pick one self-experiment from the chapter that's relevant and interesting to you.

Why Self-Science Can (Sometimes) Give You Better Information Than General Advice

Sometimes it's unnecessary to rely on general advice to figure out what you should do. Case in point: Umpteen articles will attempt to tell you how long you should work before taking a break. However, that's something you can (and should) test for yourself to find out what works for you.

Frustratingly, general advice sometimes lacks nuance. Even sound principles applied rigidly may have downsides. For example, you might gain benefits from sticking to a habit, up to a threshold. Perhaps up to 80 or 90 percent consistency in how often you stick to a habit, the more consistent you are, the better. Beyond that, the effect of rigid consistency might become detrimental. Research studies don't always pick up on subtle patterns. You can, through self-science.

Self-science can help you understand why adopting general advice is more complicated than it appears. One personal observation that has shocked me is that when I enact my ideal on-target week, it leaves me feeling flat. Objectively, I should feel a great sense of accomplishment, but I don't. Even when I take generous breaks and love the work I'm doing, too much consistency in my work schedule doesn't feel pleasant to me. Also, I've noticed that I don't enjoy the much-heralded feeling of flow. I don't like emerging from a work session in which hours have passed in a blur. These are trade-offs I'm willing to make sometimes, but not always.

Habits work for me as the research says they should. They make sticking to routines easy. Unfortunately, they have an unexpected negative consequence too. Being on autopilot flattens my mood. My wiring and your wiring aren't the same, so you might have a different experience! My point is that humans are complex. And furthermore, it's not wise to take research from one niche within psychology, such as habits research, and turn it into a general model of how all people should live and work.

Finally, your data may be more convincing to you than other people's data. You may need to see a pattern reflected in your data to convince you to make a needed change.

Ultimately, combining published science, self-science, and insights you pick up from others will give you the best results.

How Self-Observation Can Help You Do Challenging Work

Through self-observation, you can find what helps you have stickability. You could study your behavior and emotions systematically, but most people won't have the energy or inclination for that. Instead, you can do it in a way that's a bit more art than science, by generally tuning in to yourself. For example, gently observe your productivity patterns (your behavior): whether productivity clichés are true for you; when in your week you're up for a challenge and when you're not; what affects your focus; and what your thoughts and emotions are.

The best way to show you the potential this has is through examples. Here are five observations that have made a massive difference in how I work. Your observations don't need to be earth-shattering. They simply need to be personally relevant. When you learn through observing yourself, you'll see how this is necessary to understand yourself fully. You can't wholly rely on understanding general science or other people's systems for getting things done.

I've noticed:

Observation 1

Surprisingly, the emotional state I'm in when I start a session of work has little bearing on the quality of work I do.

I can concentrate on writing for about two to two and a half hours. This is true regardless of whether I start the session feeling focused or distracted, happy or flat or anxious. At this point, I'm conditioned to write or read for this length of time. My emotions don't negatively affect that.

If anything, I work better when I'm feeling upset or vulnerable. When I'm anxious or sad, my work is sometimes more empathic. I take more risks in writing, putting my ideas out there, rather than just summarizing research.

This observation has helped me not to fear these emotions.

Ironically, the one emotion that does consistently negatively affect my concentration is excitement.

Observation 2

I can do about an hour of busywork in the mornings before I knuckle down to deep work, without its affecting how much deep work[2] I do in the day.

This observation has stopped me from resenting admin tasks so much or fearing they'll get in the way of more important work. If I plan to do admin tasks after my deep work sessions, I'm usually too tired and don't do them, so doing them beforehand is usually better.

Observation 3

I write about twice as much as I publish. If I want to publish 1,000 words, I need to be prepared to write about 2,000.

Accepting this has helped me feel less stressed over it.

Observation 4

If I get interrupted early in a work session, I can snap back to focusing. If I've already been working for an hour or more and I'm interrupted, I struggle to regain focus. I can discipline myself to struggle through the rest of my session, but my concentration feels broken and fragmented.

Curiously, though, there's a twist. If it's my five-year-old who interrupts me, I can often snap back. I know she is interrupting me because she misses me when I'm hunkered down. If my spouse interrupts me, I get steaming mad, because the intrusion is thoughtless and uncaring. I struggle to recover my concentration after being steaming mad, more than from the interruption per se.

As you might guess, this has helped me control my emotions when I get interrupted. Also, I try to protect myself from intrusions in the second half of my work sessions.

Observation 5

Writing I do past my normal two to two and a half hours in a session isn't high quality. I get writer's diarrhea and produce rubbish I end up cutting later.

Pushing myself to do long writing sessions isn't helpful.

EXPERIMENT

What do you already know about your productivity patterns? Spend ten minutes writing some bullet points as I've done. You might know quite a bit about yourself already but not had the confidence to structure your work habits around those observations. Articulate why each observation matters. How does your insight into your patterns help you be more productive? By reviewing what you already know about yourself, you can focus on learning new insights and allowing what you know to influence how you structure your days and expectations. Also, note questions you'd like to answer or your hypotheses.

IMPORTANT!

When you observe your productivity patterns, make sure you don't equate productivity with when your work feels frictionless. For example, when people work in diverse teams, the work can feel more challenging, but ultimately it tends to be higher quality.[3] Work that feels easy is often only moderately productive.

A day you spend doing familiar tasks in a focused manner might feel like a productive day. In reality, it might not be as productive as a day in which you spent an hour doing a novel task. Even if you spend the rest of the day feeling scattered, you still may come out far ahead. Doing hard, innovative, counterintuitive work often leaves us feeling on edge.

Make sure your self-observations aren't tainted by motivated cognition or confirmation bias. Some of your observations should surprise you or be patterns you'd prefer not to be true. For each pattern you observe, consider multiple explanations for it before you settle on one. For example, I've noticed I concentrate well when I drink electrolyte water. Maybe drinking electrolyte water helps me concentrate better. But perhaps it's just the water itself, not the electrolytes, and I drink more of it because it tastes better. Maybe it works because it cues my deep work habit (more on this coming up soon). Or maybe I drink electrolytes mainly when I know I have to concentrate to meet a deadline, and it's the deadline helping my concentration. Once you think you've identified a pattern, look out for any data that doesn't fit your explanation. I still revise my explanations of my patterns. It's normal to jump to some wrong conclusions initially and need to revise your ideas, but what's important is that you don't blindly attach yourself to wrong or incomplete ideas. If learning about yourself feels messy, that's to be expected.

It should take you only a week or so to gain some useful insights from self-observation, but you'll gain more if you tune in to yourself on an ongoing basis when you're feeling strong emotions or a lot of stress or when you're procrastinating. Writing down your observations will help you remember them. Make sure you note how an insight helps you, as I've done in my examples. Alternative: If you don't want to write observations, video yourself talking about them.

Track Your Computer Activities

I apologize that this section won't be relevant to all readers. It's for readers who spend their workdays on their computers.

To understand someone as thoroughly as possible, you should look through different lenses to get the most complete picture. For example, when psychologists get to know clients, they typically interview them, give them questionnaires, observe them, and perhaps talk to others who know them well.

The same principle applies when you do self-science. To get the fullest, most accurate understanding of yourself, you should look at yourself through as many lenses as possible. One of these should be introspection, as we've already covered. Another obvious option is some light self-tracking. In the modern world, a good way to understand how people use their time is to see what they do on their computer. Metrics can help you see patterns you miss with the naked eye, but it's important you don't think of this as surveillance. You're not doing it to beat up on yourself.

I use the free version of the app RescueTime to track how I spend my time on the computer. I let RescueTime collect my data in the background. I then dip into it (very) occasionally when I have a question about my workflow.

What I learned from RescueTime surprised me and changed my strategy for being more productive. My data shows that I almost always focus well on Mondays and Tuesdays. I get my focused work done without special effort on those days.

My productivity falls off on Wednesdays and gets worse by Friday. Although I could've guessed this, I was stunned by how stark this pattern was. Thankfully, it also revealed a solution that hadn't been obvious to me before. I realized I don't need to be policing myself at the beginning of the week, which was an immense relief. I need strategies to stay focused Wednesdays through Fridays, when I'm more tired.

Knowing I don't need strategies for Mondays and Tuesdays made improving my focus feel much more manageable. When you look at your data, try to find a similar insight—one that changes your strategy for how you approach your productivity. Hopefully that will help you do it in a targeted way.

Make the goal of this data tracking to learn something that surprises you, takes the pressure off rather than increases it, and provides a clear course of action. This should be your focus rather than robotic optimization of every minute of your workday or giving yourself a time management makeover.

EXPERIMENT 1

Download RescueTime and let it track you for a month. Check in on it after a couple of days to make sure all the data is being collected as it should be. Once you have at least two full weeks of data, poke around in it.

RescueTime lets you see your data from hourly, daily, weekly, monthly, and annual perspectives. You can also look at all your instances of doing a particular activity, like checking email. Approach your data like an explorer. Be open to what it exposes. You can use the following questions as prompts for what to look at, to the extent they're interesting to you.

- What are the head and tail of your activities like? How many major activities make up 80 percent of your time use (the head)? How many make up the other 20 percent (the tail)? How much time did you spend per week on each of your core activities?
- What are the day-of-the-week patterns you observe in your data?
- What are the time-of-day patterns?
- What is your concentration span for different activities? This can help you with timeboxing, should you choose to do that.
- What surprises you in your data? What were your positive surprises? For example, do you spend less time on social media than you thought you did?
- Examine times you're not productive during times you usually are. What went wrong? How could that have been avoided?
- Look at a single session when you're doing focused deep work. Look at the detailed hourly view to see what you did within that time. Did you self-distract? What were the patterns of this? For example, how long did you focus before the first time you self-distracted? Were you self-distracting out of habit or because you needed a mental refresh?

- Do you have dead zones? Maybe you run out of steam thirty minutes before lunch every day and do nothing during that period.
- How bitsy is your time? Do you have lots of slots of less than an hour that are too short to start anything substantial?

EXPERIMENT 2

Identify one actionable insight from your tracking data.

Take a return-on-investment perspective on the time you spend looking at your self-tracking data. Say you spend twenty minutes digging into your data. You gain an insight that results in your doing twenty more minutes of focused activity each week. You've gotten your investment back in a single week. Beyond this, you'll get diminishing returns from over-analyzing. If you develop excellent systems for how you choose what you work on, it won't be necessary to measure the outcomes constantly.

If you're okay with letting RescueTime continue collecting your data, keep it turned on. If you let it keep running in the background, you'll have long-term data available to you, which will give you a distinct perspective and fresh insights.

Consider How a Self-Critical Person Would Do Self-Science. Do the Opposite.

Imagine the approach a self-critical person might take to self-tracking. They'd be on the lookout for all their imperfections. They'd have unrealistic expectations that they were going to be on-target at all times. They'd look at their best day and think every day should be like that. That is not how life works. Humans have ups and downs.

Treat self-science how a psychologist would approach assessing a client. You want accurate information so you can make sound plans. You're not doing it to dump on yourself.

Don't Confuse Symptoms and Causes

Contrary to popular belief, self-science shouldn't be focused on how you can reduce your time spent on distracting websites and apps.

We've all had the feeling of being immersed in an absorbing project and realizing we haven't checked email or other communication tools for hours. Behaviors like using social media are often more of a symptom than a cause of suboptimal productivity. For instance, you might jump on social media when you're avoiding deep work. Perhaps you're not conditioned to do it and it makes you uncomfortable. Your lack of conditioning to deep work is the issue.

When we do something hard (or even contemplate doing it), it can bring up inner experiences we want to escape. This is similar to how physical exercise makes novice exercisers emotionally and physically uncomfortable. A new exerciser isn't used to those sensations of effort. They lack trust in their body. The experience brings up ruminative thoughts like "Why aren't I better at this? Why have I let myself get so out of shape?" or "This was so much easier when I was sixteen."

A similar constellation of thoughts and feelings can pop up when people attempt to do deep cognitive work. We sometimes feel a strong urge to escape the negative feelings that hard, deep work stirs. The ways people escape (Twitter, incessant email checking, Slack) aren't particularly germane to solving the problem. Once you train yourself up to concentrate for reasonable periods of time, and if the work you're doing feels meaningful enough, you'll feel much less need to escape from the effort of focusing.

The Lock and Key Model of Behavior

This model will help you resolve stubborn patterns you've been unable to change.

Think of your behaviors as locks and keys. The messy human part is that you don't know which behavior is a lock and which one is a key. For instance, Marie Kondo-ing your house might give you a fresh start. That clean slate might be what you need to start a consistent habit of doing deep work at the same time every day. In this example, decluttering is the key that opens the lock of deep work.

Alternatively, when you start a deep work habit, you might find you have an urge to declutter. Pottering away at cleaning might be what you feel like doing after you've mentally exhausted yourself. In this case, deep work is the key that opens the lock of having less clutter in your life.

A fun aspect of self-observation is when you observe behaviors that improve other behaviors, without directly targeting those.

I could've tied myself in knots devising a system to help me prioritize better. It turned out I didn't need to. Having strong, deep work habits (two sessions per day of book writing) has effortlessly solved most of my problems with prioritizing. I have little energy left over after these two sessions. Consequently, I let more small and medium opportunities pass me by that shouldn't have been a priority anyway. (As I said earlier, this pattern of working also makes me feel flat if I do it too long, so it's complicated. You can expect you'll be complicated too!) So in this case, my deep work sessions are a key to unlock my prioritization system.

This effect isn't unique. Generally, when you have strong positive habits in one area, it helps you in others simultaneously. When people exercise, for instance, they become better regulated in many diverse areas of their lives. This happens even without targeting those other areas.[4] If you closely observe yourself, you might notice that when you exercise regularly, you're more organized. These are the patterns you can pick up on through observation. I've noticed doing deep creative work makes me crave exercise. I need the release. For me, deep work is a key that unlocks both better prioritizing and doing more exercise.

If there is any aspect of self-regulation you struggle with, consider that for you, it might be a lock, not a key. You might need to unlock it with another habit. I thought better prioritizing was a key, something I needed to target directly to accrue other benefits. As it happened, I was wrong. It was a lock. A behavior that's a lock for you might be a key for someone else.

As you observe yourself, pay attention to how your habits influence your other habits.

EXPERIMENT

Note any productivity problem that:

- is impossible to solve,
- you approach using convoluted or punishing plans, or
- you make plans to change, but never stick to those plans.

Now switch your view of the problem. Instead of seeing it as the key that will unlock other benefits, try seeing it as the lock. Find another habit that you can more easily target that will effortlessly improve (not necessarily completely solve) that problem for you.

How to Develop a Deep Work Habit

Everyone needs habits of doing challenging, focused deep work. These could be permanent habits, or habits that last the length of a particular project or life phase.

You can take a direct approach to this. How? By establishing a routine of it. Cue the start of the routine in the same way each time.[5] For example, when I start writing, I set three timers on my Google Home for 60, 90, and 120 minutes. I have a quick chat with my kid, get a drink of water, and physically set myself up in the same spot. If you enact the same routine (close to) every weekday consistently, it'll start feeling much less effortful after a few months. Your habit will become a safe space to return to when other aspects of life are out of your control.

To increase your habit resilience, create a fallback in case an aspect of your routine fails. For example, if I don't set the timers, I can check the revision history on my Google document to see when I started working. This way, I can still make sure I complete my session without overdoing it.

Tip: Keep some elements of your deep work routine solely for when you are committed to doing a deep work session. I'm not always doing focused writing. I save my routine of setting Google Home timers for when I am. That way this trigger is exclusively linked to that behavior, strengthening the connection. (In the same way, I listen to specific songs only for long runs.)

Some people feel psychological resistance to having consistent deep work habits or they have practical challenges, like lack of control over meeting times. No judgment. If you fall into this category, you can try an indirect route. You can use the lock and key model to find another habit that will indirectly flow on to doing more deep work. For example, you could try improving your habits of switching off from work and enjoying more relaxed personal time. When you're better at switching off, your focus while you're working will improve. Designing a better habit for switching off might be the key you need to unlock deep work. In chapter 15, "How to Think Like an Expert," I give tips for breaking free of rumination, which is a common stumbling block people experience when they attempt to switch off from work.

Insights You Can Gain from Natural Experiments

You could measure the impact of going to bed earlier on your productivity by going to bed late one week and early another. Or you might be interested in the effects of exercising in the morning as opposed to exercising in the evening. A true experiment is usually defined as when you purposely change a particular behavior and attempt to isolate its impact.

In reality, that's more work than most people want to put in. Another option is to learn through natural experiments. Natural experiments give you another lens to view your behavior, just like introspection and self-tracking. In fact, a surprising number of scientific discoveries come about by accident.

- A patient is given a drug for one condition. It unexpectedly helps an unrelated condition.
- A researcher observes an odd reaction between chemicals in the lab or strange patterns in their data. In science, unexpected observations can turn out to be more interesting than the original purpose of the research!
- A student misunderstands some instructions and comes up with an inventive method.

Natural experiments can be either accidental or forced. A forced experiment is when an outside circumstance forces a change in your behavior. Forced experimentation can also result in fresh ways to get things done.

Back in 2004, there was a strike by London Underground workers. This resulted in some stations, but not all, being closed. A sizable proportion of people needed to take a different route to work. Most commuters use electronic cards to enter and exit the Tube system, and researchers could track behavior through these cards. When their habits were disrupted, many commuters found a more efficient route to work. Astoundingly, economists estimated that the value of these more efficient routes outweighed the value lost from the disruption.[6]

During coronavirus, I took a forced break from my side hustle. This revealed how much time and focus it was taking away from my core work. I enjoy it, so I hadn't wanted to see this. The forced experiment made recognizing it unavoidable. Ultimately, this was helpful.

Forced experiments are more common than you might realize. They occur, for example, when someone you worked closely with leaves their job. Working with someone new becomes an experiment. It often requires you to examine your processes and can give you new insights, if you're open to them and observant. A new teammate is becoming frustrated with you? This might reveal an inefficiency in your work that you were overlooking. Forced experiments can help us reexamine how we work and make changes we didn't know we needed to make.

As you may have noticed, these points dovetail with the earlier material about how disruption in your routines can promote new thinking. Being an open observer can help you turn disruptions into opportunities. To accrue all these benefits, you need to be adept at observation and self-reflection. You need to notice differences and deduce cause and effect. Then translate your insights into a new routine.

EXPERIMENT

Over the next few months, keep an eye open for a natural experiment and see what you can learn from it.

Observe When You're Most Creative

Knowing what improves your focus is a modest aspect of understanding what helps you be productive. Observing what makes you more creative will allow you to engineer more pivotal moments that shape your trajectory. A good measure of when you're in a creative state is noting the times when you see something anew. Here are some examples:

- You notice something you've never paid attention to before on a walk you take every day.
- Your view of yourself, someone else, or a topic changes.
- You see a new application for your existing skills or knowledge.
- You recognize the value of other people's knowledge in a way you haven't previously, or you see the value of their perspective for the first time.
- You suddenly see a solution to a vexing problem.
- Right upon waking up in the morning you spontaneously have new insights into work problems.
- You become open to a solution you've stubbornly resisted.
- A path that felt murky becomes clear.

Whenever you have a lot more of these creative insights than usual, what's going on? What are you doing differently that's precipitating it?

Keep an eye out for any observations that provide a clear, practical course of action. They don't need to be fancy.

I've noticed that I often have fresh ideas right after I wake up, if I allow myself to lounge in bed before getting up (without reaching for my phone). So I know to hang out in bed for five or ten minutes. That's a clear, doable action that my observation points to. I've also noticed that if I'm stuck or overwhelmed with my work, those problems are almost always cured by taking the weekend off. When I'm fresh on a Monday, problems that felt difficult to solve on a Friday suddenly have easy and obvious solutions.

Walking, and especially walking in nature, have been shown to boost creativity. At the extreme end, four days of backpacking improved scores on a creativity test by a whopping 50 percent.[7] But any activity that allows your brain to work in the background, like painting a fence or mowing your lawn, should work to an extent.[8] Try noticing if this is true for you.

It's Okay If You Can't Solve Every Problem Right Now

Don't panic if solutions to all of your productivity stumbling blocks don't come to mind immediately. Throughout the rest of the book, you'll learn ways to help you find creative solutions. What you've done in this chapter is assess the lay of the land.

Your Takeaways

1. What surprised you from this chapter? Did you learn about a potential benefit from self-science you hadn't considered?
2. What's your plan for how to make that insight useful to you?

PART 2

....

Improving Your
Repeatable Systems

C ongratulations! You've now reached part 2. This part of the book
is about having effective, efficient, repeatable systems. These contribute to productivity. On the other hand, they're not the be-all and
end-all. So in order to adopt a realistic view of their role, let's debunk
some myths about efficiency.

Myth 1. Being Efficient Will
Result in Being Less Busy

....

You may have gravitated to this book because you're overloaded. People
often see becoming more efficient as the solution. This is a seductive
thought, but largely wrong. Being efficient can help you succeed, but it
won't make you less overwhelmed. Why? Being more efficient usually
leads to becoming busier.[1] For example:

- The more emails you write (including replies you send), the more emails that will generate.
- The more efficient I am at writing guest articles for blogs, the more I'm asked to do it. I get busier.
- The more efficient someone is at real estate, the cheaper their projects will be. With those lower costs, more projects will be profitable. Hence this person is likely to do even more projects.

Being inefficient is possibly an unconscious defensive strategy some people employ to reduce the volume of work coming at them. Strangely, being inefficient gets reinforced by having less work to do. The side effect, however, is it sabotages your success.

There is one way that becoming more efficient will reduce over-burden. How? Eliminate unnecessary urgent tasks. I covered this topic in my last book, *The Healthy Mind Toolkit*, so I'll only recap it here. Briefly, use strategies like batching and redundancy. For example, get a spare key. If you lose your key, looking for it doesn't become an urgent problem. Keep extra supplies on hand so you don't need to run to the store for a single item, like you need a single bubble mailer that day. You can also reduce your unimportant tasks by empowering others to decide rather than coming to you for input. Apply this principle broadly, say, to your spouse and kids. If you're a parent, you can invest in helping your children learn to play independently.[2]

Urgent tasks are a threat to maintaining your good habits and routines. The less you must deal with relatively unimportant yet urgent tasks, the more you can devote yourself to deep work. You can establish routines that become automatic, without fear of your habits being disrupted.

Reducing your urgent tasks through being well organized and empowering others creates a positive spiral. The fewer urgent tasks you have, the less time you'll spend in chaos. The less chaotic your life is, the more energetic and clearheaded you'll be. You'll have the energy to become even more well organized.

All that said, the most critical solution to becoming less over-whelmed is to adopt better (practical and emotional) strategies for handling challenging tasks. You'll learn those throughout this book, including in our next chapter.

Myth 2. Speed Is Always Important

Do you believe it would be ideal if you could do everything faster? If yes, that's pointless pressure.

What you do will have a far greater impact on your productivity than how fast you work. The direction you are rowing will determine where you will end up more than how frenetically you paddle.

When work is especially meaningful, speed rarely matters much. Even doubling the time you take to complete a task might not matter in the grand scheme of things. If the work you're doing is important enough, it often doesn't matter if you complete it in two hours or four hours, or in six months or twelve months. Sure, sometimes it might. Speed matters if you're an athlete and half a second is the difference between first and last. Speed matters if you're rushing to create a gene therapy for a deadly disease.

Most of the time, what matters is whether you do something, rather than how fast you do it. Sometimes people think speed matters because of first-mover advantage—the idea that people who speed toward a discovery first (or get a product to market first) will succeed the most. However, first-mover advantage is overestimated.[3] Getting there second often doesn't mean you'll have less success.

As a general rule, speed will matter more for moderately productive activities than for highly productive projects. If a house flip is going to make $15,000 profit, it becomes much more important to complete the job quickly. If it's going to make you $100,000, this matters a lot less. Working more slowly increases costs, but that'll matter less for highly productive or intensely meaningful activities.

Deadlines can be useful if they help create boundaries for how long you spend on a task, ensuring that you don't overcomplicate it. They can create useful pressure. However, when you have a mix of tasks with short and long deadlines, this wreaks havoc on the way you prioritize. We'll address all this in chapter 7.

Doing some things faster will free up some time, but you shouldn't automatically assume you need to do everything fast. There are plenty of examples of people who've done remarkable work at a leisurely pace, like Susan Cain's spending seven years to write her national bestseller, *Quiet*.[4]

Don't let self-imposed pressure to work quickly deflect you from doing innovative or far-reaching work if you're only capable of doing it slowly and inefficiently.

Myth 3. Goofing Off Is the Biggest Enemy of Productivity

For most people, the number one enemy of meaningful work is not goofing off. It's expending all your energy doing moderately productive work.

When we're goofing off, we're aware of being off-task. On the other hand, marginal and moderately productive work provides a psychological crutch. It helps us maintain a comfortable yet false sense we're achieving, but with an enormous opportunity cost. It's robbing you of opportunities to do more impactful work.

If you're doing only moderately productive work, you'll need to do vast amounts of it to achieve success. Under this pressure, you won't have mental space and free time for mind-wandering and decompression, and without this, it's much harder to conceive and design impactful projects. It becomes a negative feedback loop.

Part 3 of this book has many tips for how to make your work more impactful.

Summing up: It's useful to recognize the ways efficiency can and can't help you. By taking a realistic view, you won't be disappointed if becoming more efficient doesn't make a dent in how busy you are. Or if becoming faster at moderately productive tasks doesn't on its own make your work impactful. You can become more successful by approaching tasks systematically, but your goal doesn't need to be to do everything fast or be on-task all the time.

Finally, don't be too hard on yourself about having inefficient processes in your life. The truth is that there's a yin and yang cycle to life in which people alternate between simplifying and complicating.

Imagine you simplify your life by living in a small apartment that is within walking distance to work. However, you then complicate it by having a baby, which means you have to move because you need more space.

Or you embrace minimalism and cut down on possessions but then take on a large DIY project you need many tools for.

Try accepting that alternating between simplifying and complicating is part of life. Imagine how boring a too-simplified life would be! Accepting this aspect of human nature will lower your frustration with your inefficiencies. Surprisingly, this can make you more open to working on them (because doing so stirs fewer unpleasant emotions).

In the upcoming chapters of part 2, we'll cover creating effective, repeatable processes that work even for new-to-you tasks. We'll tackle prioritizing, procrastination, and psychological resistance to changing your behavior.

CHAPTER 6

Create Effective Processes You Can Repeatedly Exploit

To recap, for all these quizzes, scoring mostly As and Bs means you can probably skim the chapter. If you score mostly Cs and Ds, read in more detail. Choose the best answer. If no answer is a perfect fit, choose the closest.

Quiz

1. How often do you come away from a task wishing you'd approached it more systematically?

   (A) Rarely. I have good procedures.

   (B) Occasionally.

   (C) Sometimes.

   (D) Often. Other people around me wish I would do this too!

2. Do you have repeatable formulas for success that work well for you?

    (A) Yes, I have a niche, and systems to exploit my capacity to crush it.

    (B) I do, but I could define my niche or formulas for success better.

    (C) I have systems for minor tasks, but I wouldn't say I have a formula for my success.

    (D) If I do, I'm not aware of it.

3. Do you consider more than one approach before starting an unfamiliar task?

    (A) Always. I pause before starting and consider different ways I could approach it.

    (B) Sometimes.

    (C) Rarely.

    (D) Never.

4. Do you resent unfamiliar tasks because you find them stressful?

    (A) No, I have excellent strategies for how I approach unfamiliar tasks.

    (B) A little, but I muddle through those tasks. I stumble on strategies through trial and error.

(C) I find new tasks stressful, but I don't excessively put them off.

(D) Yes. I avoid any task if I don't have an existing system for how to do it.

5. When you create a new system, do you automatically think about how you could reuse elements of that system for other tasks?

(A) Yes.

(B) Sometimes.

(C) Rarely.

(D) No, I only think about my systems on a superficial level. I don't think about the principles that might transfer across different tasks.

This chapter will guide you about how you can create reusable processes. A small portion relates to money and passive income. Having reusable processes that improve your finances is one of the main ways you can free yourself up to be your most productive. While this isn't a book about strategies to create passive income, relieving yourself of money stress is important for thinking big picture. When you have money stress, it creates a lot of urgency and inefficiency.

We'll then switch our focus. I'll help you learn to recognize when you've stumbled on winning reusable strategies for approaching projects efficiently that you can use in other contexts and projects. Lastly, we'll dive into how you can create a reusable system for approaching new-to-you tasks.

Money Stress

If you lack spare money, it's tough to feel any breathing space. Around six out of ten adults report that money and work are significant sources of stress.[1]

If you're juggling finances, it creates extra work to manage your life. Imagine people who have enough cushion to put all their bills on autopay without worrying if they can cover it. This person employs a reusable process (automatic payments) to ease stress. Contrast this with others who need to juggle their bills ad hoc, so their bank balance doesn't dip into the negative. Lacking the reserves to autopay your bills, buy in bulk, and so forth results in having urgent tasks more often. As previously mentioned, it's easier to do serious work when you're not burdened with never-ending urgent and short-deadline tasks.

Money angst isn't merely personal stress, it's also interpersonal. Lack of shared money goals and values can create relationship fault lines. And not only that—schisms and lack of trust about money undermine your capacity to use your relationship as a secure base for your growth.

Emotions and Beliefs About Money

Money is an emotional minefield. People harbor strong feelings about it. Some folks endure shame and regret about money mistakes they've made. Some people worship money. Other people associate money with greed and injustice and have a general distaste for it.

It can feel invalidating when financial gurus or self-help writers give practical solutions for emotional topics. There's nothing written here on passive income that will make you a better person than you are now. Great artists from history who were broke were still great artists. This section is merely about smoothing your path and removing the stress of money.

People who've made money are often beneficiaries of the halo effect.[2] Everything about them is viewed more positively because they've succeeded in that way. If you've cracked the passive income code, you'll get credited with an especially giant, glowing halo. The halo effect can make these folks seem more different from you than they are. You might feel inadequate or lacking if you haven't made those same achievements.

Money talk affects people differently. Let's say a bunch of folks all read an article about the one percent. Some folks light up with excitement over that. They don't think of the problematic aspects of it. Their brain flashes "goals."

For others, reading about the one percent stirs thoughts about systemic injustice and broken systems. When people associate accruing money with injustice, practical tips about starting passive income streams are inadequate. Since people's negative beliefs about money aren't baseless, it's critical to acknowledge that.

EXPERIMENT

Try reading this vignette. Reflect on how you react to it emotionally. There isn't a right answer, but it should help you understand your emotions about money and your money beliefs. If you're middle class, you might've grown up in one of two types of families. And/or these families might reflect your current situation.

Two families are neighbors on the same street. Both own their homes. For one family, the Smiths, their home and cars are about all they own. They've made modest contributions to their workplace retirement funds, but they're burdened with various forms of debt. They owe money on their mortgage, car payments, credit cards, and student loans.

Our other family, the Carters, might have similar incomes, but they're the millionaires next door. They're not servicing debt. They've got investments. They've made slightly different choices than the Smiths, but ended up in a dramatically different position.

The Carters got a head start. Unlike the Smiths, they graduated from college without crushing debt because they got scholarships by working as golf caddies. Through their respective parents, they'd heard about this quirky opportunity from people who had done it themselves.

Subtle differences in decision-making, habits, and opportunities drive gaping differences in trajectories over time. Some differences in decision-making are related to privilege. Not everyone has family connections that lead them to hear about unusual scholarships.

People with money trauma, like those with overwhelming student loans or a family history of money problems, can develop complex money beliefs. The Smiths, the family with less money, subtly avoid accumulating money. In some ways they see it as a source of evil and believe accumulating more than you need in your lifetime is greedy. Another family in a similar position might equate money with status and spend above their means to convey that status. The Carters, our millionaires next door, are less likely to harbor either of these beliefs.[3]

Rewrite Your Money Beliefs

Before you can jump into practical strategies for improving your finances, you may need to tweak your psychology first. If you've heard plenty of money tips before and not acted on any of them, your core beliefs about money might be the reason.

Almost everyone reading this will have emotional baggage related to money. Virtually no one is immune.

EXPERIMENT

Think about how you'd like to rewrite your money beliefs. What would you like your money attitude to be? How can you adopt a money attitude that serves you but also acknowledges any complicated feelings you have about the topic, such as those related to injustice?

Your approach to money doesn't need to mirror any culturally pre-scribed notion, but it needs to work for you and sit well with your values.

Give Yourself Some Psychological Breathing Space by Automating Earning Income

You might think that automating income is only for entrepreneurs, but it's not. You can do income automation even if you're in a salaried job and don't have an itch to run a business. Here's a simple example.

Every year, my bank deposits $240 of free money into my checking account. Why? My spouse and I each hold a credit card that works like this: If you pay the statement in full each month, you get $30 per quarter. The math is: $30 per quarter × 4 quarters × 2 people = $240. You don't get the quarterly rewards if you don't pay your statement entirely or don't make any purchases.

This is a small but sweet amount of money. It certainly wouldn't be worth the mental effort to remember to make a small purchase every month. Instead, I trigger the bonus automatically by using the cards to pay a recurring $5 monthly charge. Every year, my spouse and I get $120 of free stuff ($5 × 12 months × 2 people), and an additional $120 of cash for holding these cards. Sure, this example is incredibly minor. But we've had these cards for years, and I've automated our system. Unimpressive but simple. If passive income isn't something you've ever succeeded with, this is the type of place you can start. Over the years, I've accumulated many mini-systems like this.

Even if you don't care about automating income earning at the outset, once you do it, the benefits become self-reinforcing.

Let's stop talking about money and shift gears to other types of reusable systems. If you want more ideas for automating income, see the book's resources page on AliceBoyes.com.

Moving On from Money—The Invest-and-Accrue Approach to Efficiency

How do systems for automating income relate to efficient systems more broadly? They fall under a rubric I call the invest-and-accrue approach to efficiency.

The personality quality most consistently associated with great life outcomes is conscientiousness, possibly because conscientious people take an invest-and-accrue approach to life—they sow seeds that will pay off in the future.[4]

Conscientious people practice future-oriented behaviors, like studying hard and investing in relationships. They experience a wide range of benefits from this approach, within and across domains. For example, learning work skills helps people do their job better. As a result, they get promotions and gain flexibility in their job options. Having a better job might result in better access to healthcare and ultimately better health. Their dependable job might help make them attractive to highly desirable romantic partners, meaning they marry a partner who is also healthier, smarter, and more emotionally stable.

The benefits they experience further encourage them to keep being conscientious. It's a positive feedback loop.

Developing efficient systems is similar. The more you do it, the more the benefits will spread out and touch many aspects of your life.

Even if your personality is naturally conscientious, you can always further optimize your processes. If you don't think of yourself as naturally conscientious, the fact that you're this deep into a fairly demanding self-help book about productivity suggests you're being too harsh on yourself. It's common for conscientious people to mainly see their flaws and imperfections and not to see themselves as others do.

If you lack conscientiousness in some areas but are diligent in others, the problem is often that perfectionism and anxiety are interfering with your natural conscientiousness. The skills you'll learn through this part of the book will help with this, and if it's a special interest for you, I've also written on this topic extensively for the *Harvard Business Review*. You can find these articles online and I'll include them on the resources page on AliceBoyes.com to make that easier.

Psychological Knowledge Won't Help You Unless You Embed It in Systems

Throughout this book, I've made the point that psychological knowledge is critical to our productivity, and much more so than any hacks or time management strategies. Your psychological knowledge includes what you know about managing emotions, planning, making smart decisions, and interacting with other people. To extract the most benefit from your knowledge, you need to entrench it in your systems.[5]

For instance, in some hospitals, they teach staff members to simply reply "thank you" and comply when a coworker reminds them to wash their hands.[6] People tend to respond grumpily to this type of reminder. The system counteracts this by removing the negative emotional impact a question like this may trigger. It helps set the culture and prevents patients from getting unnecessary infections. Systems like these require up-front investment, but then become self-perpetuating when they become the norm.

You can use systems like this for planning, deciding, managing others, and managing yourself. When you design simple systems for managing your thoughts, behavior, and attitudes, over time, they'll become your personal norms. Your internal culture will change. Your new attitudes, approaches, and ways of responding will become permanent and much more automatic.

Take a Broad View of What Systems You Can Improve. Get Creative.

Recently, I was listening to an episode of Gretchen Rubin's podcast, *Happier.*[7] Her listeners shared strategies for refereeing squabbles between their kids about whose preferences would get priority (e.g., about what flavor of ice cream the family would buy or who would get the window seat on a flight). The strategies were simple but ingenious.

- Rotate which child gets their preferences each week.
- Give preference to one child on even number days of the month and the other on odd days.
- Assign a number to each child (e.g., oldest = 1, youngest = 3). When disputes come up, ask a voice assistant to pick a random number between 1 and 3 to determine who gets what they wanted.

For any area of friction or underperformance in your life, you can improve it by creating repeatable systems. The better you get at improving your systems in any area, the better you'll get at it in every area.

Capture Your Winning Systems

If you think that developing a kick-ass system starts with staring at a blank Google Doc, you're making this process too hard. You can do it organically using self-observation instead. This concept links back to the last chapter, when we discussed natural experiments. If you notice times you're more productive or efficient than usual, you can extrapolate what allowed you to be so. This will be personal. For example, if you tie yourself in knots with perfectionism, then you would attempt to notice any times when you were willingly less perfectionist than usual. You'd try to systematically create those conditions on a regular or semi-regular basis so that it's easier for you to periodically drop problematic perfectionism.

Sometimes your observations will be related to your emotions, and sometimes they'll be far more practical. I mentioned in the last chapter that I notice that I do particularly good writing when I'm sad. I'm obviously not going to engineer feeling sadder, but this observation has helped me realize I can use writing as an antidote to sadness (since doing good work perks me up). My observation also encourages me to write from a more vulnerable position more often. This is what I naturally do when I'm sad and is why my writing connects better with people when I'm feeling that way.

A practical example is that I notice that I'm really productive in the few days after returning from a trip. That observation reminds me that breaks that are longer than a weekend help my productivity and encourages me to take these more often without fearing it will hurt my output. I know it will actually help. No amount of reading research about the value of rest has as great an impact as observing this pattern in myself.

Whenever you do anything new, you'll stumble on winning strategies. Don't forget these when a project ends. Spell out what you've discovered and how you could use those strategies for other projects.

Example: My spouse and I recently replaced the drywall in several rooms of our house, by ourselves. Drywall sheets are heavy and cumbersome. At the beginning, we grumbled and swore at each other. By the end of the project, we had a smooth system.

At a specific level, our strategies related to hanging drywall. At a conceptual level, the strategies we discovered related to how we:

- can work together without getting angry (or at least recover quickly when we do).

- fitted a DIY project into our day without ignoring our five-year-old.
- avoided losing steam and motivation.
- handled missteps.
- learned how to do it and found the necessary resources.

Another simple example—you thank someone for their feedback and explain to them why it was so helpful to you. You observe that this results in them offering you more opportunities (or more help). You could then make this a routine you do whenever someone gives you feedback, thus creating a system.

EXPERIMENT

The next time you take on a tricky task, codify how the strategies you used could help you in other projects.

The more you think conceptually, rather than about the specifics of the project, the more you'll find successful strategies that will work across diverse new situations.

Make sure you think about what you learned about managing your thoughts and feelings and other people's personalities, and about navigating unfamiliar problems.

To get you started, here are two specific strategies that will improve virtually any system.

Get Your Tools and Materials Ready Before You Start

Imagine this scenario: You're starting a DIY project at your home on a weekend. Come Saturday morning, you realize you've run out of something you need or you can't find your tape measure. You're delayed in starting the job by an hour while you schlep, irritated and frustrated, to a store.

In contrast, if you get everything set up before Saturday, you'll become aware of anything you've forgotten. Get your ladder set up, your extension cords out, and so forth before Saturday. For anything you can't physically set up, visualize the steps you will do. Imagine yourself doing each action. You'll get a flash of insight about anything you've overlooked. It'll save tension and many unnecessary hiccups. To make visualizing more manageable, you can visualize in more detail for your first steps and in less detail for later steps.

This principle of setting up your tools and materials before you start applies to many processes, like mise en place in cooking. Everyone has an instinct to take this approach for some tasks, but you forget to use it in other situations. You'll be less likely to forget if you think of this as a universal strategy.

I like to take this strategy a step further. For any project, I typically do the first small step the day before I'll start the bulk of the work. For our drywall project, we planned to start on a Saturday, but we hung one sheet on Friday night. This helped us develop a more realistic plan for Saturday. Emotionally, it also got us over the hump of starting.

Consider a Second Option

This insanely useful, universal efficiency strategy is also one of the simplest. People make better decisions when they consider a second option.[8] You can use this principle to save you from work you don't need to do. How? Before impulsively starting anything, consider more than one approach you could take.

I still sometimes fail at this. Recently, some code I was using stopped working. I was using the code to access an API, but the company changed their API. I'd originally found the code on a blog. When the code ceased to function, I started googling, trying to figure out how to modify it myself. An hour later . . . I was still messing around. It then occurred to me to email the blogger to ask if he had an updated version. I should have paused and considered at least one additional approach before I spent an hour on it. I might've considered that option earlier.

I like to go one step further and apply this principle by using the rule of three. To do this, define three different ways you could approach a task before impulsively starting down a track.

Another way I use this strategy is that when I'm frustrated with how a project is going, I will revisit alternative options for how I could approach the project. Mentally, I go back to the drawing board and reconsider my full range of options.

Often, once we start down one particular route, we close ourselves off to other options. Having chosen one route initially, we become mentally committed to that route. We get myopic and cannot see that choosing another approach is still an option. Some options you initially ruled out might be more attractive when you give them a second look. Having tried one route, you possess more data and experience through which to evaluate all your potential options.

EXPERIMENT 1

When would it be useful to consider more than one approach before you start? How could this save you extra work? Think broadly.

EXPERIMENT 2

These aren't the only efficiency strategies that work across diverse tasks. Think of a principle of efficiency that you like, such as eliminating work before you optimize how you do that work. Brainstorm three different manifestations of the principle. Here's an example. Cull unused household items before organizing your cupboards. If you've thrown an item out, you no longer need to figure out where to put it.

This experiment will help you think abstractly and transfer your psychological knowledge from one domain to another. If you start with a principle you already like, you won't need any encouragement to buy into it because you already understand and like it.

Create a Niche by Reusing Your Successful Systems

Consider any TV series you love. The show isn't completely reinvented with each episode. The creators reuse successful processes and follow a formula for creating each new piece of work.

One reason to reuse systems is that people like familiarity. If a system has familiar elements, other people involved will feel more comfortable with it. This has an evolutionary basis. Familiarity allows us to put our guard down.

Reusing your winning systems will establish your niche, the specific focus of your work. In real estate investing, it's common to have a niche and a formula. For example, your formula might be "I buy properties between $X and $X, spend between $X and $X rehabbing them, and then they appraise for $X to $X."

Creating a niche can help you feel less flooded by too many opportunities or too much choice. A narrowed focus can also help you see opportunities to remix work you've created or processes you used for creating it to produce new work. Your niche could be as simple as a skill that many colleagues come to you for help with, automating networking for you.

I'm not suggesting you restrict yourself to a niche. Establishing effective, repeatable processes within a niche can give you more freedom to explore outside that niche. We'll discuss this later in the book when we work on enhancing your creativity.

EXPERIMENT

What brilliant systems could you reuse to create new work? How might doing so help you create a niche?

Optimize the Parts of a System That Matter Most

It would be easy to feel overloaded if you tried to optimize every aspect of a system. Think about what elements of the system matter most. What most hurts your efficiency?

If you're disorganized with a DIY project and need to make extra trips to the home improvement store for materials, that's incredibly inefficient. Each of those trips takes an hour. Or if a piece of essential equipment on your production line breaks, your capacity might be dramatically reduced until you can repair it. Target the inefficiencies that matter the most first. Likewise, target the parts of a system where improvement would be most beneficial. It's much more impactful for me to labor over the title of an article than over the twenty-third sentence.

EXPERIMENT

Pick a recurring task you do. Have you optimized the most influential elements, like your call to action, first impressions, and so forth? Do this. Approach this from the perspective of systems and processes you can create and reuse.

Even if you don't think of your work as having these elements, it does. For example, teachers and doctors ask students and patients to do things; thus a concept like a call to action is still relevant in those fields. When a doctor asks a patient to take a medication, that's a call to action. When a teacher asks students to contribute to a class discussion, that's a call to action.

Use Data to Make Your Work More Impactful

My blog articles for *Psychology Today* follow the 80/20 rule almost exactly. About 60 of my 300 articles contribute 80 percent of the reads. Typically, those articles appear prominently in Google results for commonly searched phrases like "how to help someone with anxiety."

Other articles with fewer views overall attract disproportionate attention from journalists looking for comments on stories. I pay attention to which articles work for that purpose too.

I also like to look at Google Trends data to see how the popularity of certain topics is evolving. Interest in topics like anxiety and self-care is growing, whereas interest in other topics is stagnant or declining. I assess the Venn diagram between what's popular and what I've got helpful, uncommon things to say about.

You too can use data to better understand which aspect of your work is the most influential.

- You're a teacher. You count how many children contribute to each class discussion and use that information to gauge which of your lesson styles your students find most engaging.
- You're an accountant who works with nomadic entrepreneurs. You look at the returns of the 20 percent of your clients who pay the lowest taxes to see how similar strategies might help the other 80 percent of your clients.
- You're a business coach. You identify the 20 percent of your clients who grow their businesses the most while working with you. You survey how they implement your strategies and what additional strategies they employ, and use this information to influence your work with all your clients.

Experiment: How can you use data to work more efficiently? What can data tell you about what to focus on the most?

Efficient Processes for Approaching Novel Tasks

The last section of this chapter is about how to be efficient in approaching a task that's new to you.

People think of efficiency as being about optimizing their recurring tasks. However, often the to-dos that most intimidate us (and trigger procrastination) are those we haven't done before or don't do regularly. To help with this, develop a system for unfamiliar tasks.

Recently my pool pump failed. Buying a pump was a new-to-me task and out of my wheelhouse. I'll use this example to illustrate the system I use.

1. Try a Premortem

A premortem is when you project yourself into the future. Imagine you completed a task and it went badly. Come up with hypothetical reasons it went wrong.

There were three things I worried about going wrong when buying a pump: (1) getting grossly overcharged; (2) the pump not being powerful enough to run a pool cleaner; and (3) the new pump breaking down after a short time but being denied warranty coverage.

My premortem helped me identify what questions I needed to ask. You can use this premortem strategy for any task. It's most useful for unfamiliar or high-stakes assignments.

2. Consider More Than One Approach

As discussed earlier, consider more than one approach before you start. The possible tacks I identified were (1) call pool pump installers, (2) call a company that sells but doesn't install pumps, and (3) do research online.

Doing your premortem first will help you evaluate the options you come up with.

3. Find Quick Ways to Test Your Assumptions

I suspected that buying the pump myself and having it installed would be much cheaper than buying it from an installer. It turned out I was correct. I looked up the most popular variable speed pump on Amazon. Next, I called one company and asked the cost to buy that pump from them and have it installed. They said it would be about $1,400, whereas install only would be $250. The cost of the pump on Amazon was only $700. It would've cost me an extra $450 to buy it from them. This validated my assumption that buying from an installer would mean buying at an inflated price.

4. Decide How Much Effort to Go To

Near the start of your task, estimate how much time you should reasonably devote to it. I was willing to spend up to 45 minutes researching and making calls for each $100 that I saved. Up front, I had guesstimated that doing my own research would save about $400, which turned out to be bang on. According to this calculation, I should cap the entire process at 3 hours.

5. Cut Down on Research

If I could buy from a local company at a similar price to online, I would. Knowing the online price for one particular model of pump helped me find a local supplier with good prices.

The manufacturer's website for that pump had a list of local authorized dealers. I found one that sold the pump for only $25 more than the online price. From that, I guessed that prices for all their pumps would be similar to online prices. I called and asked their opinion of that pump. They had encountered problems with people trying to run pool cleaners with it and recommended another one. The one they recommended was $400 more but twice as powerful. I also asked them to recommend an installer who would install pumps purchased from them.

6. Enhance the Reliability of the Information You're Getting

I'm always skeptical of being upsold. My approach to this is to triangulate information. If three people tell me the same thing, I will go with it. Here, I decided that if the installer also recommended the more expensive one as necessary, I would go with it. The installer wasn't 100 percent sure, but he called his supervisor, who said he thought the cheaper one was a "heap of junk." I had my decision.

7. Check for Any Remaining Gotchas Related to Your Premortem

Early in my research process, I googled around for gotchas related to companies not honoring warranties and found many. Although I'm capable of self-installing a pump, that would void the warranty. And if I didn't pay for professional calibration, I wouldn't get a $220 rebate from my energy company. So installing the pump myself wasn't a great option.

To give myself an extra year of warranty, I checked my credit cards that offered extended warranty protection to see which would cover a pool pump.

Choosing the pump took about 90 minutes. I felt fairly satisfied I'd done my best to avoid the potential failures my premortem had turned up.

8. Move on Quickly from Strategies That Don't Work

Here I glossed over strategies I tried that didn't work. For example, I tried checking the tech specs for the pool floor cleaner to see what pump I needed to run it. That info wasn't in those specs.

EXPERIMENT

Try these strategies yourself. Bring to mind an unfamiliar task you anticipate needing to do in the next year. Pick something that's at least a moderately big decision. Strategize about how each of the principles mentioned in this section would apply to solving that problem.

You don't need to adopt my system. The point is to create a general system for approaching unfamiliar tasks. That way decision fatigue about how to start will not lead to procrastination. Following your system will become a habit.

You may find a creative way to simplify my system. Or your system might diverge completely from mine, since your personality is different. My system is slanted toward avoiding mistakes because that's my personality.

As we close out this chapter, a reminder: The strategies in this chapter won't make life less busy. Achieving that requires a more deliberate choice to forgo some opportunities to make way for unassigned time. Without that separate decision, any space you make by becoming more efficient and organized will only get filled by more doing.

Your Takeaways

1. What broken process in your life most needs attention?
2. What are the obstacles you face in fixing it? How could you overcome those?

CHAPTER 7

Prioritizing—The Hidden Psychology That Drives Your Decision-Making

To recap, for all these quizzes, scoring mostly As and Bs means you can probably skim the chapter. If you score mostly Cs and Ds, read in more detail. Choose the best answer. If no answer is a perfect fit, choose the closest.

Quiz

1. Do you diligently beaver away on moderately productive tasks but leave projects with much more potential on the back burner?

    (A) No. I frequently do work that has the potential to change the trajectory of my success.

    (B) Sometimes, but I branch out to do challenging work.

    (C) I dream about getting to my long-term projects but rarely do.

    (D) My workweek consists only of moderately productive work.

2. To what extent do time-driven but unimportant tasks make up your workday?

> (A) I've structured my working life so I have few unimportant tasks with short deadlines.

> (B) About a quarter of what I do in the day feels urgent but not important.

> (C) Over half of what I do in the day feels urgent but not important.

> (D) My days are filled with tasks of low importance that require timely attention.

3. How aware are you of how you prioritize your tasks on a day-to-day basis?

> (A) I have strong habits that eliminate most thinking about prioritizing. I've already done the work of prioritizing and entrenched those values in my habits.

> (B) I have systems that ensure I do a sizable chunk of impactful work, but low priority tasks also creep into my workday.

> (C) Prioritizing feels like a constant juggling act.

> (D) I just do what comes at me.

4. Do you overcomplicate tasks that have long or no deadlines?

    (A) No, I'm good at keeping unstructured tasks from becoming unwieldy.

    (B) This happens occasionally.

    (C) My perfectionism comes out when I have a task with no or a long deadline.

    (D) Yes. I get overwhelmed about where to start when a task has no or a long deadline.

5. Do you put off tasks until they become urgent?

    (A) No. Every week I do proactive maintenance or other important tasks that don't have deadlines.

    (B) This happens only a few times a year.

    (C) In domains in which I lack confidence, I ignore looming problems (e.g., my air conditioner making an odd noise). When these become urgent (e.g., it breaks), they end up being more disruptive than they needed to be.

    (D) How did you know? I do this with minor and major tasks.

This chapter is about prioritizing. It's not about how to eliminate your need for downtime. It's also not about time Tetris—how you can squeeze in a productive task in the fifteen minutes you have between finishing a phone call and the start of a meeting.

Those aren't pleasant or effective ways to approach the goal of using your time productively. If you try to do everything fast and avoid any wasted time, you'll be distracted. If you have everything tightly scheduled, you'll feel intense time pressure. You'll often think about the next project when you're trying to concentrate on the current one. That's not conducive to focus.

Instead, this chapter will help you understand why people often do something with moderate value over something with much higher potential impact. As previously discussed, using your peak focused time for moderately productive activities is often more of a productivity problem than wasting time. Doing moderately productive activities will cause you to stay on the trajectory you're on now—not accelerate or change your trajectory.

By the end of the chapter, you'll understand how to prioritize more impactful work. You'll learn what your biases are when you're prioritizing. You'll learn how you can overcome these using metacognition, which is your knowledge of how you think.

Our Hidden Decision-Making Rules

People have unconscious rules for how they prioritize. A common one is "disappoint or anger the fewest people." Imagine that in one workday, ten people each make one request of you. At home, your spouse wants you to do ten things. You end up doing none of what your spouse wants because you've used up all your energy to placate your ten colleagues. Unconscious rules can cause you to be least responsive to those you love the most. The same pattern can occur if your implicit rule is "disappoint the people most likely to forgive me first."

When you articulate your unconscious decision-making rules, you can look for unintended consequences.

EXPERIMENT

What's an important item on your to-do list that you struggle to get around to? How might unconscious rules for prioritizing be undermining that? If your rule is "I'll focus on the big picture after I've done everything else on my to-do list," you'll never do it!

How Deadlines Affect the Way We Prioritize

Humans are like moths to a flame when they have tasks with short deadlines. It's logical that we might prefer tasks with short deadlines if those are easier. However, research has shown that people will choose a task with a shorter deadline over one with a longer due date, even if the one with a longer time frame is just as easy and has more payoff.

The deadline for a task influences our perception of it. When a task has a longer deadline, we perceive it as more difficult. This is termed the *mere deadline effect*.[1] Even when everything else about the task is the same, people commit more resources to tasks with longer deadlines. Long deadlines put us at risk of overcomplicating tasks, procrastinating, or bailing. The take-home message here isn't to shorten deadlines. It's asking yourself or your team "How can I/we simplify this task?" when you have a long deadline.

You may notice you also have the same problem of overcomplicating tasks that don't have deadlines at all.

Why We Prefer Short Deadlines

I've argued that people are far more likely to contribute to the world if they commit to demanding long-term projects that require building tremendous skills over time. On the other hand, there are a bunch of reasons that gravitating toward short deadlines makes some psychological sense. By understanding these, you can achieve the best balance.

Sometimes a bird in the hand is better than a bird in the bush. Because of compounding, rewards we accrue now are often worth more than the same rewards in the future. Let's say I interrupt my day to handle a media request. Publicity leads to increased publicity. It's more valuable for me to lock in those benefits now than to get the same benefit in a month. Or let's say your boss's recognition will lead to your moving up within your company. Showing your talent on a quick project might lead to your being put on a team that's highly innovative or creative. That will further accelerate your success. Accruing your boss's recognition as a standout performer earlier rather than later has benefits.

Furthermore, tasks can be dependent upon one another. Failing to complete a task now can result in missing out down the line. If a reporter contacts me and I don't reply promptly, they're unlikely to reach out again. Working on a long-term project with uncertain payoffs can also be risky. If you work on a start-up or write a spec script for a TV pilot, there's risk to that. And sometimes we miss out on opportunities for early feedback when we devote our attention to longer projects.

Understanding these benefits can help you figure out which short-deadline tasks are worth doing.

EXPERIMENT

How can you ensure your short-duration tasks accrue a long-term benefit? Ask yourself: Will doing this short-duration task:

- attain recognition that will lead to compounding benefits?
- result in early feedback that will help me improve a skill?
- help strengthen a relationship?
- result in any other ongoing benefits? For example, if you call your internet company to negotiate your rate, then you'll have a lower rate from now on.

Furthermore, ask yourself if this task has any true urgency, such as if you're a doctor who needs to review patient test results in a timely fashion.

If a short-duration task doesn't check any of these boxes, then maintaining focus on your long-term projects makes the most sense. At minimum, you can enhance a short-term assignment so that it will provide a long-term benefit.

Metacognition—A Defining Feature of Humanness

Although humans have biases and flaws in our thinking, we're also equipped with metacognition. This is a big word for a simple concept. It means we can think about our thinking. You can use metacognition to overcome your automatic biases, including with prioritizing. Thinking flaws matter a lot less if you have systems for negating them.

Here are some examples of people thinking about their thinking.

- You know you're a worrier. You know you worry about things that don't happen. Therefore when you worry, you discount that. You might think, "My new colleague Daphne didn't chat with me while we were waiting for our meeting to start this morning. That made me worried she doesn't like me. However, I know I jump to those types of conclusions, so I'll remind myself not to read too much into tiny things without other evidence."
- You need to make a relatively minor decision but recognize you could easily spend several hours waffling over it, so you decide to limit your time researching and deciding to thirty minutes.
- You're deciding on a purchase. You have lots of wants, but you list your top five criteria to help you narrow down your decision.

- You love yellow, but you know not everyone does, so when you want to change your company branding to yellow, you check out others' reactions to this first.
- You know you react negatively to feedback initially, so you ignore those initial reactions. You give it a day and reread the feedback with fresh eyes, and your reaction is almost always different.

People who are better at reflecting on and regulating their thinking think better. This includes being more creative.[2]

You can turn your metacognition into mini-systems by using heuristics. I'll explain how now.

Use Heuristics to Prioritize

Heuristics are a way you can overcome self-defeating patterns of prioritizing. A heuristic is a quick and easy rule aimed at making sage decisions most of the time.

These are some examples of heuristics that can help with prioritizing. To prevent you from spending too long on a task:

- I won't spend over two hours doing X (where X is one of your recurring tasks).
- I won't include more than five distinct points in a presentation.
- If a reporter sends more than six questions, I'll answer the six I'm most interested in and skip or minimally answer the others.[3]

To counteract perfectionism:

- If I get the urge to take a perfectionist approach to a task, I'll ignore it in 7 out of 10 cases and give into it in 3 out of 10. (You don't monitor this; you just use it as a ballpark.)

To focus on the big picture and not be nitpicky:

- If I want to push back on changes an editor has made to an article, I'll usually limit it to two to four points.

To prioritize the most important people:

- If my spouse asks me to do something simple and it's not during a deep work session, I'll do it straightaway.
- If my child signals she needs my attention, I'll give it to her willingly, even if this interrupts my deep work session. During deep work sessions, I'll give her brief attention and get back to work.

To help stay focused during deep work:

- During deep work sessions, I will ignore everything except my child, including the two-minute rule. (This is the rule that if something will take less than two minutes, do it straightaway.)[4] If something I need to do pops into my mind, I will ignore it and risk forgetting about it so as not to interrupt my focus.

To counteract a tendency to overcomplicate tasks with long deadlines:

- Before starting a task with a long deadline, I will ask myself: (1) "How would I do this if I had only a week to finish it?" (2) "How can I get this project done to an acceptable standard in half the time?" (I like to leave the other half of the time for improving it, or as slack for parts that take longer than expected.)

As you will have noticed, developing heuristics requires self-knowledge. Your heuristics should be directly linked to your observations about what self-sabotaging patterns you need to overcome.

Experiment

What is a heuristic that would help you prioritize better? Start with one. Add others once that one feels established. I've got lots of heuristics now, but I've evolved them over years, not months.

Don't overthink your heuristics initially. Expect to tweak, discard, or revise them after you've tried them in the real world.

Prioritizing Involves Tolerating Regret, Anxiety, Guilt, and Other Powerful Emotions

To prioritize well, you need to acknowledge the emotions that come up in doing so. I gave the example of how I limit how much I push back on editors' changes to only a few points. Occasionally an article goes to press with a statement an editor added that I don't ultimately feel comfortable with. I regret not challenging it. Prioritizing inevitably involves tolerating difficult emotions. Then again, so does *not* prioritizing well and experiencing the emotional fallout of not having accomplished anything.

Experiment

If you are going to prioritize effectively, what emotions are you going to need to tolerate? How will you do that? What will you do with bubbling guilt or other emotions? My general approach is to let the emotions recede on their own. A good approach is often to acknowledge an emotion and simply allow it to exist, without either fueling or pushing it away. When you do this, emotions will only bubble up without bubbling over.

You might prefer another approach like meditation, or learning other techniques derived from psychological therapies, like cognitive behavioral therapy or acceptance and commitment therapy, to help train up your capacity to let thoughts and emotions go.[5]

Having sufficient downtime can also help with prioritizing. It gives you a buffer to process any difficult emotions that arise. That way, those emotions don't result in doing tasks of lesser importance to go easier on yourself.

Career-Specific B.S. Ways You Prioritize

We've addressed how humans generally prioritize. The norms within your field of work and social circles will also influence you.

Every career has certain norms for how to measure success and productivity. For example, a scientist's success is customarily measured by how many papers they publish and how often those are cited by other scientists. However, someone can do well on those metrics but still not have much effect on people's lives or the history of their field.

Sometimes people do work that is too obvious or too obscure to matter much.[6] Or they get drawn into trendy but crowded areas within their field. Working in an unpopular area might offer more opportunities to be innovative. This is especially true if your world view or experiences give you a unique perspective in that area.

EXPERIMENT

Consider these questions: How are productivity and success defined in your field? What are some alternatives to that? In what ways do you need to step back from those conventions? Think independently about what to prioritize to maximize your impact.

Consider how acting the role of a productive [insert your career] and being productive might differ.

Use Estimation to Judge Potential Impact and Prioritize Your Activities

Let's revisit estimation—a tool we already discussed back in chapter 3. Estimation can help you prioritize.

Simple estimation can help you decide between alternatives. When I was a clinical psychologist, I would spend an hour with each client. I loved that work and sometimes miss it, but it's hard to ignore how much greater an impact I have through writing.

Let's say I spend three hours writing a blog post. Imagine 30,000 or 300,000 people read the article. If only 1 percent of these readers are helped by it (absolutely not what I'm aiming for!), then that's still 300 or 3,000 people. I'd need many lifetimes of clinical practice to have an impact that's similar to what I achieve through writing. How can you estimate the impact of your work?

Should You Exploit a Successful System or Explore New Frontiers?

Prioritizing often involves a choice of whether to exploit a successful system you've already mastered or to explore new frontiers. This is not a simple issue.

In some respects, you are probably not exploiting your successful systems as much as you could be (as discussed in the last chapter). In other respects, you're likely not exploring new frontiers enough.

People often do what's familiar and comfortable over what could have a greater impact but feels scarier. Doing more of the same feels productive but isn't satisfying. Imagine if Beyoncé kept pumping out songs similar to "Single Ladies." That might've been efficient but also stifling, and the world would've missed out on *Lemonade.*

What do you do that's productive, but not as productive as it could be? Do you repeat similar projects or work in the same way or with the same people? What aspects of your work feel like a production line?

I gravitate toward writing more articles for the same outlets rather than reaching out to new ones. When I write for the same outlets, I know the drill and expectations. It's faster. It's less mentally exhausting. I can write more.

Creativity research has shown that the volume of work people produce can predict whether they will do great work.[7] Therefore, there are some benefits to this approach. There are also downsides. By repeatedly writing for the same outlets, I reach the same readers and grow less, and my network remains small. Getting input from editors and adapting to the new styles required by different outlets causes me to grow more as a writer.

Experiment

When do you choose familiar, moderately productive behaviors over less familiar but more impactful behaviors?

But How Will I Fit in My Short-Deadline Tasks?

There's an elephant in the room when people talk about doing the important over the urgent. What about all those minor tasks that either have imminent deadlines or pile up if left unattended to? For many people, keeping your job will depend on getting some moderately productive things done, like a committee you need to be on.

Take a long-game approach to this. Gradually, over time, eliminate as many minor and moderately important tasks as you can. When you can't eliminate them, use strategies like batching tasks to make these disruptions occur less often. For example, pick up medication every ninety days rather than monthly, or have it delivered. And do short-deadline tasks in a way that has long-term value, as previously discussed.

It's possible to take these suggestions too far. People do better mentally when they do a mix of easier and challenging activities. For this reason, incorporate some activities into your day that aren't cognitively demanding. It's not ideal to have only two modes: being fiercely engaged with work or crashed out. This is when an activity like folding your laundry or weeding your garden can help provide some balance to your days. Therefore, keep some activities in your life that give you a mental break from cognitively taxing work, providing your mind with a chance to wander and decompress.

Initially, you might not see a vision of how unimportant, unwanted tasks could become a minor feature of your life. The more you succeed with eliminating or reducing minimally and moderately important tasks, the more you'll learn from those successful systems and can extrapolate from them. The fewer of these tasks you have, the less fragmented your days will be.

What Are Your Existing Systems Optimizing For? Is It What's Ultimately Most Important?

In the book *Algorithms to Live By,* the authors describe what's known as the secretary problem.[8] This problem relates to deciding among applicants for a secretary position. They outline some math that points to the best average strategy. What is it? The first step is a search phase. Evaluate 37 percent of the candidates but commit to choosing none during this phase. Then, after that 37 percent mark, pick any candidate who exceeds all the others so far. In math lingo, this is known as an optimal stopping problem.

The book outlines similar math aimed at making optimal decisions in other circumstances, like whether you should try a new restaurant or keep visiting your existing favorites. Their advice on prioritizing and choosing from alternatives is worth a read. All the examples they give will help you reflect on your systems for making decisions. Regardless of whether you adopt the authors' suggestions, you'll benefit from making your unconscious decision-making processes more conscious. From there, you can devise your own systems.

We often unconsciously optimize for what isn't most important. For instance, you optimize for never making mistakes, never being disappointed, or never expressing a bad idea publicly, rather than for maximum overall positive impact.

Experiment

Answer these questions:
- What do your existing systems optimize for?
- What should you be optimizing for? What would bring you closer to the life and productivity you want for yourself?

Your Takeaways

1. What's the project you're not working on that has the biggest potential to improve your life?
2. What single point about *prioritizing* do you most want to take away from this chapter? How can you translate this insight into a new step in your systems?

CHAPTER 8

Procrastination

To recap, for all these quizzes, scoring mostly As and Bs means you can probably skim the chapter. If you score mostly Cs and Ds, read in more detail. Choose the best answer. If no answer is a perfect fit, choose the closest.

Quiz

1. How's your mental game for overcoming procrastination?

   (A) I know myself well. I know how to navigate what I find difficult.

   (B) I have strategies that work for getting past procrastination, but using them feels like a battle.

   (C) I don't have much of a mental game. I mostly rely on external factors like hard deadlines or other people harassing me.

(D) I'm depressed about how much I procrastinate and it causes conflict with other people, such as teammates or family members.

2. Do you have a gut sense for when procrastination is helpful to you? Do you know when you need to take a longer-than-usual break from a big project to get some perspective or renew your energy?

(A) Yes, I know when I need to take longer breaks to recharge and refresh.

(B) Sort of, but I have a super hard time trusting that I will come back stronger after a longer break.

(C) I've never considered this, but now that you mention it, there are times I resolve stuck points in projects after procrastinating.

(D) No.

3. How many strategies do you have for overcoming procrastination?

(A) Six plus. Different strategies work in different situations.

(B) I have four to six.

(C) I have one to three.

(D) None.

4. How well do you understand the thinking processes that trigger procrastination for you? How skilled are you at adjusting your thoughts?

(A) I know I procrastinate when I make tasks harder in my head than they are in reality. And I procrastinate when I'm resentful about doing a task. I can work successfully through these thoughts and feelings.

(B) I can do this about 50 percent of the time.

(C) I have some insight into this, like I know I have perfectionistic tendencies, but it's a struggle to overcome them.

(D) I don't understand the triggers or have strategies.

5. When a project feels difficult, do you have the urge to put it off?

(A) No. Most of my best work doesn't go smoothly the whole time.

(B) Occasionally, but eventually I will do it without outside prodding.

(C) A lot of the time, but not always.

(D) Yes. I really only want to take on tasks that are guaranteed to go smoothly.

Right Now, You Can Probably Think of at Least a Half-Dozen Tasks You're Putting Off

In this chapter, I'll outline the psychology behind procrastination and then give you lots of specific practical strategies for overcoming it. I'll also elaborate on why not all procrastination is a bad thing.

Procrastination is more complex than people make it out to be.[1] There are several popular explanations for why people procrastinate. One is that the root of the problem is the absence of strong habits. This story goes: If you had strong habits, you wouldn't need self-control and would eliminate some decision fatigue. So you'd eliminate procrastination. A second view of procrastination is that it's an emotional problem.[2] We're intolerant of tasks that trigger boredom, self-doubt, impostor syndrome, social comparison, and so forth, so we put them off.

There's plenty of truth in these explanations, but neither is the full story.

Here's the critical piece people miss when they describe procrastination as an emotional problem. People procrastinate about doing tasks they feel overwhelmed by. This begs the question of what makes someone feel overwhelmed by a task. One criminally overlooked factor is that people lack skills and confidence for planning tasks.[3] You might feel confident when doing a narrow range of work every week. However, when you are faced with a new task, deciding how to approach it feels overwhelming. If this is you, use the strategies you learned in chapter 6 about dealing with unfamiliar tasks. You can apply those strategies to ambitious projects that are outside your wheelhouse, like "If I wanted to run for office, how would I fundraise and campaign?"

Another overlooked factor is that people don't ask themselves how they can channel their difficult emotions into greater focus rather than being distracted by them. Mistakenly, people often think about how they can reduce strong feelings rather than how they can use strong feelings. We've covered that too.

Explanations of procrastination also sometimes miss that there are a bunch of different types of procrastinators.

The stereotypical procrastinator will get an assignment with a deadline, but instead of getting started, they do something fun and distracting.

Procrastination isn't just that stereotypical variety. Often it's fatigue-related. You've been at work all day, and your kids are finally in bed. You know you could work on a plan for addressing your debt, run on your treadmill, or learn a new skill, but you watch a crime procedural instead. That might be the only relaxation time you've had all day. People who can see themselves in this scenario don't have a procrastination problem, they have an overload problem. When you diagnose the problem accurately, you can treat it more effectively.

Procrastination can also be related to being curious and excitable. If you're a curious person with many interests and ideas, you might find it hard to pick only one pathway. You might get caught up in thinking about all the things you would like to do, but you have difficulty settling on one to pursue. You have FOMO. You can't decide if you want to escape the rat race and take up #vanlife or get aggressive about increasing your income so you can live in a $4,000-a-month New York City apartment. Instead of choosing one of these, you keep up the status quo.

Be kind to yourself when you have more things you'd like to do than you have focus for. Curious people are often self-critical about all the dreams they'd like to pursue but have a super hard time getting around to. Observe whether being more accepting of this helps you get to more of the dreams on your list. Recognize that it's understandable to want to choose everything. Having abundant avenues you'd like to pursue is better than the opposite problem—that nothing sounds fun to you. Also, recognize that choosing not to focus or commit to anything isn't a great solution to the problem.

Sometimes people feel like they're procrastinating when they're not. You might spend all day doing things that are personally or professionally important. However, you still don't accomplish a fraction of the things you would like to get to. This can feel like procrastination when it's not. What you label as procrastination might be your overestimating how long it's possible for you to focus intensely in a day. Your "procrastination" problem might actually be having unrealistic expectations of yourself.

Why You Shouldn't Try to Eliminate Procrastination Completely

Like almost all maligned aspects of human behavior, procrastination has its upsides.

If you expect a lot of yourself and you're attempting to do innovative work, you'll hit a wall at times. You'll need to zone out. You'll need to take a few days or even weeks away from your projects at unexpected times. Observe your patterns. I often do fantastic work after taking an unplanned week off. Even when I've felt angst about being unproductive, a break that's longer than a weekend still helps me regain focus and perspective. Sometimes procrastination reflects an unrealistic expectation that you can be innovative and creative or deeply focused with absolute consistency. You can't. You need breaks. You may need more or longer breaks than you think you should need based on your image of how a productive person acts. If you label all these needed breaks as procrastination, it'll lead to self-criticism.

Sometimes the most impactful work we end up doing is when we're supposed to be doing something else! It's when I'm too tired or distracted to write that I get around to browsing studies on a question I've been mulling or reaching out to colleagues I haven't communicated with in a while. These times end up being surprisingly productive.

If you're prone to procrastivity[4] (doing something productive that isn't objectively your highest priority), evaluate whether for you this is a net positive or negative. If you reclean your already clean house, it's a negative. If you do other important tasks you would normally put off or not get around to, it might be a net positive. This is another example of when you can observe what's true for you rather than for the collective. You don't need anyone else to tell you whether procrastivity is positive or negative. For me, it's net positive!

As I mentioned way back in chapter 1, people's creativity often benefits from an incubation period. It's often better to take a short break between when you're presented with a problem and when you try to solve it.

These reframes can help you be more accepting of harmless forms of procrastination and be less self-critical. This attitude shift should have a paradoxical effect. It should help reduce your urge to go on procrastination binges. If you see short stretches of procrastination as warming up into your focused work, it will make it easier for you to snap into focusing before you've procrastinated too long. I've noticed that if I skip my pottering time of checking email and Slack in the mornings, I feel more overloaded at the end of the day. See if that's true for you.

If you have strong habits of doing deep work most days, then you can trust that any craving for downtime is what your brain needs.

Whether you are doing some impactful work is far more important than whether you procrastinate. Optimize for increasing your ultra-high-value behaviors, not for a decrease in "time wasting."

Mental Tricks for Procrastination—Address Your Specific Thinking Patterns

As I said earlier, strong daily habits of doing deep work will go a long way toward reducing procrastination. If you missed it, tips for conditioning yourself to do deep work are included in chapter 5. But most of us will still need strategies to manage our mental game. If you find at least six anti-procrastination strategies that work for you, that should cover most situations. Here are some to try. Pick those that strike you as most relevant.

A good way to know if psychological blocks are contributing to your procrastination is if you quite enjoy (or at least get a sense of satisfaction from) a task once you start working on it.

Use Effective Self-Talk

When I procrastinate, it's often because I want to do an exceptional job of that task and I'm psyching myself out about my capacity to do that. How do I overcome this performance pressure? I remind myself that working on the thing is the best way to do a good job!

I do this in a kind, gentle way, so it's self-compassionate. I say to myself, "I'm anxious about doing a good job and that's making me hesitant. That's a normal and understandable feeling. The best way to do a good job is to plod away. Even if I make missteps, it's still the best way."

Find and then reuse self-talk that works for you. It should address the psychological mechanism of why you're procrastinating, so you'll need to identify what that is. If you're not sure what the mechanism is, the material in the rest of the chapter should help you figure it out.

Don't Aim to Work on the Task All Day

When a task is important or we've already been putting off doing it, we often think we need to do marathon work sessions to nail it or make up for past procrastination and lost time. (This happens a lot when people are depressed and are feeling guilty about lost productivity that was due to their depression.) Attempting to catch up rarely works. Why? The thought of slogging away on a challenging task all day will inevitably trigger more procrastination.

You can try one of two strategies to navigate this: (1) Plan to work on the task you're avoiding for ten minutes today and pick it up again tomorrow. Doing a little today will get you over the emotional hump of starting. Or (2) plan to work on it for ninety minutes today and cap it at that. If you're reasonably conditioned to deep work, it's likely you can get yourself to work on almost anything for ninety minutes. The reasonable goal will make it much easier to start.

You can adapt this principle any way you like to suit yourself. For example, you might prefer a strategy like adding an extra ten minutes each workday to the time you work on the task, until you get to two hours total. This is like training yourself as you'd do for an endurance exercise. The specifics are unimportant, but use the principles.

How to Overcome Confidence Wobbles

Certain thinking patterns can give you the confidence wobbles, which can lead to procrastination or overthinking tasks.

Your specific thinking patterns will be deeply personal, and another reason self-knowledge is key to productivity.

One of my thinking patterns is that when someone tells me they like a particular piece of my work (such as a book chapter or article), my brain jumps to the conclusion that my other work is no good. For example, if my spouse reads several of my book chapters and says her favorite is chapter X, my brain screams, *All the other chapters must be terrible! She must not like any of them.* Look out for when you jump to nonsensical conclusions, when you add 1 + 1 and get 3.

You'll need to pay attention to your emotions and work backward. Notice shifts in your emotions, like a dramatic surge in self-doubt. Then ask yourself what has happened recently that might've triggered that emotional shift, and then hunt for thinking errors.

Identify Aspects of the Task You Don't Feel Anxious About

When you feel the confidence wobbles, a good way to overcome procrastination is to start with any aspects of the task you don't feel anxious about. You don't always need to do the hardest aspects of a task first. Do some easy aspects and let momentum propel you. If you're doing big, complex projects, this can be easier. Usually there are lots of simple to-dos within a big, complex task.

Sometimes anxiety about one small aspect of a task can block you from starting (or continuing) the whole thing.[5] For example, you need to reach out to someone you're intimidated by. People often make the mistake of labeling themselves as globally anxious about the task, when only a few aspects are spiking their anxiety. Notice if you're doing this and label your emotions more accurately. For example, you might say "I'm confident with 60 percent of this task and nervous about 40 percent of it" (or whatever is true for you). Doing this can reduce boiling emotions to a simmer and make it easier to find a place to start.

What to Do When Your Emotions About a Task Are Intensified by a Past Experience

A well-organized colleague of mine whose job involves managing large projects recently told me she was feeling very stressed out about moving, in particular about how her daughter would cope with their family's moving to a new state. I asked my colleague if she had had any experiences herself that were making her more worried about her daughter's coping. She said she had moved to a new part of the country as a nine-year-old and found it emotionally difficult. As an adult, this colleague had all the project management skills to navigate the move, but she mentioned how destabilizing it felt to unmoor herself from the comfort and predictability of her current home. She felt ambivalent, even though she knew moving was a great decision overall.

When strong emotions are being triggered by a task, you'll have lots of worries and ruminations about it, but handling these will often feel overwhelming. When there are many things you could do, it can be hard to pick one. Get practical. In order to get past this block, this mom identified the top thing she could do to help her daughter cope with the move. She did the same for herself, identifying the number one thing that would help her cope emotionally with the move. Once she put these top solutions into practice, only then did she choose a couple more solutions for helping herself and her daughter cope.

When you implement some solutions to lessen the chance of a feared outcome occurring, it will help reduce stress and pointless overthinking without action. Once the mom addressed her emotions and worries, getting on to the nuts and bolts of the moving process felt easier and less fraught.

For situations like these, you can also use the technique for emotionally processing old memories and hurts that I included with the material on growth mindsets in chapter 4.

How to Handle Tasks That Are Both Boring and Anxiety-Provoking

We avoid tasks that are boring, and we avoid tasks that make us anxious. What if a task is both? Doing my taxes is the quintessential example of this for me. It's tedious, but I'm also nervous about making mistakes. When this happens, each of the feelings (boredom + anxiety) intensifies the other.

It's that combination that often ties us in knots. Disentangle your feelings. Identify each feeling separately. Ask yourself how strong each feeling is out of 10. For example, "This task is 6 out of 10 boring, and 7 out of 10 anxiety-provoking." Then you can address each. Research shows that simply identifying your specific emotions in a granular way (using accurate single-emotion words, like anxious), helps soothe them.[6]

Once you identify specific feelings, solutions will become more obvious. Problem-solve boredom. For example, work for discrete periods, like ninety minutes, followed by a planned activity you enjoy, like taking a walk in the sunshine. Then problem-solve your anxiety. For example, perhaps start with the familiar elements of the task that trigger the least anxiety.

What You Do After a Deep Work Session Matters

When we do focused work on a long-term project, we tend to stop each work session at a point when we get stuck or exhausted. If you're trying to pick back up at a stuck point, it's hard to restart, which can trigger procrastination. One solution to this is to stop mid-flow, so you're not pausing work at a stuck point. However, sometimes people can't help working till they're stumped or exhausted. A work-around is to do an activity after your focused session in which you can let your mind wander to whatever you're stuck with. (I like to drive to do an errand or go for a walk.) If you allow your mind to drift back casually to your work, you will often have a brain wave about what you should start with when you do your next session—perhaps you think of a solution to the problem that stumped you. Clearly knowing what your next steps are will reduce your urge to procrastinate.

Try the Thought Experiment "What If the Obstacle I Think Is Stopping Me Is Imaginary?"

Let's say you want to write a TED talk. These are about 2,000 to 2,500 words. The standard advice for preparing talks is to rehearse your delivery for one hour per one minute of content, so an eighteen-minute TED-style talk would require eighteen hours of rehearsal.[7]

You could guesstimate you might put in eighteen hours writing it and eighteen hours rehearsing. It's a commitment, but not a crazy one. You've wanted to do this for years but have never written a word toward it. Why?

People often have a specific obstacle in mind. They ruminate on a particular thought, like "I need to be funny to write a TED talk. I need to know how to write jokes," or "None of my ideas for topics are good enough to change the world."

Most of us have an automatic bias toward believing thoughts we have. We assume they're true. What if these weren't true? What if you didn't need to know anything about writing jokes before you start? What if you've already had several great ideas and you just need to pick one?

Sometimes people think what's stopping them is a lack of information or connections. For example, you'd like to make an estate plan, but you have no one to ask for a referral to a dependable lawyer. Do you absolutely need a personal referral? Your block could be that you think you lack a particular skill or talent. It could be a personal quality you think is stopping you—maybe you see yourself as not charismatic or engaging. Blocks like these occur when people consider only one way of accomplishing a task. Their focus has narrowed too much around one perceived obstacle or method of accomplishing it.

EXPERIMENT

Think of some valuable work you have wanted to do for some time but have never made a start on. What is the imaginary factor stopping you?

Without logically evaluating whether your thought is valid, go with the assumption it is not an impediment to starting. If you were to start, what are the first steps in the process you could take/accomplish?

Write those steps out in chunks that correspond to an hour of work.

Don't gloss over steps. The first step of writing a TED talk might be to spend an hour understanding the anatomy of a TED talk. TED talkers usually include a personal story, one that reveals them as vulnerable, and a smattering of funny moments. If you spend an hour looking at transcripts, you'll understand the format.

During your second hour, you might collect all your ideas for topics, check for other TED talks on those and pick one of your ideas.

In your third hour, you might work on recalling stories related to your topic that show your personal vulnerability.

If writing out all the steps feels overwhelming, write out the first three steps. Complete those three steps and then outline your next three steps.

Redefine Your Task in a Way That Makes It Less Procrastination-Inducing

Throughout part 3 of this book, I'll help you see how to use creativity to get things done and solve everyday problems. At its heart, creativity is about seeing something in a new way. A practical application of this principle is for you to creatively redefine tasks, which will lessen the urge to procrastinate.

One way is to link an unfamiliar task with one you already do expertly. For example, writing a TED talk is a lot like writing a blog post. It has some similar elements: telling a story, getting to the point fast, and making a few points clearly.

Sometimes the mental shift you need is to see a task in a more inspiring way. When people feel inspired by self-improvement books, it's often because they help us reframe behaviors that might otherwise trigger procrastination. For example, they recast good but boring habits, like doing daily push-ups, as a step in developing our superpowers. Or they frame everything in analogies to sports. This primes us with the identity of "athlete." In turn, this helps us take a positive view of practice and drills. You can inspire yourself by reframing tasks in a way that feels empowering, rather than panic- or boredom-inducing.

If we go back to the TED talk example, you might reframe "writing jokes" as "telling a self-deprecating story" or "recounting a story about a time I felt foolish." You might reframe your task as helping the audience feel included. You can do this by telling a relatable tale or involving their emotions.

In essence, creativity is a great antidote to procrastination. Use your creativity to view your task in a slightly different way. A subtle difference in how you view your task will often lead to different subsequent thoughts, emotions, and behavior. Find the reframe that changes your attitude to "I can do this." There's an art to reimagining tasks. Play around with what redefinitions inspire you.

EXPERIMENT

Here's a similar way to reframe, but in reverse. Try reverse brainstorming as a strategy for finding a manageable way to approach scary tasks. Ask yourself, "What would be a way of thinking about my task that would make me terrified to start? What way of thinking about it would make it feel impossible and out of my capacity?"

You might experience a thought like "I need to do this task just as inspirational expert person X would." That might terrify you and make it insurmountable. Generate thoughts that would make the task more daunting. Use these as your seeds to come up with opposing thoughts that would make your task more doable.

First, Make Your Minimum Viable Product

This is a strategy for perfectionists.

If you work in tech or have used lean start-up methods, you'll be familiar with this concept. A *minimum viable product* is a product with just enough features to satisfy your early adopters.[8] In some situations, you might be the early adopter if you're building something for yourself.

A commonly cited example of how a minimum viable product evolves is fire. Humans need a light source when it's dark. First, we had campfires. Then we had portable fires in the form of lamps and candles. Then we had battery-powered incandescent lightbulbs. Then the electric grid.[9]

You can take this minimum viable product approach to anything: baking a birthday cake, creating a training manual, starting a YouTube channel, or coming up with a scientific or tech innovation.

Perfectionists sometimes complicate products to the point that they're less useful, like creating a training manual that's so onerous the critical points are lost.

EXPERIMENT

What's a project you're putting off because you're thinking beyond your minimum viable product? For example, you're considering a full vegetable garden with raised beds or a greenhouse. In reality, planting some herbs that are expensive to buy at the store would be a satisfying start.

Acceptance Will Reduce Procrastination

Procrastination may look like a passive process, but sometimes it is an active form of defiance.

When we procrastinate, often we're defiantly resisting that a task needs to be done. Or resisting all the messiness and imperfection that doing it will involve.

You have a piece of work to do. You know it will require slogging through the stages of being confused, getting things wrong, taking directions that don't pan out, and feeling uncertain. You say to yourself: "I'd be happy to do my work, but only if I can do it perfectly, in a way that avoids all that messiness and is guaranteed to work." Or "I'm happy to do my work, but I'd like to avoid emotionally brutal feedback. I want to avoid scenarios in which I do my best and then someone comes along and points out the flaws in my work, and I have to retool. I don't want to go through that."

In these cases, the person isn't accepting that doing something requires intrapersonal (inside their head) and interpersonal (with others) messiness.

Sometimes you might resent having to do a task at all. You resent needing to fill in an expense report because there should be a more efficient way to handle that than doing it manually.

Sometimes we procrastinate because we're not willing to accept the truth about what we can realistically get done. We want to bite off a huge chunk of a task and we can't (because of other commitments or the natural limits of our focus and energy), so we don't do any work on it. In these scenarios, you can try self-talk like "I would prefer to get more done in a day, but I'm going to accept what I'm realistically able to do."[10]

EXPERIMENT 1

Bring to mind an impactful to-do that you've put off. Ask yourself, "What would I need to accept to actually do it?" Sometimes it might be accepting regret over not having done it earlier. Sometimes it might be accepting a messy process or an uncertain outcome.

To help you better accept uncertainty, think back to the timeline you made in chapter 2. Identify when accepting uncertainty has changed your life. I had anxiety about whether I would like my child's personality or if I would end up stuck living with someone I didn't like for eighteen years. But I accepted that uncertainty, and I love her to bits.

Another tack to better accept uncertainty is to consider whether any sense of certainty you have is just an illusion anyway. Isn't the reality that *everything* is uncertain? Radical acceptance of uncertainty is accepting that nothing is certain. Any sense that anything is certain is an illusion.

EXPERIMENT 2

Use the following technique to learn how to better tolerate specific emotions, like regret over not having handled a problem earlier. Try writing the emotion word on a piece of paper—for example, write *regret*. Stick the piece of paper in your pocket or bra for the day. Go about your day as normal. This exercise symbolizes that you're willing to feel that regret. You can let that emotion literally exist on you without being derailed by it. You can still go about your day purposefully with the emotion existing. You can choose any emotion word where you need to experience taking purposeful action with that emotion present. For example, if you resent having to do a task, write *resentment*. Let that emotion be present and take purposeful action anyway. This technique is adapted from a well-researched form of treatment called acceptance and commitment therapy.[11]

Identify What's Enjoyable About Each Stage of a Project

Here's another way to handle intense emotions, like anxiety or doubt. Try this: Tune in to the more subtle, calmer aspects of the experience of doing hard work. For instance, the beginning of projects is hard, but the possibilities at the start of a project are also exciting. The middle parts of projects can test our persistence, but they're also sometimes easier than when we're starting from a blank page. During the later stages of a project, we might feel tired and sick of it. But we also get to enjoy seeing the project come together.

EXPERIMENT

When you're breaking down a big project, identify in advance what you expect to enjoy about each phase.[12]

How to Handle When Important Work Feels Dissatisfying

I've said that moderately productive work sometimes feels more superficially rewarding because it's frictionless. It's more predictable and often of shorter duration. As mentioned earlier, you must not equate the fact that work feels frictionless with productivity. Doing work that matters will sometimes leave you wanting to cry. You might think you're messing it all up and making terrible decisions! I rarely feel this way when I'm doing moderately valuable work but often feel this way when I'm doing life-changing work. Is the same true for you?

How can you handle it when you've shown up to do impactful work, but it hasn't felt blissful? You haven't had any epiphanies. It feels messy,

like a slog. You're wondering whether, despite all the effort and dedication, you've achieved anything productive at all. It crosses your mind
you might've been better doing something minimally or moderately
productive; at least you would have achieved a small win.

This is a scenario in which trusting your gut less can be helpful.
People often extrapolate too much from their feelings. For example,
someone with OCD feels dirty despite having washed their hands for
forty seconds. They think they're at risk of illness from germs based on
their feelings and not their actions. This is called *emotional reasoning*.

If you showed up to do important work and approached it as strate-
gically as you could, you will have made progress, even if it doesn't feel
like it.

The more tolerant you are of friction-filled work, the less you'll
procrastinate.

Want More Strategies?

. . . .

In one of my previous books, *The Healthy Mind Toolkit*, I wrote twenty-
one specific, practical strategies for procrastination. I won't reinvent the
wheel here. You can read seven of them online in an excerpt of that book
published by *Fast Company*, which I've linked to on the resources page
on AliceBoyes.com.[13]

Here's a particular favorite of mine from that list, one that's not in
the online excerpt. Plan to ask for help, but you don't necessarily need to
follow through. A colleague and I were recently laughing about how
when we write an email asking for someone else's suggestions, we often
solve the problem for ourselves before we even hit send (or thirty seconds
after). Preparing to ask for help causes you to frame your questions clearly
and concisely. Doing that is often enough to spark your thinking and
get you over whatever barrier is making it hard to get started. To use
this strategy, mimic what you'd do if you were going to ask for help. For

example, imagine you are asking for help from a particular person. It can even be a person you don't have access to. When you think about who has the expertise to answer your question and why, it will often help you solve your problem. (Of course, you can follow through and actually ask for help if you want an additional perspective.)

When You Finally Do an Important Action You've Put Off

Whenever you finally carry out an important action you've put off, figure out why. What was the change in your thinking or approach that led to it? Closely tune in to what your thinking shift was. Once you figure this out, you can turn your insight into strategies for future use.

Examples

- You accepted that the task you'd been avoiding was not going away and no one else was going to do it, so you got on with it.
- Perhaps after a break from working on the problem (when you were procrastinating), you spontaneously had new ideas for how to do it, or you thought of places where you could get that information.
- Perhaps something triggered a sense of desperation or urgency for you. This may have caused you to revisit a way of approaching your task that you'd considered but ruled out.
- Perhaps you made a small step. It didn't go as badly as you feared, so you pushed on.
- You got a boost of confidence from somewhere. This translated into you having more belief in your capacity to do a good job at your task.
- You revised any unrealistic expectations you had of yourself.

In closing, I want to reiterate that always being productive, like a robot, isn't the ideal here. As I've said many times, there are lots of scenarios in which pushing yourself to be productive in every nook and cranny of your week will not be the most effective choice.

Yes, you need some skills for overcoming procrastination, but don't expect robotic performance of yourself. Don't label all unproductive time as procrastination, even when you have a giant list of what you'd like to get to. When you accept your need for some unproductive time, this should have a paradoxical effect. When you're not constantly critical of yourself, it'll help you take a more strategic approach to being focused.

Your Takeaways

1. Did anything you read in this chapter change your view of procrastination?

2. Which specific strategy for reducing procrastination do you think will be most helpful to you?

CHAPTER 9

. . . .

How to Customize Your Productivity Solutions and Break Through Psychological Resistance to Change

T o recap, for all these quizzes, scoring mostly As and Bs means you can probably skim the chapter. If you score mostly Cs and Ds, read in more detail. Choose the best answer. If no answer is a perfect fit, choose the closest.

Quiz

. . . .

1. When you're psychologically resistant to a change you think you "should" make (like going to bed earlier), what happens?

   (A) I acknowledge my feelings and identify strategies that won't make me hate my life.

   (B) I give strategies a shot, but I don't feel fully committed to them.

   (C) I try to make the change work for me but resent it.

   (D) I get defensive and ignore any advice about the topic.

2. How actively do you try to solve your productivity problems?

    (A) If I've got a problem, I define it and come up with a range of options.

    (B) I've improved some problems but have some recurring ones that never improve.

    (C) I try, but either the only solutions I generate seem like they won't work or I don't want to try them.

    (D) I don't.

3. Do you know techniques to help you brainstorm a wider range of solutions to problems?

    (A) Sure, I know a bunch of cool ones, like forced analogy and assumption reversal.

    (B) I know one method beyond a basic list of ideas, like mind maps or reverse brainstorming.

    (C) Occasionally I will use basic brainstorming.

    (D) I don't do any brainstorming.

4. Can you find simple, doable versions of productivity suggestions, or does most advice feel overwhelming or unappealing?

    (A) I rarely use other people's systems or advice as suggested. I can usually find a simpler version.

(B) Sometimes, but frequently productivity advice feels unattainable.

(C) I mostly find productivity advice unrelatable. I find it difficult to see how it might fit with my lifestyle and responsibilities.

(D) Productivity advice feels too hard.

5. Bring a particular productivity problem you have to mind. How easy is it for you to think of at least two different ways of viewing the problem, and at least ten solutions that don't all feel like variations on the same theme?

(A) Sure, I can do that.

(B) I'd give it a crack.

(C) I'd try, but struggle and get discouraged easily.

(D) That feels too hard. I wouldn't try it.

Some productivity tips won't resonate with you. Or they'll seem impossible. Hearing the same advice again and again can be downright nauseating.

You've probably heard productivity experts talk about using smart switches to kill their internet automatically at ten P.M. each night. Or they keep the power cord for their TV in an inconvenient place. Most people can see the point behind these ideas. They're still not willing to do it. Or someone they live with isn't.

How useful is advice if most people ignore it? Often it makes the recipient feel like a self-control failure. It's not that these tips are bad or won't work, but reaching the point where you want to do those things requires getting to a unique psychological place. Some tips never appeal to a particular individual. We're not behavioral psychology robots. We have thoughts and feelings too.

You can see the limitations of pure behavioral psychology if you think of it this way: When psychology experts change their own behavior, it's not like they learned a principle and applied it later that day. Chances are they learned the principles twenty years ago, in their first year of college psychology classes. It's not until much later that the alchemy of life brings them to a moment when they make those changes. And there's a reasonable chance they may not keep up their new routine forever. I switch up strategies often.

If you're going to make a behavioral change, to some extent, that epiphany needs to come from within. It needs to seem like your idea.

Understand the Principles Underlying Specific Tips

I have colleagues I respect greatly who swear by self-imposed rules like switching off from work at eight P.M.[1] And I have colleagues who say that when people are working from home, they should get dressed in work attire and under no circumstances work from bed. However, none of these tips are right for me.

Take, for example, the advice to wear work attire when working from home. This is based on the principle of conditioning. Work attire signals to your brain you're about to be in work mode. But there's nothing unique about work clothing. You can pick any cues to signal you're about to start concentrating. Any cue you consistently pair with working will become associated with it.

Advice might be aimed at problems you don't have. For example, if reading work emails before bed doesn't disrupt you from getting to sleep, you don't need a solution for that. A tip like "stop looking at anything work-related after eight P.M." might work great for many people, especially if they go to bed early. If it's not great for you, concentrate on the underlying principle instead. If you want to be optimally restored for work, have some consistent times in the day when you're separated from work.

It's Not Just You. "Simple" Suggestions from Experts Often Feel Overwhelming.

This week I listened to a podcast in which the hosts and guest talked about how switching up your routines can improve your creativity.[2] The hosts mentioned how "simple" advice, like boosting your creativity by doing a new activity on the weekend, feels overwhelming.

However, some ingenious solutions are truly doable. The guest, Professor Scott Barry Kaufman, pointed out research showing that even a tiny switch in routine can lead to better performance on creative tasks. How simple? Changing up how you do any everyday routine, like the order in which you construct a sandwich.[3] Or putting milk into your cereal bowl first, rather than starting with cereal. I kid you not.

You could hear the relief in the hosts' voices. Someone had suggested an intervention that felt achievable to them. They hadn't been assigned yet another thing to feel guilty about never getting to.

There's a doable version of virtually any advice. It can take time to see it.

Behavior Changes That Don't Last Can Still Have Value

I recently heard *Eat Pray Love* author Elizabeth Gilbert talk about a daily routine she has had for twenty years. She writes herself a daily "letter from Love" and has spoken about how this helps her work through emotions and decisions and have greater clarity.[4]

When I hear about daily routines like this I (genuinely) think, *Wow, that's impressive and amazing.* I also think, *There is no way I would like to do that.* Recall from chapter 1 that some people thrive on long-term consistency of habits and others on more variety. Your temperament matters. One temperament is not better than another. And whether or not you generally thrive on routine, strong routines might be critical for certain phases of your life or projects, but not for others.

Every habit is constraining. Even a daily deep work habit has some downsides. It prevents you from having any clear days in which the whole day stretches before you. You can't leap out of bed and deep dive into a project if you've got a decades-long habit to keep up.

I mentioned that switching up your routines is beneficial for creativity. Thus there's an argument that short-term changes have the most creative potential, since those involve frequently switching up your routines.

Play with your routines, without the pressure that you're trying to find an ideal routine for life. Doing this can help you keep up an exploratory and experimental attitude toward your rhythms.

EXPERIMENT

Consider a behavior change you don't want to make permanently. A change that you know would be wrong for you in the long term. For example, perhaps you're an extreme night owl. Switch to an early bird schedule for a while. See what different work you produce in that different routine. Or every so often, go to bed when your kids go to bed. See what your performance is like when you wake up feeling refreshed an hour or two earlier than usual. I've said that I'm an extreme night owl. However, I love an occasional day in which I go to bed early and get up early.

How to Improve Your Productivity Problems Your Own Creative Way

What are human productivity problems like?

A while ago, I watched a YouTube video in which Elon Musk gave a tour of a Tesla factory.[5] He spoke about the continual optimization of their production process. This included:

- removing unnecessary steps in the process (the eliminate before optimizing principle).
- tweaking equipment so it could complete its task at a faster speed.
- better handling of cumbersome handoffs of whole cars from one giant robot to another.
- minimizing delays that happen when equipment breaks.

Human productivity problems have a lot more psychological complexity than a production process at a factory or warehouse. They're often not the types of problems that traditional productivity advice, like to write shorter emails, have much bearing on.

These are examples of common human productivity problems:

- The volume of work I'm expected to do doesn't leave room for anything other than relentless grinding to get through it.
- I end up watching TV late at night, not getting enough sleep, and then feeling tired the next day. I stay up late because I crave personal downtime, and that's the only time I get it.
- My area of work isn't my CEO's top priority. They have other pet areas that get more resources and attention.
- There is a mismatch between my organization's view of what successfully executing my work role is and what would be more meaningful. For example, I'm a lawyer and my company's priority is how many

client hours I bill. Or I'm a teacher and my school district's focus is on kids passing standardized tests. I would like to focus on more meaningful outcomes than that.

- My working environment isn't focused on doing anything innovative, just on our executing existing systems and processes. For example, I work at a family doctor's office. The focus is on seeing the patients who show up and treating them in typical ways.

- My team environment isn't conducive to creative risk-taking. People share nothing but fully formed, conventional ideas. Sharing more out-there, incomplete, and potentially bad ideas will result in a loss of social standing within the group. It could even result in hostility or ridicule from other group members.

- I have a personal quality that results in bias against me, and I need to work twice as hard to get half as far.

- Colleagues who have better social skills are getting opportunities over me.

- I've had five colds this year because my child is in daycare and is always sick.

- There's something about my life that makes it hard for me to be at my best for work. For example, my spouse is an alcoholic. Or I'm dealing with domestic violence.

- I procrastinate in doing activities that it makes no sense to procrastinate with.

- I'm successful, and that attracts crazy people. The emotional toll of this impacts my productivity. For example, I'm a successful YouTuber who gets abusive comments or stalkers driving by my house.

- I feel paralyzed by social comparison. I want to come out of my shell in my career, but my peers and competitors all seem better than me.

- I have an efficient process (e.g., a cash cow or work I can do with my eyes closed), but I've lost interest in that work.

Some productivity problems are common. Others affect a smaller segment. General productivity advice doesn't scratch the surface of the less common dilemmas. If I were to identify what my major problem is, I'd say this:

My largely solo working style is conducive to deep work. I get the benefits of a lack of distractions and disruptions. I don't have to manage social dynamics much. However, I know more collaboration would benefit me. I should use my expert status and platform to collaborate more with other experts. My hesitation is that I feel protective of the routines I've created for doing deep work. I'm nervous to upset the applecart by introducing the added complexity of other people.

As you can see, my most pressing problem isn't too much email, too many distractions, or too many pointless meetings. Everyone will have a mix of some common and some less common productivity problems. This is why you need skills to solve your own unique set.

There aren't one-size-fits-all solutions. A phrase I use often is "one person's lightbulb moment is another person's eye roll." A solution that's a genius idea or a slam dunk for you might be unappealing to someone else, and vice versa.

Furthermore, an idea that gives you the urge to roll your eyes at one point in your life might hit you as an epiphany at another. Sometimes all of a sudden a person becomes a devotee of deep working, getting sleep, meditating, investing in relationships, surrounding themselves with diverse teams, or completely switching off in the evenings. It might sound like I'm mocking that type of conversion, but I'm not. That's how people's evolution often works. You can take it any way it comes.

And if you remove the pressure of making permanent lifelong changes, you can experiment more.

A Guide to Brainstorming Solutions to Your Productivity Problems

Your constellation of productivity problems and preferred solutions will be unique to you. Therefore, you'll need a reusable system for finding solutions.

Creative solutions come from generating a lot of ideas. If you ruminate about a productivity problem, you probably think of the same three to four solutions over and over. Instead, try some formal brainstorming techniques to come up with more diverse solutions. When you do this, you'll eventually find one that's doable. Solutions are sometimes instantly appealing. Or you come around to them by periodically revisiting your ideas.

Fundamentally, if you are stuck for fresh ideas, it means you haven't found the right model or perspective from which to view your problem. You need to see different analogies so you can see new solutions.

EXPERIMENT

Pick two productivity problems to practice this method with, for variety. Start with one of these.

Step 1: Define your problem in different ways. For example, if your passion is not your CEO's priority, you can frame your problem as either bringing your CEO around to your way of thinking or figuring out how you can do what you want without the CEO's buy-in.

If several definitions seem helpful, you can take one at a time or work on them together. Write your problem definitions on a large piece of paper or in a new computer doc. If you use physical paper, you can more easily branch ideas off other ideas (mind map–style). But it's up to you.

Step 2: Use a formal brainstorming strategy to diversify your ideas. Here are some to try.

Reverse brainstorming. As previously mentioned, identify what you'd do to make your problem worse. Then come up with opposites. For example, if you wanted to do the most meaningless, low-impact work, what would you do?

Assumption reversal. Identify your assumptions about how your problem will be solved and challenge or reverse these.

Say you're a night owl who gets your most creative work done between nine P.M. and eleven P.M., once your kids have gone to bed. After this, you still need some switched-off time to feel ready to work again the next day. You end up staying up till one or two A.M. You assume that problem will be solved by either not requiring that wind-down time or retraining yourself to do your peak work earlier in the day. If you were to break those assumptions, you might come up with a solution like having your two hours of me time during the day.

True assumption reversal takes it a step further. What if you could make emails more productive by writing longer ones rather than shorter ones?

I'll link an article with more examples of this approach on the book's resource page on AliceBoyes.com.[6]

Random input. Pick something random, like a bird, a storm, or vegetable gardening. List the attributes of your random choice. Think about how those attributes might relate to solving your problem at hand. Google "random input brainstorming" for more info, if this strategy appeals.

Forced analogy. Pick a random problem, like a problem that was faced and solved in the past. If your problem could be solved in a similar way to the historical one, how would that work?

Creative solutions arise when you find another paradigm or analogy you can relate to your problem. (I'll show you how to do this in a myriad more ways in part 3.)

Step 3: Set a timer and generate as many ideas as you can without evaluating them. You pick how long, but not over ten minutes. Try to get to at least ten ideas. Brainstorm somewhere different from where the problem occurs (e.g., home versus work versus a coffee shop, park, or library), to give you some distance and reduce anchoring.

Step 4: Repeat your ten minutes of brainstorming when you're in a different mindset and a different physical place. If you first tried this when you're focused, try it when you're tired. If you tried it in a sunny mood, try it when you're sad, or vice versa. If you first tried this at home, try it at a coffee shop. If you first tried it inside, try it outside. Attempt to get to twenty ideas in total.

Don't attempt to think of ideas in between your brainstorming sessions, but if you do, add them and count them in your total.

Coming up with a lot of ideas will mean coming up with some silly ones. Allow yourself to do that. Silly ideas may be transformed into good ones. I call this the bunny hop.

Step 5: Take a break and then evaluate your ideas. Let your ideas rest for a few days. Designate a time and a place when you'll pick this back up. Then come back and evaluate any that have potential. Shrink ideas that have potential but are too onerous. If you're prone to making complicated plans, you may need to employ strategies that help counteract this tendency, such as by using the question *What if I could only solve this problem through subtraction and not addition?*[7]

Prioritize ideas that require just a one-time effort rather than necessitate creating a habit.

Make a specific plan for executing one idea. When you implement your idea, you might run into unexpected problems. Your expectations will sometimes turn out to be unrealistic. If this happens, tweak your solutions until they work.

Be open to any outcome from this. For example, this process might cause you to come around to trying a traditional solution or one you've previously considered but rejected. That often happens to me! Or you might identify a small twist on a traditional idea that makes it appeal to you.

Extension. Swap problems with someone else who also wants to do this exercise. Without first looking at each other's ideas, spend ten minutes generating as many ideas as you can for your friend/colleague's problem. Remember, they don't need to be practical (yet!). When you swap back, add in any of their ideas that interest you or spark your thinking.

Solving Smaller Workflow Problems

Make a Bug List for Your Workflow

Let's drop down a level from the big productivity obstacles and challenges we've focused on so far. You'll also have some niggly inefficiencies in your workflow. These problems are more like the production line at a factory scenario.

I try to avoid computer metaphors when describing human productivity, but here's one I like. A *bug list* is a term from computer programming. It refers to programmers hunting down and systematically fixing bugs in their code. Bugs in code either cause the code not to execute or lead it to do things the author didn't intend. The concept of bug lists is also used in design thinking. Product designers use it to identify aspects of a product that make it clunky to use.[8]

EXPERIMENT

You can use the concept of a bug list to gradually and systematically improve parts of your workflow that aren't optimized. Write a bug list over a week or two. Note any bug as it comes to mind or as you encounter it. You don't need to commit to fixing any of them initially. You're not prioritizing. You're just generating the list.

Be an intricate observer. Be human-centered about this process. To illustrate, here's a sample of what I'd put on my list.

- Sometimes I don't record where I read or heard ideas. For example, I'll remember whose idea it is and that it was from a podcast interview, but not which one. This creates problems when I'm quoting material. I need to hunt for the specific reference. For podcasts, this often means relistening to find the quote and to make sure I'm getting the reference right.
- I enjoy going for walks with my spouse and daughter as a break from working. I cannot get my spouse to be ready to go at a specified time. If we plan to go at, say, 2:00 P.M., it's guaranteed to be 2:20 P.M. before we get out the door. This lost time drives me nuts. Often over half the time I'd intended for my break is consumed by waiting.
- I occasionally waste time on ridiculous things, particularly deciding how best to use expiring rewards.

A Guide to Creating Your Bug List

Thoroughly mine each theme. Once you identify one bug, you're likely to have others that fall into the same category. Here are some possibilities:

- Not being in optimal physical condition for work (sleep, fitness, food)
- Double-handling (when extra steps are added to a process unnecessarily, like if materials are dropped off at a construction site in the wrong place and then someone else has to move them)
- Open loops that suck up mental energy (unmade decisions, guilt about tasks you haven't gotten to, periods when you're waiting to hear back from someone)
- Tasks you do manually that could be automated

- Things you're doing that aren't worth doing at all (projects you've been roped into that wouldn't make your cut if you found out you had only five years to live)
- Miscommunication or excess communication
- Distractions
- Equipment failures
- Lacking tools or knowledge
- Reinventing the wheel
- Problems with other people, like colleagues who annoy you
- Attitude problems
- Competing priorities
- Fragmented days (if you haven't already addressed this)

Don't be afraid to outline thorny issues. You're not stupid. For instance, adding in references after the fact is time-consuming. However, doing it as I write disrupts my creative flow. Outline what the tension is rather than criticizing yourself. Doing this will point you to solutions, like "How can I make it easier to reference as I go, without losing flow?" Or "Should I be spending an hour looking for a specific reference? Would it be better to use another example to make the same point to skip the hour looking for the reference?"

Your problems and solutions shouldn't all feel like variations on the same themes. Try seeing radically different angles. Don't let lack of knowledge about a solution prevent you from noting the bug. If you compile your bug list over a week or two, you might miss events that come up less frequently than this. Add those later when they come up.

Finding Solutions to Workflow Bugs

Here are some solutions, and if you want to make them into habits, you will need an if-then rule to trigger the solution. "When X happens, I will do Y." For example, if my family isn't ready to go for a walk at an agreed time, I'll walk around the block and swing back to see if they are ready.

Use any of the strategies we've previously discussed to find solutions to your workflow bugs. You can try:

- Reusing other solutions that have worked for you previously, perhaps in other domains
- Creating new reusable systems that will help you solve more than one bug of the same type
- Using brainstorming techniques
- Using data to guide you
- Utilizing your knowledge of your nature to come up with creative ideas
- Using acceptance to see a problem differently

If doable, creative solutions aren't coming to mind, revisit the problems you've identified in this chapter when you're working through part 3 of the book. Apply those suggestions to the problems you've defined here.

If you're interested, here are some example solutions to the workflow bugs I mentioned earlier.

- Increasingly, if it will take longer than ten minutes to relocate the source of an example or quote, I will omit it rather than spend the time hunting for it. You may have noticed that this reflects the principle of considering more than one path before starting down a particular one. In this case, I consider the path of not using the example/quote.
- I've found that I can put distinctive terms into Google Scholar and it will find the article I'm looking for. That's how I relocated the Gwyneth Paltrow example I mentioned earlier. I searched "Gwyneth Paltrow willpower" in Google Scholar. Astoundingly, the academic paper that included that example showed up.

- Some problems I've chosen to accept, like my spouse's never being ready when we've planned to go somewhere.
- I've gotten a lot better at making unimportant decisions quickly. When I label the decision as unimportant, I can make a reasonable decision quickly and move on.

Your solutions don't need to be brilliant or exciting to anyone else. They just need to solve your problems in ways that suit you.

Advice for Perfectionists

Perfectionists are bothered by problems with a seemingly obvious solution that they struggle to implement. Let's say you think doing a seven-minute workout at lunch would help your afternoon energy, but you can't get yourself to do that.

Perhaps you tell yourself, "I'll start with a minute of jumping jacks." It never happens, or it happens a few times and then doesn't. If you cannot get yourself to do something, accept that evidence. Move on. That solution isn't a smooth fit for you. Try a different route to your broader goal.

How to Get Around Psychological Resistance

Consider this hypothetical case study.

Tamika knows that getting more sleep would help her focus better. However, she bristles at advice like turning off all electronics at eight P.M. to start winding down for an early night. She resents people suggesting she give up the most pleasurable part of her day. Yet, on the other hand, she's sick of struggling through the workday tired. When she's worn out, she is focused only on making it through the day. She has no energy to consider whether she is doing pivotal or meaningful work that day.

When people feel resistant to particular advice, they often get their backs up and stop there. Tamika doesn't want to give up her me time. When people tell her she should go to bed early, she hears: "Are you saying I don't deserve the meager personal time I get?"

Imagine this. Instead of focusing on advice that doesn't work for her, she tries to get creative. Becoming a person who goes to bed early isn't a goal she wants to adopt. Instead, she frames the goal as getting more sleep, which is her actual goal.

Let's say instead of trying to get an extra hour of sleep, she aims for an extra fifteen minutes each night. She could find either one strategy that gives her fifteen minutes of extra sleep or three that each give her an extra five minutes. With this attitude change, some ideas she might hatch are:

- Getting her kids off to bed closer to their bedtime, instead of their always being fifteen to thirty minutes behind their schedule. She recognizes that if she starts dinner on time, the other elements of her kids' wind-down routine run on time. When they get to bed earlier, so does she.
- She also remembers she previously thought about getting blackout shades for her kids' bedrooms. She thinks these would help them get to sleep earlier and wake up later during the summer months, which would lead to her getting more sleep too.
- She's fine with turning on the blue light filter on her devices and setting her phone to turn on "do not disturb" mode automatically at a certain time each evening. That tip is one she has read in self-help articles, and it doesn't make her bristle. However, she didn't implement it because she was resistant to the overall prospect of going to bed early.
- She considers if there is a way for her to sleep five extra minutes in the morning. Perhaps she sets her clock for 7:00 A.M. because it's a round number, but realistically she could get up at 7:05 A.M. and still have plenty of time to get ready.

- She realizes that if she didn't have to be reminding her kids about as much in the mornings, she could also get up a touch later. She strategizes for how to make this happen.
- She lets go of guilt she has felt about wanting me time in the evenings. Instead, she closely observes what activities do the trick for helping her feel as if she has had the time she needs. There might be some activities that give her the sense of being restored that she is craving in a slightly shorter time frame. Perhaps she observes that some of the activities she does during her me time aren't restorative at all. She can drop those without losing anything.
- She tests taking more me time during the day. Tamika investigates whether taking a walk during her lunch break helps her need a smidge less me time at the end of the day.

When her goal is smaller, she can find solutions she doesn't feel resistant to. She can test out her favorites and find the combination that works in practice.

Additional Tips for Bypassing Psychological Resistance

Consider seasonal or other nonpermanent changes. Perhaps it's easy for Tamika to feel like she is getting me time on her lunch break whenever the weather is pleasant, but it's harder during the winter months. You'll have more psychological resistance to a permanent life change than to a temporary one.

Try dropping your focus on immediate change. Hustle culture will tell you it's essential to act on ideas immediately. Hesitation is seen as the enemy of productivity. But personal change often involves a contemplation stage.[9] Even if you have ideas but don't act, all is not lost. Rush into implementation if you want to, but it's okay to mull over changes.

Try returning to all your ideas several times. Add new ones, modify your existing ideas, or attempt to see what you've considered already from a fresh vantage point. Eventually, something that feels doable will emerge.

Try coming up with a solution to a different problem that will flow into this one. Back in chapter 5, I mentioned how strong deep work habits solve most of my problems with prioritizing. I'm too tired to do much else. If no solutions that directly address your issue appeal, you need a work-around. Change another aspect of your behavior or routine that flows into and improves the problem you're stuck with.

Your Takeaways

1. What's the single problem you most want to apply the tips from this chapter to?
2. Can you approach that problem directly? Or do you have too much psychological resistance for that? Do you need to approach it indirectly by changing another habit or aspect of your environment?

CHAPTER 10

. . . .

Free Yourself from Repetitive Computer Tasks Through Automation

To recap, for all these quizzes, scoring mostly As and Bs means you can probably skim the chapter. If you score mostly Cs and Ds, read in more detail. Choose the best answer. If no answer is a perfect fit, choose the closest.

Quiz

. . . .

1. Do you use automated solutions for boring, repetitive computer tasks (like formatting or finding and sorting information)?

    (A) Yes, I already automate anything repetitive.

    (B) I use a few automated solutions, but I have some repetitive tasks I do manually.

    (C) There are many inefficiencies in how I work.

    (D) No.

2. How confident are you in finding automated solutions to reduce unnecessary manual labor?

    (A) Very.

    (B) Moderately.

    (C) I'm savvy with the technology I use in my job, but I don't seek out novel forms.

    (D) Not confident.

3. For repetitive computer tasks, does it occur to you to seek an automated solution?

    (A) Yes.

    (B) Sometimes.

    (C) Occasionally.

    (D) I do everything manually without considering if I could automate it.

4. Have you ever hired a programmer to automate part of your workflow or business?

    (A) Yes, multiple times successfully.

    (B) Yes, once successfully.

    (C) Only unsuccessfully.

    (D) No.

5. Does data help you see your results and opportunities? Or does it feel messy, overwhelming, or confusing?

> (A) I have automations that extract just the data I need. These give me a much clearer picture than I could get with my naked eye.

> (B) Yes, but there's room for improvement.

> (C) I have useful data, but it isn't in a format that allows me to see patterns easily.

> (D) Huh?

This chapter is about automating boring computer tasks, either with code or software that's prebaked for you. I suspect that for most readers, this won't be a chapter that feels up their alley, but some readers will find it their favorite. So whichever way you jump, that's cool. You can take or leave this chapter.

Advice to learn to code is right up there with advice about sleep and exercise as the most clichéd advice I could give in a productivity book. But I'm not really suggesting you learn how to code. Let me explain.

I have a side hustle in which many of my colleagues can code. It opened my eyes to how to automate repetitive tasks in my workflow. Initially, I started by learning how to run code friends had written. Then I made small tweaks to their code. Next, I learned how to find code on the internet and slightly adapt it for what I needed it to do. I still don't know how to code. I can code as well as a two-year-old kid can speak—barely. However, I now know enough about automating repetitive tasks to see what the possibilities are.

Surprisingly, the biggest barrier to using automation in your workflow probably isn't the tech element. What is? Lack of awareness of how automation could improve your life and work, and of the tools available. You don't know what you don't know.

Some automation solutions don't require any coding knowledge. Others do. Once you understand the potential, you can get someone to help you create a script that does what you need it to do. Or use an off-the-shelf tool. Many times there will be a prebaked solution for tedious tasks, but you're clueless it exists.

How Negative Assumptions Can Get in Your Way

Some of the most useful solutions are simple ones. Almost embarrassingly so! This is a funny but exasperating story. At college, I was taught to do two spaces between a period and the start of a new sentence. This was the norm at the time for writing drafts within psychology. It became so ingrained that I still do it automatically. But everywhere I write now, one space after a period is preferred. For years, I wasted time manually editing out extra spaces—that is, until I found a way of automating it. Now I use "find and replace" to find any instances of two spaces and replace them with one space. It's that easy. I can fix my entire document in under a minute.

The point of this story? I've used the "find and replace" function often. However, I assumed it would not work for spaces. The day I tried it and instantly solved my problem, it was magical. (Thinking back on all the manual effort over the years was also heartbreaking!)

You won't know how automation can help you until you try it, but people don't try. If you have reasonable tech competence and a willingness to give things a go, and you're proficient at searching for information, you can figure out automation. Don't let psychological barriers get in your way!

Examples of What You Can Automate

Here are some ways I've used automation. If these seem complex, don't panic. After this, I'll give some simple options that even the least tech-savvy person can use. For now, I'll illustrate the potential that exists, even if you don't work in tech.

- *Isolating what most needs improvement.* If I'm practicing a talk, I will use a speech-to-text dictation tool to make sure I'm speaking clearly. Anyplace where the tool misunderstands a word, I can work on saying that word more clearly. This method helps me quickly target where the problems are. It makes me less sensitive about people misunderstanding words spoken in my native New Zealand accent because I can isolate specific problems and fix those. I don't need to worry about all the parts that are already clear. I automate finding the problem words.
- *Pulling information at scheduled intervals.* Google Apps Scripts is a programming tool from—you guessed it—Google. I use a Google Apps Script (adapted from two scripts I found online) to pull the Amazon sales ranking for my books once an hour. The script will alert me by email if the rankings go too high (bad) or too low (good!). This helps me see which publicity helps my book sales.
- *Getting alerted early.* One of my side hustles involves reselling (don't judge me!). When in-demand items are discounted, they often sell out quickly. Companies will often announce the date of a sale but not the time. I use a free app called Distill.io to monitor webpages for changes. The app lets you isolate elements on the page. Once the sale starts, a button on their website will change from some version of "not available" to "add to cart." It's possible to set up an automation that will recheck that page every five minutes to see if that element on the page has changed, and to receive an alert when it does. I use the same app to monitor when out-of-stock items come back in stock.

- *Finding discounted stock.* I occasionally use the website BrickSeek to find items that have gone on heavy clearance at stores like Walmart or Target. I purchased my TV this way. It was on 70 percent clearance at a Walmart across town. When stores put items on clearance, most stores may not still have the item. With this tool, you can see if any stores in your local area still do. It's not 100 percent accurate, but it's worth a shot. I also use the website CamelCamelCamel to alert me to price drops on Amazon for certain items that I regularly purchase or that are on my wish list.

- *Making sales data more useful.* Google Sheets is spreadsheet software similar to Excel. I use advanced features of it to automate aspects of my side hustle. The advanced formulas help speed up processing inventory coming into my business. They also make it easy to see trends and patterns. By combining advanced formulas and pivot tables, I can see how fast items sell and which variations of similar items sell the fastest and for the best prices.

- *Monitoring supply and demand.* For a website I sell items through, I use their API and a Google Apps Script I wrote to pull the lowest price for particular items. Each hour, my script pulls the price and puts it on a Google Sheet, along with the date and time. If the price goes above or below a certain threshold, the script will generate an email to tell me. This helps me see whether prices are increasing or decreasing. I can better judge how long to hold my inventory. If the price suddenly drops, it typically means the item has gone on sale somewhere. This presents a potential opportunity for me to buy items in that sale.

How to Get Started with Automation Without Coding

Whatever level of tech-savvy you are, you'll be able to automate some aspects of your workflow.

Simple Examples

- Use web-based calendars to show your availability and allow people to book or change their own appointments.
- Set recurring calendar events, like tax due dates.
- Write surveys and quizzes using Google Forms. These will autoscore and give you the responses in a standardized format.
- Schedule emails, like a series of orientation emails that get delivered at intervals. You can do this with email services like Mailchimp.
- Create QR codes to simplify opting into receiving information—e.g., for people who want to sign up to your email newsletter after a workshop.
- You can use tools like Grammarly and ProWritingAid to improve your writing. I use the free version of Grammarly and pay for ProWritingAid. Each has a web editor tool into which you can paste your piece of writing, which is how I prefer to use these services.

Automation Can Be Frustrating

It would be a big fat lie to imply that automating boring tasks is a matter of a quick Google search, finding exactly what you need, and having it work perfectly. It rarely happens like that for me. There's much more trial and error. I googled editing apps on at least three or four occasions before I found the combination and workflow I currently use. I was stop-start about it. I'd spend fifteen minutes looking into it, get frustrated, and bail. Then a month later I'd think, *I should look into that again.*

Remember that getting things done in the end matters most. If you can only tolerate something that works perfectly efficiently, you might opt out of worthwhile challenges that require muddling through. It's okay if your learning process is sometimes messy, imperfect, and frustrating. If you expect that, it's easier to handle.

Other frustrations can occur too when tools you rely on stop working. This happens frequently. Automation isn't frustration-free—but the question is whether it's a net positive.

You may not always experience incredible time savings because of the work it takes to find or develop automations. Some of the time you'll hit the jackpot and find a solution that saves you a great deal of time, or that enables you to improve your performance in a meaningful way. Even when this doesn't happen and the time savings are smaller, you'll free yourself from the drain of tedious, repetitive tasks. The more you practice finding novel, creative automated solutions, the better you'll get at it.

As with any other tool, once you've used it in one particular way, you'll think of other ways the same tool would be useful in different contexts. That happens with scripts you write or use too. If a piece of code is useful for one task, you'll realize you can use the same approach for other tasks.

Benefits of Learning to Use Code

Are you interested in going further? Learning to code a tiny bit (or even to run code) can help you think more systematically.

When you want a computer to do something, you need to tell it exactly what to do. You have to specify each tiny little step. If you attempt to write or adapt code, you get great practice at thinking through each step of a task.

This has transformed the way I approach projects. In college, I always struggled to outline essays before starting. I'm now much better at thinking through the most logical order in which to do steps of a task and figuring out how I can eliminate unnecessary steps.

As a beginning coder, you'll start with building whatever parts of a script feel achievable. Then you'll figure out the unfamiliar bits.

This hands-on experience can help you approach other challenges the same way.

Learning to think like a software engineer has many transferable benefits. It will make the way you think and how you approach projects more systematic, efficient, and understandable to others. Engineers are fantastic at breaking down projects into chunks. They're highly focused on writing efficient code. And good programmers use clear comments in their code to explain it. This way, someone else can easily work with it in the future.

Sharing Useful Code Is a Great Form of Networking

Chances are what's insanely useful to you will also be handy to your colleagues.

If you write a basic script for automating your workflow, you can share it with many colleagues. I've given scripts to others, and I've been given scripts in return. Every time I use someone else's code that saves me from tedious work, I feel a sense of connection to the person who generously wrote and shared it.

Learn Enough to Outsource Your Projects

If you understand even a little about coding, it can help you outsource your coding projects. You don't need enough knowledge to do a project yourself. You simply need to know what is possible to do with code. When you do, you can create a scope of work, understand how much work it involves, and hire someone to do it. You'll be a better judge of whether a contractor you're considering has a proposal for the project that makes sense.

Knowing what clean, efficient code with clear comments (explanations) looks like will help you recognize if you are getting this when you hire a programmer. You'll speak the language of coders well enough to ask smart questions.

Your Takeaways

1. What repetitive tasks would you like to automate?
2. How much effort does it make sense to put into doing so?

> ### QUICK TIPS FOR GREATER FOCUS AND PERSISTENCE
>
> To close out part 2, this box summarizes points about how you can focus and persist. I've gathered a condensed version here so you can easily refer back to them when you need a reminder.
>
> **Train your focus and persistence as you'd train for physical fitness.** The more you have "muscle memory" for focused work, the easier it gets.
>
> **Designate more tasks as unimportant.** Perfectionists often struggle to designate tasks as unimportant.[1] Labeling a task as unimportant gives you the freedom to move on from it quickly (or not do it). You don't have to give it your all. This shift will help you keep up your focus on tasks that have the potential to influence the trajectory of your success. You can't devote excessive effort to unimportant tasks without that having a cost.
>
> **Work in a way that reduces dead ends.** For example, if you get a no from someone, make it a habit to ask questions so as to

still get value out of the interaction. Get turned down? Ask: "Who else would you suggest I try?" Say you make a pitch that gets rejected. But you get handy information about why it was wrong for that outlet. How can you respond in a way that strengthens your relationship with the person who just gave you helpful information? When your missteps aren't dead ends, it helps keep your momentum up. It doesn't feel like you're back to square one. You've moved forward, even if the leap was smaller than you'd prefer. Think diversely about how this principle might help stop you from getting blocked.

Avoid cold starts. After a deep work session, do an activity in which your mind can wander. Your brain will naturally help you resolve stuck points and plan your next steps. This will help reduce any urge to procrastinate starting your next session.

Ask questions that will help you approach your task diligently and eliminate errors. Ask open questions to illuminate gaps in your knowledge. For example, "What do people commonly overlook with this?" Or "If you were in my situation, would you do X, Y, or something else?" Asking people for their advice strengthens connections and makes you more memorable.

Your work sessions should have a meaningful, focused goal. "Put in two hours of work on . . . (your project)" will not be as focused as having a specific plan. A plan can be exploratory, like "spend two hours understanding as much as I can about . . ." Or it might be "spend two hours creating an outline for . . ."

If a focused approach is too hard, commit only to showing up. Occasionally, you may need to take the opposite approach of committing only to showing up for a set time—for example, if you don't know how to start a particular task. Remember it's okay if a task feels like it has friction. That's not a reason to panic or worry you're not making progress. That feeling is part of progress for some unfamiliar tasks.

Alternate your focus between the big picture and the work session right in front of you. Sometimes in order to concentrate, you need to narrow your focus. Plan what you can get done to advance your project in your next single work session. Temporarily put everything else you could or should do aside.

Refine your strategies for dividing your attention effectively. Some people's work is focused on one project at a time. Other people have several distinct roles or projects. For example, there's Elon Musk, who oversees Tesla, SpaceX, and The Boring Company. Or, say, you're a college professor who teaches large classes and does research. Or you're a parent who is splitting their focus between raising kids and another work role. You'll need to strategize and experiment with what sort of routine helps you best focus on one role at a time. Prior to his move to Texas, Elon Musk apparently worked on Tesla several days a week in the Bay Area and SpaceX several days a week in Los Angeles.[2] That geographic split likely helped his brain focus. Other people structure their schedule so they focus on one project for big chunks. College professors sometimes cram all their teaching into one semester so they can focus on research the rest of the time.[3] Develop a strategy, test it out, and optimize it.

Sometimes choose to do things the hard way. We often have choices like "I could figure this out or I could throw money at it." I've sometimes heard it said that success requires learning to love solving problems. I wouldn't go that far. However, you'll gain tremendous self-knowledge from tackling problems that require gritty persistence. If you always choose the easy, convenient, low-stress option, you'll miss out on this. If you habitually ask other people to take care of hard problems for you or leave tough decisions to others, you'll miss out on gaining skills in gritty persistence. The more experience you get solving hard problems, the better you'll become at it. And you'll develop an identity as someone for whom this is a strength.

Use strategies for habit lapses. Everyone needs methods for getting back on track when they've lapsed with a good habit for a few days (or longer). Habit lapses can be because of circumstances (e.g., travel, out-of-the-ordinary responsibilities). Or they can be due to fatigue. If I feel intimidated about getting back into a work habit after a break, I often do some online learning for thirty minutes as a warm-up. That's enough to get inertia working for me rather than against me. Figure out what works for you.

PART 3

. . . .

How to Be More Creative and Visionary

Despite all of what I've said so far, some readers of a book on productivity might still not understand how creativity is relevant. So let's do a quick overview of the benefits of this final part of the book.

In this section, I'll help you feel less anxiety about creativity and better understand your potential to be creative, even if you don't currently see yourself that way. Every life is a creative life.

The effort you put into being creative and daring will be a bigger factor in your success than how much effort you put into being efficient. But outside of the arts, many people don't put any effort into being creative or innovative.

Sometimes people aren't creatively open because they're psychologically crunched. They're compressed by a crushing weight of too many things to do. Or someone might not be creatively open because they've lost touch with that side of themselves.

Let's start with a quick quiz to assess how open to creativity you are.

You can use this quiz to set goals and gauge your progress through this section of the book.

Quiz—How Creatively Open Are You?

The format of this quiz is different from that of the other quizzes at the beginning of each chapter. Rate the following statements from 1= strongly disagree to 7 = strongly agree. Write your rating next to the question. You can also find this quiz on the book's resource page at AliceBoyes.com.

After you've answered the quiz below, highlight any answers that are lower than you'd like. Use the strategies outlined in the following pages to improve.

- I find creative activities energizing rather than exhausting.
- I do novel activities on a whim.
- I feel playful and engage in playful activities.
- I search for answers to questions that have piqued my curiosity.
- I use empathy to better understand a situation.
- I see familiar sights with fresh eyes. For example, I make an effort to notice unfamiliar aspects of the scenery I walk past every day.
- When creativity strikes, I see opportunities differently. I suddenly see them as applicable to me or see my path to taking that opportunity more clearly.
- When I'm doing activities unrelated to my work, like showering or driving, useful solutions and ideas arrive in my mind out of nowhere.
- I possess a sense of self-efficacy, an inner confidence that I have creative ideas within me. I believe I have innovative ideas that will contribute to my life, my workplace, my field, or my community.
- I'm more interested than usual in art, artists, science, or nature.

Why People Who Care About Productivity Should Care About Creativity

If you're overwhelmed by your workload, you might fear you don't have time for creativity, or that it will detract from the limited energy you have. However, you're just as likely, if not more likely, to find solutions to your feelings of overwhelm from reading this part of the book compared to the chapters on efficiency. Solutions to being overwhelmed often come from creativity.

Regardless of how busy you are, acting creatively should help you feel more enriched and alive, which you will see when you tackle the experiments I've laid out in this part. There's satisfaction in acting as your complete self, in bringing all the elements of your nature, knowledge, and creative spark into your life and work.

The more you practice trying to be creative and innovative, the better it will feel. Problem-solving and facing mental challenges will feel more playful. This can happen even if, at the same time, it also feels hard to attempt to be creative.

The longer-term benefits of this section will be that you will have better ideas that you can execute. You may not notice those benefits straightaway, but you will notice your thinking has been freed up. You'll learn to perceive stuck points from new perspectives and find new angles. The rewards will accrue when you apply a more playful, creative approach to challenges and puzzles, broadly defined, when those arise.

These principles of creativity apply whether you work in corporate America or are an educator, a healthcare provider, or a solopreneur. Whether you're a scientist, an engineer, or a government worker, these tips are universal. Our focus will be on how to innovate in ways that don't require extensive R&D. I'll help you have novel ideas you can conjure up and implement on the same day. If you make creative thinking a habit, you can begin to apply this to longer-term projects.

If you don't like the word *creative* because you associate it with fields like the visual arts or marketing, then reframe it. Conceptualize creativity as thinking differently or solving problems creatively, if you'd prefer.

Focus most of your effort on creativity, not on discipline. Being more human, not more robotic, is the key to greater productivity.

How Creativity Can Help You If You Feel Overwhelmed

If you feel overwhelmed, it's understandable that your main concern will be with that. Here are just a few of the ways creativity can help you feel less overwhelmed.

- You'll come up with creative solutions to your workflow bugs and bigger productivity problems, and you'll be less likely to feel psychological resistance to your own solutions than ones others have developed.
- You'll network creatively and find better support.
- Problems will seem more like achievable challenges than insurmountable mountains.
- Creativity and innovation will lead to greater success, more agency to choose your projects and schedule, and better access to people who want to help you succeed.
- When you find creative ways to step out of your lane in your career, it can help you reduce your concern with those career metrics that don't really matter.
- When you're succeeding in innovative ways, how much work you do and how fast you work will matter less to other people.
- A more playful, creative attitude to your work will lessen your urge to procrastinate.

Anxiety About Creativity

People have great anxiety about creativity. On the one hand, we fear that we're not creative enough. Original thinkers drive breakthroughs rather than just incremental growth. Managers and leaders know this and value creativity (at least on the surface). This can make people fear that they're not naturally creative enough.

On the other hand, while creative ideas get many accolades once they're successful, until they've proven themselves, novel ideas tend to be judged negatively. If being creative intimidates you, you're not alone. Around 60 to 80 percent of people report that they find creative thinking exhausting.[1] Much of this is because it's such an unfamiliar endeavor for many of us. People who practice it more find that it energizes them rather than wiping them out.[2]

Earlier I argued that lack of discipline isn't the core problem getting in the way of most folks being more productive. For most of us, we expend the majority of our effort being disciplined. We spend it meeting deadlines, showing up on time, returning emails and phone calls. This far outstrips the time and effort we devote to attempting to be creative, innovative, and visionary.

How creative we are is highly influenced by how much effort we devote to practicing it. Successful innovators spend around 50 percent more time attempting to be creative. They agree with statements like "I creatively solve challenging problems by drawing on diverse ideas or knowledge."[3]

Along the same track, people underestimate how persistence can help their creativity. In one study, comedy artists were asked to generate ideas. They were then asked how many more ideas they expected they could whip up if they were given another few minutes. On average, their estimates were 20 percent lower than reality.[4]

Creativity Is Extremely Easy to Ignite

In many ways, modifying your own psychology is tricky. Surprisingly, it's ridiculously easy to help people be more creative. Experiments show that you can induce a creative mindset in minutes. This is termed *priming creativity*.

If you prime a creative mindset before giving people a puzzle, they're more likely to solve it. For example, researchers have used priming techniques before giving study participants insight puzzles. These are the type where the answer comes as a flash of insight. You experience a sense of "aha" when you know you've found a solution.

Here's an example of creative priming. In one study, all participants were given a set of five words (e.g., *sky, is, the, why, blue*) and asked to form a four-word sentence out of them (e.g., *the sky is blue*). Some participants were given word sets that included words associated with creativity. Terms like *original, inventiveness, novel, new, innovative, invention, creativity, ingenious, imagination, originality,* and *ideas*. This task was just a prime; it wasn't the task participants would be judged on. Participants were then given insight puzzles. What happened? Folks who had been primed with creativity-themed words did better on the subsequent insight puzzles. They beat out people who'd been given word sets that had nothing to do with creativity.[5] Merely thinking about creativity will make you more creative!

Keep all these principles in mind as you peruse the rest of these chapters about creativity. The primary tool you need to be more creative is to dedicate time and effort to being creative. Use your metacognitive capacities (your ability to reflect on your thinking) to overcome any insecurities you have about your creativity. Factor in that you will underestimate the creative benefits of persistence. Factor in that if you don't view yourself as creative, that's a misperception.

As a reminder, the upcoming chapters contain lots of ideas, but these are not a to-do list for you. You might run with only two or three ideas from this part of the book, ideas that will impact the trajectory of your success. Embrace the serendipity of that. Notice any ideas that spark your curiosity in the abstract, but you can't envision how they apply to you yet.

Highlight a few ideas now as you're reading the text for the first time. Come back and reread it when you're in a different mood. Reread the material when you've got different pressing projects or worries, and fresh goings-on are influencing your mindset. See what pops out at you in that mindset. Remember that your life is a journey of self-exploration, not a fixer-upper or makeover project, or a grueling Ironman!

Remember, do a short filler task between reading the instructions for any experiment and trying it. As I mentioned way back in chapter 1, this will help you have more creative ideas. It will help prevent your thoughts from being anchored to the examples given.

CHAPTER 11

. . . .

Loopholes and Work-Arounds

To recap, for all these quizzes, scoring mostly As and Bs means you can probably skim the chapter. If you score mostly Cs and Ds, read in more detail. Choose the best answer. If no answer is a perfect fit, choose the closest.

Quiz

. . . .

1. How easy is it for you to think of a resource (item, skill, service, relationship) you use unconventionally? For example, I sometimes get work done at the gym by utilizing their drop-in childcare.

    (A) I'm resourceful. I use my skills and other resources in unconventional ways often.

    (B) I do this, but I usually get the idea from someone else.

(C) I'm drawing a blank. I suspect I do this occasionally, but I can't think of anything specific.

(D) This is a waste of time. Conventional thinking is the way to go.

2. When was the last time you used a work-around that made solving the original problem unnecessary? For example, instead of figuring out how to buy an item cheaply, you found someone to borrow it from.

(A) Recently. I always see problems from multiple angles.

(B) Sometimes I stumble on these ideas, but it's not a deliberate strategy to think that way.

(C) The distant past.

(D) I never think much about how to solve problems, either unconventionally or conventionally.

3. Do you notice opportunities that other people miss?

(A) Yes. Other people often overlook potential I can easily see.

(B) I can do this within my narrow area of work expertise, but not outside this.

(C) I'm receptive to this if someone helps me, but I find this difficult to do on my own.

(D) The opposite! Even if someone draws circles and arrows for me, I still fail to see opportunities other people can see.

4. Have you ever benefited from an opportunity that seemed too good to be true?

(A) Yes. When these come along, I jump on them, fast and at scale.

(B) I've stumbled into situations like these. When I've realized it, I've enjoyed it, but I've looked back and regretted not taking full advantage.

(C) I don't notice opportunities like this. Where do I find them?

(D) That must be a scam. If it seems too good to be true, it must be.

5. Have you ever stacked deals together?

(A) Sure, like negotiating a discount at the store and getting a manufacturer's rebate on top of it. I can think of times I've stacked three deals together!

(B) I've done this in my personal life but not in my work.

(C) Only on small things. Never in any meaningful way.

(D) That sounds difficult. I like to avoid anything that might be hard or confusing.

Everyday creativity is often creative problem-solving. That's what we'll focus on in this chapter. Everyday creativity can be a building block for other types, which is why we'll start here.

If you find loopholes and work-arounds that accomplish goals in unconventional ways, this is a great way to train your creativity. This skill has many practical uses and can get you out of a jam. To be visionary or paradigm-shifting, people often need to think of work-arounds. It requires you to see past the barriers that have stopped other people from doing whatever you want to do! The more you think about loopholes and work-arounds, the more routine that will become.

As I noted, if you attempt to think creatively only sporadically, it'll feel excessively effortful. If you do it routinely, it'll become more fun, like figuring out a puzzle. It'll feel much less taxing.

Remember, if you have sticky productivity problems left over from chapter 9, try applying the strategies from this part of the book to those.

What Do I Mean by Loopholes and Work-Arounds?

Let's start with a simple example of a work-around.

Something unexpected comes up and you need to cancel a reservation at the last minute. You can change your reservation for free. However, if you cancel within 24 hours of the date you've reserved, you need to pay a cancellation fee. To avoid the fee, you change the reservation to a future date. You then cancel, without cost.

Ethics

Okay, very sneaky, but isn't that dishonest? What about ethics?

You'll notice that some examples of loopholes and work-arounds are ethically gray. Work-arounds and loopholes require considering ethical or even legal issues. When you're brainstorming, it's helpful not to consider ethics at that stage. You can bring in ethics once you move past idea generation to idea evaluation. You can potentially transform your unethical idea into a more ethical version. If you're too closed initially, you'll miss that opportunity. If you assume that using loopholes and work-arounds is inherently bad, that will hold you back creatively.

As you read the examples, try to put aside whether you agree with the specific behavior. The goal is to learn about this thinking style. Then you can laser in on applications that are a smooth fit for you.

People who have antisocial personality tendencies are sometimes extraordinary at thinking of loopholes. (In psychology, antisocial = rule-breaking, whereas asocial = less social.) However, people with this wiring can push it too far and get themselves in hot water![1] Don't do that!

A Puzzle to Try

Later in the chapter, I'm going to discuss the puzzle below. If you've never seen it before, have a go at it before I spoil the answer.

Instructions: Look at the image below of nine dots. The puzzle to be solved is this: Without taking your pen off the page, connect all nine of the dots with only three straight lines.

We'll come back to this shortly.

Types of Creative Thinking

. . . .

Alternative Thinking Type 1. Use Your Tools, Skills, and Other Resources in Nontraditional Ways

Have you ever used a chair or a box to keep a door open? Of course you have. Then you already have innate skills for overcoming functional fixedness, which means seeing an object as being for only one intended purpose. If you view a chair as nothing more than something to sit on, that's functional fixedness.

Creativity is often measured by testing functional fixedness. These assessments are called Alternative Uses Tests (AUTs). Researchers ask people to think of a common object, like a brick or a toothpick. They then ask them to come up with as many creative uses for it as they can. The researchers measure the number of ideas the person thinks up, and how diverse and unusual their ideas are. Someone who comes up with variations on only a few themes will get a lower score.

Dreaming up novel uses for objects doesn't sound like an exciting route to real-world creativity. If you broaden this, the concept becomes more exciting. Don't just think of objects. Consider alternative uses for services, tools, skills, relationships, and any other resources available to you.

One particular example of an alternative use for a service has had a significant impact on my life in recent years. It's been important for me to be a stay-at-home mother throughout my child's preschool years. I don't need all-day or even half-day daycare. What I love is that my gym offers childcare for up to two hours per day, included in the membership. I can drop in during any hours it's open and the only restriction is that I need to stay in the building.

The intended use is obviously for parents to work out. But I use it to work. You'll find me walking at 2.5 miles an hour on a treadmill or looping the track. I read studies, answer emails, or peck out outlines for blog posts on my phone. Our family membership is $50 a month. It boils down to paying about $1 per hour for on-demand childcare. Plus, I get a free family gym membership thrown in.

When it comes down to it, this type of creativity is about resourcefulness.

Experiment

Can you think of an item, service, or relationship you use atypically?

Alternative Thinking Type 2. Change the Problem You're Focused on Solving: Solve Problem B Rather Than Problem A to Get to Your End Goal

If you change the way you view a problem, you may eliminate the need to overcome the obstacle you've been worried about.

The best way to explain this concept is through examples:

- Imagine you're packing for a trip. You've tried a bunch of ways to get your clothes into your suitcase, but it won't zip. You conceive of your problem as "How can I fit everything I need for my trip into this suitcase?" Instead, you might change the problem you're trying to solve to "How can I acquire a bigger suitcase before my trip tomorrow?"

- Bob wants to become an Airbnb host but doesn't own any property (Problem A). Another approach is to rent property on a long-term lease and sublease it on Airbnb with the owner's permission. Someone might think, "Why would the owner permit that?" Finding an owner open to this is an alternative problem you could solve (Problem B).

- You need a coalition to win a vote. Your first idea is to look to moderates on the other side as your best potential coalition partners. Problem A is how to convince them to come to your side. Problem B might be to find another angle to appeal to people with radically different views than yours. For instance, people on the far right and the far left might both want to vote for a bill, but for different reasons.

- Plant "meat" producers like Impossible Foods didn't solve the problem of converting more people to being vegetarians and vegans (Problem A). They made a product that appeals to nonvegetarians who will choose plant-based options sometimes (Problem B).

- Let's say you're in a catch-22. You need to hire someone to help you with your tasks. You estimate you'd need to spend at least twenty hours hiring and training that person. Finding that time feels impossible (Problem A). You see your problem as "How can I find twenty hours to hire and train someone?" What if you decided not to train them in how you'd like the work done? What if you let them work their way? Or what if you didn't interview anyone? What if you came up with five tricky scenarios the person is likely to face in their work for you? You ask applicants to write step-by-step answers about how they'd approach those. Coming up with the scenarios that would help you identify the best candidate becomes Problem B.

EXPERIMENT

What's the problem that's most hampering your success? For example, you think "I want to do X and I don't know how to do it. I don't have the skills or resources." Using the principle we've worked on here, how can you change the problem you're focused on? Generate ideas. They don't need to be good or even make sense. Just practice.

We often psychologically attach ourselves to solving problems in set ways. We then prematurely close off to other ways. A quick way to shift your perspective is to imagine an aspect you've designated as crucial actually isn't.

- "What if making long, perfect videos isn't an essential component of an online course?"
- "What if doing everything my peers do doesn't matter?"
- "What if finishing this project in six months isn't critical?

Alternative Thinking 3. Exploit Offers in Unintended Ways

One of my hobbies is travel hacking. The basic gist is to travel extensively using miles and points. However, a love of travel isn't the only reason I'm attracted to this hobby. Partly I do it because of the community of creative thinkers it immerses me in. If your job doesn't have a strong emphasis on creative thinking, travel hacking is one avenue that can help you develop those muscles. For anyone interested in this hobby, I'll provide some up-to-date information on the resources page at AliceBoyes.com.

In the travel hacking community, people don't widely share live deals. Therefore, what I share here will be dated. There is a lot to learn from dead deals, as learning the structure of these can lead you to find live ones.

Around 2008, the U.S. Mint wanted to get $1 coins into circulation. They offered $1 coins for purchase for $1 and would ship them free. Travel hacking enthusiasts used this opportunity to earn free miles and points (or cash back) from their credit card providers. If a person ordered $10,000 in coins with a credit card that earned miles worth 3 percent, they'd profit $300. The folks who scaled this the most didn't purchase $10,000 in coins—they purchased up to $696,000 in $1 coins.[2] What did they do with the coins? They schlepped them to their banks and deposited them like any other deposit.

Another famous dead deal involved earning miles for buying qualifying food products. The cheapest of these was single-serve pudding cups. The miles earned outweighed the cost. Another similar deal involved cheese. The value of the miles earned exceeded the cost of the cheese.

A quirky promotion I took advantage of involved a hotel chain. The standard way to enter the promotion was through a hotel stay. A careful reading of the terms revealed an alternative way to enter. You could fill out an index card and mail it in. They allowed each person something like ninety entries. The published rules of the promotion stated that most entries would receive a minimum number of hotel loyalty points. Some would receive higher prizes. It was possible to calculate an expected minimum return.

As it turned out, this would far outweigh the stamps' cost. My spouse and I bought index cards and completed the maximum number of entries. The value of the hotel points was around $1,000 for a couple of hours of effort. It was a lot of fun and created a hilarious family memory of odd things we've done for earning points and miles. This wasn't a loophole. The index card method was hidden in plain sight in the terms, but it wasn't the primary way the promotion was advertised.

One way to exploit offers in unintentional ways is to stack deals that allow stacking but don't advertise or intend that. This is what extreme couponers do, but you can apply the same principle for more important purposes, like buying equipment and supplies for a business or accruing tax advantages.

What Stops People from Thinking of Loopholes and Work-Arounds?

To get better at noticing loopholes and work-arounds, understand the barriers that prevent folks from doing this.

Imagined Barriers or Rules: Imposing Constraints on Yourself That Aren't Part of the Rules

Let's return to the nine dots problem from earlier in the chapter. If you haven't tried it yet, now is your last chance before I spoil it.

Okay, fair warning, now I'm going to spoil the answer.

To solve the nine dots problem, you need to recognize that you can extend your lines beyond the bounds of the box created by the dots. Solving it literally requires thinking outside the box. Need to see this visually? Here's one answer, and I've linked to a few more on the resource page at AliceBoyes.com.[3]

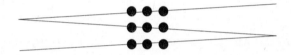

Many of the examples in this chapter have a similar structure to the nine dots puzzle. People read constraints into the problem description that aren't there. This same issue comes up extraordinarily often in life.

People bypass opportunities. They see an opportunity as not applying to them, or they see it as not scalable and therefore not worth their time. The more you think outside the box, the less you'll make this mistake. You'll grow a collection of analogies. You'll notice how new opportunities are analogous to imaginative thinking you've already done.

Here's an example. When browsing for a new gadget, you see an offer. You can get a $300 discount on a new one if you trade in an old one. However, you don't own an older model. You write off the offer as irrelevant to you. You see a constraint of needing to own that item.

Let's say a quick check of eBay shows that for $100 you can buy a battered version of the item you need to trade in. If you do this once, you'll likely notice similar opportunities to buy items to trade in.

Not seeing an opportunity as applying to you is an example of a knowledge transfer problem. Imagine you read about an amazing business strategy, model, or method. But you can't see how it applies to you (who you are, what you know, and whom you know).

You're excited by the model, but the dots aren't connecting about how you could realistically use it.

The more you practice transferring knowledge from one context and applying it to another, the better at it you'll get. Seeing how great ideas apply to your life and work now will become more obvious.

Experiment

Think about your field, or a field you are familiar with. What's a simple innovation that has become commonplace but once wasn't? For instance, in New Zealand, it's common for medical practices to have a bowl of free condoms in the waiting rooms. Before this was commonplace, anyone who thought of it might've balked: "We can't do that." They might've imagined barriers to implementing it that didn't exist.

Like the nine dots problem, don't mentally invent a constraint that may not exist in reality. In particular, notice if you are assuming that other stakeholders would be opposed to an idea, without knowing if they would be. Don't just decide that your landlord would be opposed to you Airbnbing their house a couple of weeks a year, or that condoms in the waiting room would upset your patients.

This is yet another example of the benefits of being aware of your thinking. When you look at your thoughts from a distance, you will begin to notice unjustified assumptions.

Are Loopholes and Work-Arounds Only Small and Inconsequential?

Spending too much of your mental effort on small potatoes isn't smart. However, if you're a relative beginner at this style of thinking, even minuscule attempts at it will train your brain. Attempting to hit only home runs can make inventive thinking seem much more special than it is. Players that pick up easy singles help their team (organization, family, etc.). And if you practice scaling opportunities, some of these will inevitably turn into big wins.

EXPERIMENT

Which of the three categories of loopholes and work-arounds are you most interested to try?

Too Good to Be True or Too Good to Last?

Attractive opportunities sometimes seem too good to be true. I felt that way as I filled out all those index cards for the hotel points. If you're accustomed to working hard for your money, your belief may be "the more strenuous work I do, the more I'll be rewarded." You're likely to be skeptical of opportunities in which the reward far outweighs the effort. There must be a catch, right? Sometimes there is. However, sometimes great opportunities are available for only a brief window. In these scenarios, early adopters and people who scale fast benefit the most. For example, some early Airbnb hosts profited before popular cities cracked down, enforcing regulations on short-term rentals or implementing new ones. Similarly, some people made out extremely well by becoming Uber drivers early on. For a brief period, the company paid drivers just for having their app turned on and being available for rides, regardless of whether they completed rides.[4]

Improve Your Skills by Growing Your Collection of Examples

Set your antennae for examples of creative problem-solving. When you find a cool example of creative problem-solving, identify the structure of the idea. This will help you devise other ideas with the same bones.

For instance, when I had a small baby, I would often get Amazon Prime Now deliveries to hotels. I'd get diapers, yogurts, milk for coffee, and so forth delivered for our arrival. This meant we could often still travel without checking bags. We didn't need to run out for snacks immediately upon arriving. It was a huge stress saver.

EXPERIMENT

What was the structure of this problem and solution? What other diverse problems might be amenable to a solution with a similar structure?

If You Like to Work Within the Rules, Use That to Your Advantage

Thinking creatively isn't just for people who like to break rules. Those who wade through the rules can benefit. Getting hotel points for filling out index cards is one example of this. Here is another.

Once I took an around-the-world trip involving nine countries on four continents. I had funding to go from New Zealand to a conference in the United States. An around-the-world trip cost only a few hundred dollars more than flying directly to the conference.

The fare rules for the around-the-world ticket permitted twenty flights for a flat fee. The fare depended on which country your first flight left from. Oddly, it was cheaper to start the ticket in Australia than to start it in New Zealand (where I lived). New Zealand and Australia are a relatively short distance from each other. I booked a separate ticket to Australia and then officially started my trip from there. One of my "stopovers" on the ticket was months back at home in New Zealand. I took the last flight of the ticket back to Australia for a conference I had planned to speak at anyway. Not only did I save money on the original ticket, but I only needed to pay for my flight home from the Australian conference.

More Examples of Using Loopholes and Work-Arounds

During pregnancy, I needed IV fluids because of extreme morning sickness. Where I live in Las Vegas, you can get IV fluids from services that cater to people who are seeking to recover from hangovers. This would've been much cheaper than the emergency room. I didn't do this in the end, and I'm not recommending it (it was a terrible idea and not safe when pregnant), but I considered it. The reason I've included this example is to illustrate a point. When a specific idea goes nowhere, understanding its structure can be useful. Here, the structure was "Who else provides this service?"

When I had IVF treatment, I had it out of state as it was considerably cheaper than my in-state options. Medical tourism is a work-around for high healthcare prices. People who don't want to go overseas might rule this out, but clinics in other states might be a great option.

Imagine you have a standing date to see a close friend on the same holiday weekend every year. This year, flights into your city that weekend are exorbitant. Your friend's house is in chaos from major renovations. Instead, you meet in a third city. As a rule, don't get stuck thinking either/or. Don't get stuck thinking, *Either my friend could come to me, or*

I could go to my friend. Stretch your brain by considering at least a third option.

I sometimes self-order blood tests through online services, like Ulta Lab. How does this work? You choose the tests you want, check for promo codes, place your order, and a doctor technically signs off on it. You print your orders and take them to a nationwide lab chain they contract with. Your results show up in your inbox. This is usually cheaper than if I were to pay my copay for a doctor's visit and the labs. And it saves a ton of time compared to scheduling and attending a doctor's appointment. Would I do it for anything major? No. For occasional simple tests, sure. If I'm concerned about a result, I will take that result to a doctor.

Your Takeaways

1. What's a goal or problem you currently have that could use a loophole or work-around?
2. How might the concepts from this chapter apply to that problem or goal?

CHAPTER 12

. . . .

Novelty

To recap, for all these quizzes, scoring mostly As and Bs means you can probably skim the chapter. If you score mostly Cs and Ds, read in more detail. Choose the best answer. If no answer is a perfect fit, choose the closest.

Quiz

. . . .

1. If you were to look at your Google search history, how far back would you need to go to find a topic you know little about?

   (A) Not more than a few days. I love exploring topics I'm unfamiliar with.

   (B) A week or two.

   (C) A month or three.

   (D) Many months.

2. When you dream up a cool idea related to your work, how much time passes before you experiment with it?

    (A) Under a month.

    (B) One to six months.

    (C) Six months to a year.

    (D) I don't try most of my cool ideas. They stay stuck as ideas.

3. When you look at the skills, tools, and methods you use on a day-to-day basis, how long ago did you learn them?

    (A) I'm using a method I'm still learning.

    (B) At least one skill or method I use regularly, I picked up in the last year.

    (C) One skill or method I use regularly, I learned in the last two years.

    (D) All the methods I use, I learned at the start of my career.

4. How often do you try an activity that's new to you? Think broadly: a new recipe, a new physical activity, a new skill for your job, or a collaboration with someone new.

    (A) At least once a month.

(B) At least once every two to three months.

(C) Every six months.

(D) It's been a year or more.

5. Every field has assumptions about valid ways of operating. There are norms for creating knowledge, evaluating work, and making decisions. Have you ever gone against these to accomplish a work task unconventionally?

    (A) Yes, I love to challenge the assumptions in my field about how things should be done, and I do it often.

    (B) I've done this once or twice.

    (C) I'd like to explore alternatives to standard methods or rules. I haven't thought about alternatives I could try.

    (D) Doing this has never occurred to me.

People's big wins in life often come from experimenting with novel behaviors. A novel behavior is anything you're doing for the first time. Sometimes it might be novel in the broader sense that other people haven't done it either, but propulsive novel behaviors are often just new to us.

The hurdle? Anything new requires a massive mental lift. Undertaking an unfamiliar behavior for two or three hours can take all your mental energy for that day. But this can be a worthwhile investment.

The Benefits of Novel Behaviors

Novel behaviors make you feel alive. They create emotional intensity, both positive and negative. Doing things differently leads to feeling different. Earlier I mentioned that ambivalent emotions are associated with greater creativity, and it's likely that novel actions frequently stir these. When you try novel behaviors, you'll feel strong positive and negative emotions together: fear and exhilaration, or feeling stressed while feeling proud of yourself.

Novel actions help grow your resources (skills, relationships, etc.). Over the years, the more you seek out novelty, the greater the range of resources you'll accumulate.

When you navigate a task that's new and confusing, you'll get a boost in self-efficacy. Your confidence in your capacity to get things done will grow, especially if what you accomplish is outside your typical wheelhouse or challenges the way you see your strengths. Shifts in your self-perception, even by just a few degrees, will lead to an expanded perspective on the world. A different view of yourself equates to a different view of the world, your place in it, and the opportunities available to you.

Some first-time actions are massively propulsive but don't need to be done again, or at least soon. For instance, a novice real estate investor makes a huge spreadsheet of dozens of lenders and then calls them, to learn the ins and outs of all the lending options available to her.[1] Other novel behaviors need to be repeated but become dramatically easier after the first time. When you've implemented a behavior once, it becomes a new skill in your toolkit. It gives you more options for how you approach any problem.

EXPERIMENT

Recall an action or skill that felt grueling the first time you tried it but is now routine.

Why Strong Habits and Novelty Need to Coexist

To achieve peak performance, you will need a mixture of habit and novelty. Habits reduce your need for self-control. New behaviors can change your trajectory, open up new worlds, and provide fresh ways of experiencing yourself.

Habitual behaviors are, by definition, done on autopilot. They can make life pass in a blur. Novel behaviors can produce the sense life is passing more slowly. They help provide some demarcations in your weeks and months. This can let you take the big-picture view we've talked about.

Novel experiences involve more friction. That's partly why they're associated with greater creativity. Unusual experiences shake up your ideas. They can be catalysts for creativity, even unrelated to whatever novel project you're engaging in.

Experiment

Try doing something novel and creative on a Sunday or weeknight. See if this leads to you being more creative in your work over the following twenty-four hours. Try an activity that's out of your wheelhouse. You might choose an art or craft activity, build something, or engage in a new physical movement, like trying out a rock-climbing wall. This should be an action unfamiliar to you, something you'd normally not consider doing.

If you have kids, try a creative, novel activity with them (e.g., these fun STEAM projects).[2] Make sure it's outside your norm. See if it leads to your feeling more creative.

How Novel Behaviors Build Skills, Emotional Resilience, and a Capacity to Persist

When you take novel paths, you'll spend more time being challenged. The more comfortable you become with feeling challenged and uncertain, the more familiar doing difficult deep work will become.

Novel activities involve navigating through confusion, clarity, and progress, and then repeating the cycle all over again. It might seem like doing novel behaviors will interfere with your capacity to persist with any one line of work. As long as you're completing some of the novel projects you start, that won't be the case.

Each time you complete a novel project, your resilience will increase. You will gain experience staying goal-directed, even in the face of emotions like doubt, confusion, and frustration. The more you do this, the more you'll amass diverse personal examples of succeeding at challenges. You can then draw on these emotional memories when taking on new challenges.

Try Using Novel Activities for Stress Relief

Novel activities can induce stress, but they can also relieve stress.

An overlooked benefit of novel activities is that they can be a great antidote for rumination. Rumination happens when we're obsessing about a mistake or a situation that is not going how we'd like.[3] Rumination leads to rehashing the same ideas. Often our insights about the causes of our woes (or the solutions to them) are incomplete or inaccurate.[4]

When you notice you are ruminating, you shouldn't blindly let yourself keep doing it. Intervene promptly. I recommend self-compassion (see chapter 4) or an absorbing activity. Any new-to-you activity will be absorbing. Example: While writing this book, I had IVF treatment trying to conceive a second baby. The day I found out the second cycle had not worked, I spent five hours building a solar-powered robot with my then four-year-old. It was supposed to take older children a few hours, and took me, an adult with a PhD, much longer! Sure, I dissolved into tears several times. However, it was what I needed to take my mind off my distress. If you're upset, try a short no-stakes project. Try any activity out of your norm.

EXPERIMENT

When you've been highly distressed in the past, have you used novel actions to cope? For example, after a breakup, have you found yourself getting a haircut, starting a DIY project, or making a financial change? How could you best use novelty to cope with stress or distress in your current circumstances?

A warning: Don't use novelty as an emotional escape from the psychological challenges of focusing on a long-term goal.

An unproductive route is to hop from project to project. People project-hop when they're psychologically challenged. It's an escape hatch for tumultuous emotions, like boredom, anxiety, and temptation. For instance, you start a YouTube channel about one topic. You've been working on it for six months. It's a grind. You get shiny object syndrome and start a second channel about another topic.

Your novel activities should support your core work goal. They should help keep up your energy for sticking to your goals. They should add balance and spice to your life. They should build diverse skills that will be helpful in your future. They should not be an excuse to project-hop.

Novelty isn't an excuse to avoid deep work. Don't fall into this self-sabotaging trap!

Gauge How Much You Engage in Novelty Now

Anyone who is naturally curious (if you are reading a self-improvement book, this is you!) can channel that trait into exploration.

EXPERIMENT

How much of your workweek do you spend performing novel behaviors or attempting to be imaginative? How much of your personal time do you spend doing new-to-you activities?

Remember I said that innovative people devote 50 percent more time to attempting to be creative? Think about how much time you'd like to allocate to novel thinking and behaviors. (1) What would feel ideal if you had full control over your time? (2) Based on where you are now, what would represent a 10 percent improvement in how much time you spend acting and thinking in novel ways?

The time you spend engaging in novel behaviors offers a balance to exploiting your existing systems, since novelty is exploratory.

How to Incorporate More Novelty into Your Working Life

This section contains practical suggestions for how you can incorporate novelty into the projects you already do at work.

Fundamentally, this section is about asking yourself one overarching question: "Instead of doing X the way I/people in my field usually do it, what if I did it another way?"

As you read these ideas, view them through the prism of whatever challenge you most need a creative solution for. Examples: You're an educator and your students are disengaged. You're a lawyer and the clients you'd like to help can't pay for your service. You're a children's librarian and preschoolers who could benefit from the library aren't visiting. You run a food bank and the donations you get don't match your community's needs. Identify the current challenge that is impeding your core mission the most and read these suggestions through that lens. Try to summon vision for how these suggestions might relate to your problem.

It's okay if only one of these ideas feels doable and all the others feel like too much effort.

- Take one step in your workflow off autopilot. For example, instead of writing a presentation in your normal fashion, google presentation tips and follow one of them.
- A mental model is a tool that helps you understand the world, see opportunities, and make astute decisions. We touched on this concept earlier, but I want you to think about it again in this context. Pick a mental model that already feels central to your identity. For instance, I like the 80/20 rule. This refers to the idea that 80 percent of the consequences come from 20 percent of the causes, like 80 percent of your success comes from 20 percent of your effort. Mentally scan through your goals. Ask yourself how that mental model might apply to your goals in a way you haven't considered. Ask yourself, "In what areas of my life and work have I applied this principle already? What's left?" If you already use a principle in multiple domains, you can more easily transfer your knowledge to a new area. Other examples of mental models include principles such as compounding, perfect is the enemy of the good, or you can manage feelings of being overwhelmed by going "bird by bird" (meaning one step at a time).[5] If you've found a principle helpful in one area, try applying it in others.

- Optimize for something different than you usually do. On a macro level, consider: "What if I didn't care about _____ [speed, price, quantity/scale, quality]?" Insert any variable you highly value. Imagine "What scenario would need to exist for that not to matter much?" As mentioned earlier, if work is super meaningful, within reason, speed is possibly irrelevant. On a micro level, experiment with applying a different top value to a particular piece of work. If you value being comprehensive and technically correct, try switching that up. Work as if your highest value was persuasive, zingy messaging. Ask yourself, "If what I was prioritizing was different here, how would I work differently?"

- Pick an area of self-perceived weakness and spend an hour working on it. When we perceive a weakness in ourselves, dwelling on it brings up emotional pain (e.g., frustration, anxiety, shame, embarrassment). Because doing so is painful, we avoid reflecting on it, or try to. However, the fear of those feelings is worse than the reality. When you work on a weakness, you'll realize it's not the boogeyman you worried it was.

- Work somewhere different. A physically different outlook can produce a mentally different one.

- Get feedback from someone new. Ask for advice from outside your field. If you're a scientist, you might ask for presentation tips from a friend who is a full-time YouTuber or marketer. Don't expect other people to give you 100 percent on-target comments. They may say one or two helpful things that open your mind to opportunities. Their advice might help you see when you've been overcomplicating something.

- Collaborate in new ways and/or with unique people. This doesn't mean you need to do an entire project with someone new or bring in an outside consultant. You could call customers to ask them about their unmet needs. You could ask students, who benefit from a beginner's mind, for their ideas and input.

- Hand over your decision-making to someone else. For example, ask someone else to decide how you'll spend your time for the day. Food YouTubers do this—they ask other more well-known YouTubers to pick their meals for the day.[6]
- Another way to change up your collaboration style is to try being vulnerable. For instance, if you're usually private about your finances, you might share your investing habits with a savvy investor you know and ask for their advice.
- Find a method used in other fields and apply it in yours. For example, consider decisions about how resources are allocated. Try deciding in a way that's outside the box for you or your field. There are abundant techniques of decision-making. Some examples include random choice, winner-takes-all voting, ranked preference voting, expert judgment, A/B testing, single-person experiments, large-scale experiments, focus groups, the ready/fire/aim approach, or standardized testing. You can be inventive. For example, a modified form of random decision-making has been suggested for choosing which projects will receive grants. The method? The lowest-quality ones are weeded out initially. After that, recipients are selected randomly.[7] Pick a method that's not traditionally used in your field and give it a try.
- Identify role models in your field. Pick those you admire for being the most innovative and unconventional thinkers. What contributes to their capacity to think outside the box? What traditional norms or rules of your field do they break? If the person is active on Twitter, try reading a few weeks of their tweets. Or examine their work, interviews, or writing. What does this reveal about the ways they think and act outside the norm? What qualities underlie those differences? Not all of their actions might be desirable. You can cherry-pick what is.
- Brainstorm a list of alternative uses for your most kick-ass core skill. Your ninja skill might be, for example, researching, communicating,

interviewing, organizing information, analyzing data, being persuasive, or thinking huge. Whatever you see your great skill as, come up with as many diverse, creative, innovative ways that you could use that skill as you can. Don't be practical yet. Be as wacky and impractical as you like. You can edit later. Your ideas can be inside your field, way outside it, or adjacent. Try to include some of each. Include your most out-there ideas. Once you're tapped out of ideas, review them. Look at any that spark your curiosity. Explore how they might relate to a problem in your field or to one of your productivity stumbling blocks. Even if ideas don't appear related to the problem at first, look closer. Keep your list as a permanent resource.

- Generate a lot of ideas to push past your conventional ones. Start a document called "100 ideas for . . ." Choose a crucial topic like "100 ideas for passive income" or "100 ideas for how to help my patients live healthier lives." Put down what immediately comes to mind and then add to it. Note that you can adapt this however you like. If you'd prefer a list of 50 or 75, do that. You don't need to complete it all at once, and in fact you shouldn't attempt that. Let your unconscious mind work on it in between your focused attempts.

- Make a list or mind map of 100 ways your network of contacts may be helpful to you. Keep this as a permanent resource. Once you've got your list, pick something on it that you underutilize and aim to help someone and seek help that way. Here are some examples: an introduction, a reference, feedback on an idea, or feedback on a specific piece of work. You might share tools (e.g., scripts, machinery, templates, data sets), collaborate on a project together, or benefit yourself by helping someone else. You could learn a fact or a skill from a colleague; be exposed to someone else's thinking style that highlights differences with your own; see someone in your network do something well, thus gaining insight into how you could do that; receive emotional support and encouragement; or find out how one of your contacts manages a common tension (like how they carve out time for deep work) and use that as inspiration yourself.

• Explore your least promising idea. Whenever you brainstorm a big list of ideas, occasionally, instead of gravitating toward exploring what's most promising, try to transform your least promising idea into a useful one.

HOW TO SOLVE PROBLEMS IN NOVEL WAYS—GENERATE MANY IDEAS FOR HOW YOU MIGHT COME TO KNOW THE ANSWER TO YOUR PROBLEM

When you have a problem, how many ideas do you generate to solve it? One? Three? Five? In most scenarios, it's not efficient to generate a large number of ideas. A handful of ideas is often enough to find a prudent one. In many cases, generating one idea is enough—for example, "What restaurant should we order from tonight?"

When many ideas would be beneficial, I like generating ideas for methods to solve a problem rather than ideas for solutions. For example, I could generate ideas for methods for finding a great book title. For real problems like this, devote some time to it, like three ten-minute sessions.

Experiment: Here's a fun example. Try generating ideas for how you might name a baby.[8] The point is not to generate the names themselves, but to come up with ideas for how you might go about the process. Some seeds: You could look up a list of the top 1,000 names. You could look up names based on themes, like botanical names, names from the Wild West, or biblical names. You could stand on the street and ask passersby the best unusual name they've heard recently. Give yourself five minutes to come up with as many methods as you can.

This is not an everyday strategy because it's not efficient in most cases. But when you have a vexing problem or you're dissatisfied with your typical approach, give it a try.

How to Incorporate More Novelty into Your Personal Life

Diverse experiences can keep your creative energy up. They can help you stay focused without monotony creeping in. What follows are ideas about introducing more novelty into your personal life. Use these as an indirect springboard to think more creatively in your profession. These aren't a substitute for the suggestions directly about work. They're intended to complement those.

- To access more novel ideas, sometimes you need a fresh seed. Try listening to a genre of music you don't normally gravitate toward. On Twitter, I asked for recommendations for "pick me up" songs. I got some great recommendations outside of my usual tastes. After I listened to the recommended songs, my Google Home would autoplay others based on the prior selection. I wouldn't have unearthed any of those on my own.
- Think of a resource and try a component of it you have never used. For instance, if you go to a gym but always use the weights and the treadmill, try a class or the sauna. If you always take particular classes, try a class you've never tried before. Try the class that is least appealing—e.g., try Bollywood dancing if you're "all business." Experience yourself uniquely and you'll think uniquely.
- In the book *Wired to Create,* the authors Scott Barry Kaufman and Caroline Gregoire recommend you be creative in a way that you're not normally.[9] If you're "corporate creative," try the visual/tactile

realm. For instance, watch a YouTube tutorial for origami and follow along. Remake yourself a little. Craft something. Make a miniature or diorama. Do a cross-stitch, make a homemade Christmas decoration for your tree, or make animals, furniture, or fruit out of modeling clay with your kids.

- Visit attractions in your local area. Go to the ones you've been meaning to see but have never made it to.
- Make a dish you love that originates from another culture that you've only ever bought, like pad thai.
- Try a new sensory experience. Try a cuisine you haven't experienced before. Visit a neighborhood in your city you've never been to.
- Try setting a goal that will encourage exploration, like visiting all of the ten parks closest to you, or walking every street in a neighborhood or every street in Manhattan.
- Try a mode of transportation you rarely take. It'll give you a new view of the world.
- Practice engaging in novel activities with your children. Actively teaching your children to explore novel actions will strengthen that value within you.
- Switch things up visually in your home or office. Move the furniture. Put up a new piece of artwork or a world map on the wall.

Your Takeaways

1. What's one way of injecting more novelty into your work or personal life that feels exciting and not overwhelming?
2. Which idea from this chapter piqued your curiosity, but you're not sure how it applies to you? Put this in your "incomplete ideas" file. Revisit it periodically until a practical application becomes clear.

CHAPTER 13

. . . .

How Diverse Interests Benefit Your Capacity to Be Creative and Visionary

To recap, for all these quizzes, scoring mostly As and Bs means you can probably skim the chapter. If you score mostly Cs and Ds, read in more detail. Choose the best answer. If no answer is a perfect fit, choose the closest.

Note—throughout this chapter, by *interests,* I don't mean just hobbies. It's hard to maintain an enormous variety of hobbies. Interests might be topics you read articles about, videos you watch, or podcasts you listen to.

Quiz

. . . .

1. How often do you take part in a hobby that involves creating something original? (Anything counts, including projects you do with your kids. Other examples: making a podcast, woodworking, writing songs.)

    (A) I have a creative outlet I pursue regularly.

(B) Nothing regular, but at least a few times a year.

(C) Once a year.

(D) Never.

2. How easy is it for you to name at least eight interests outside your work?

    (A) Super easy. I'm hungry to learn about diverse topics.

    (B) I can come up with at least six.

    (C) If you look at what I watch, read, listen to, and enjoy, there are only three to four topics.

    (D) I don't have any hobbies. My interests are limited to the news and one or two genres of books or TV shows.

3. How do your outside interests contribute to you being innovative in your core work? Think broadly. How have your outside interests enhanced your critical thinking, social confidence, or persistence? If you use those qualities to help you innovate, then they count.

    (A) My interests cross-pollinate how I work and make my perspective at work unique. I can point to at least two or three examples.

    (B) I can recall an example from the past but nothing recent.

(C) I can see how interests help me relax, but I can't see how they help me at work beyond that.

(D) I've never thought about this.

4. Have you ever incorporated a specific idea or inspiration from an interest into your work? For instance, perhaps you brought the way you network for your side hustle into your core role.

(A) Yes. There's an approach, model, method, or skill I was exposed to through my interests that I bring into my core work.

(B) My instinct is that the answer is yes, but I can't name anything specific right now.

(C) My hobbies and my work seem disparate. I can't see how they connect.

(D) This quiz is hurting my brain!

5. Has anyone you've met through your interests inspired you to work differently in your core role? For example, a friend from a hobby sets aside time each day to experiment. Another friend from a hobby has a fantastic way of accepting and encouraging others.

(A) Of course. My hobbies expose me to people's diverse strengths and ways of getting things done.

(B) I've picked up skills from people I know through my hobbies, but I use those skills only within that hobby.

(C) There are qualities and habits I admire in people whom I've met through my interests. I've never contemplated how those might help me in my job.

(D) There's no one I've met through a hobby who has inspired me.

You might have heard the argument that having outside interests can help you in your work. To *recreate* (engage in recreation) and *re-create* are the same word! The concept is inherently related to growth. But how do outside interests help you do unique work? How can they spark you to be innovative? We'll answer those questions in this chapter.

If creativity is joining ideas, you need ideas to connect. The narrower the path you follow, the narrower your ideas will be. The more intense a career is, the narrower its path tends to be. A medical student lives and breathes being a medical student. A PhD student is immersed in an academic environment. An engineer is taught to care about what companies that employ engineers care about. A corporate lawyer is immersed in that track.

People within a particular career path often share similar personalities, skills, and experiences. They have been trained to care most about the same set of priorities and use the same methods. When you expose yourself to smart, creative people in different arenas, you'll gain fresh perspectives. This doesn't happen as much as it should. Subfields within the same industry rarely collaborate. Neither do people who do the same job in different industries, such as nonfiction writers and screenwriters. Knowledge and methods from one domain can end up siloed from the other. This means that being cross-disciplinary can provide easy/big wins.

It's not enough to have diverse interests. You need to discern how models, analogies, methods, thinking styles, foci, and so on that are derived from your interests can inform your work. This will give you an edge and a perspective others don't have. The social connections you make through your interests matter too. People from other fields think differently about the world, and you can borrow their new perspectives in your own work.

To achieve this, I particularly like author Gretchen Rubin's concept of becoming a "minor expert" in a topic.[1] For example, minor experts might go through a phase of being intensely curious about a topic and spend a few months reading several books about it. Their knowledge becomes deep enough that they connect concepts from that topic to others. Over the years it's possible to become a minor expert in many topics.

Diverse Interests and Ultra-High Performers

Your work should leave room in your life for more than one passion. People with two passions enjoy higher well-being than people with one.[2]

Apple cofounder Steve Jobs famously took a calligraphy class in college. This offbeat class choice influenced the design focus he took with typography on Macs. It helped establish the association between Apple products and aesthetic excellence.

According to research, high achievers have more diverse interests. Ultra-high-achieving scientists are more likely to have artistic interests. Nobel Prize winners are especially likely to have hobbies related to artistic performance (like acting, dancing, or magic) or artistic crafts (like sculpting, woodworking, playing music, tinkering with electronics, poetry or fiction writing).[3] In comparison, non-elite scientists aren't more likely than the average person to express artistic interests.

Why do we see this pattern? There are lots of potential explanations for the connection between exceptional performance and diverse interests. How many of these apply to you? Which could you lean into?

- Creative hobbies strengthen the thinking skills essential in analytical professions.
- Super smart individuals might be good at lots of things, including, say, STEM and creating art.
- People gravitate toward interests that use their strengths. If the same underlying strengths contribute to being great at two different fields, people who excel at one might gravitate toward the other.
- Smart folks may be less drained by their careers. They may enjoy more leftover energy for engaging in interests outside their career.
- Intensely creative individuals and high achievers are more curious.[4] It makes sense that they're interested in more than their career track.
- Creative people often are wired with leaky filters on their attention.[5] Not only do they enjoy more interests outside their field, but they also have broader interests within their field.
- Creative interests help smart people relax and switch off from ruminating over unsolved problems in their work. This switching off and letting their minds wander contributes to having more spontaneous flashes of insight.
- High achievers are good at abstract thinking. Exceptional achievers may be better at seeing the connections between diverse interests and their work. Therefore, they might value taking part in hobbies and interests more.
- People who deliberately attempt to be creative may crave inspiration from other fields. They may look to fields that fit the traditional conceptualizations of creativity for inspiration, such as art or architecture.

Loosen Your Thinking

Research on the benefits of diverse interests has often focused on the crossover between STEM and arts, crafts, and design. But those are not the only two domains that can cross-pollinate. If you're an astute observer of yourself and the world, any mash-up of interests could be fruitful.

The following exercises are for loosening your thinking to help you connect your interests to your work. Doing these might feel like doing a physical exercise at the gym for the first time. When you're a new gymgoer, your brain isn't accustomed to asking your body to make those movements. It takes some reps to get your coordination going. Likewise, your brain isn't expecting you to ask it to make connections between different fields. It will take practice for your brain to figure out what you're asking it to do.

Another point to remember is that people don't run on a treadmill to improve their treadmill running. They do it to strengthen their heart, lungs, and muscles. The exercises in this chapter are the same. You're exercising your creativity.

At first, when you use these techniques, you may find that your ideas are semi-interesting, but nothing instantly useful comes from them. Keep it up for a few months. Many more practical ideas will flow. Take the pressure off yourself as you read. Have fun with the experiments without expecting immediate epiphanies.

What Can You Connect?

EXPERIMENT

Make a comprehensive list or mind map of all your interests and roles. Include your interests within your field and outside it. We'll use this as a base to work from for the rest of the chapter.

Note that you don't need to be an expert on any of these topics; you only need to know just enough. You'll have far more interests than you give yourself credit for initially.

To give you the idea, your list of interests might look something like this: urban planning, history, travel, New York City, "experiences," gossip, protecting the environment, eighties/nineties pro wrestling, healthcare challenges in poor countries, sport, beer, the Supreme Court, the history of . . . , desert animals, humor, politics, statistics/polling, trees, fan communities, the TV show *Survivor*, fantasy drafts and prop bets, the such and such YouTube channel, alternative living (e.g., off-grid), parenting, social policy around working parents, tinkering with code/robots, and minimalism.

Include all your interests from outside and within your profession. Include anything nerdy or technical, or about the history of your field, but don't limit it to that. If any system provokes a sense of awe in you, whether that's national parks or air traffic control, include that. It's also okay to include specific interests and more general topics alongside each other.

Practice Making Connections

EXPERIMENT

Initially, connect two of your nonwork interests. You'll find it easier to be zany if you try this first. Treat this as play. Start in creative mode rather than practical mode. The more you play with concepts that don't traditionally go together, the more interesting your thoughts will be.

Spend ten minutes connecting any two of your interests. If you want to randomize it, pull topics from a bowl or write your interests as a numbered list and ask your voice assistant for two random numbers. To explore a theme more deeply, instead of pulling pairs, you can pull one topic, and then three other topics that you will connect to that first topic. Remember, your first ideas will be your most conventional.

One way to do this exercise is to pair interests together as if you were writing titles for essays or blog posts, and then brainstorm about the points you'd make. Take the pairs you've selected and construct a title.

- A minimalist approach to polling
- A humorous approach to statistics
- The relationship between urban planning and gossip
- How would a minimalist think about . . .
- What would a Supreme Court justice think about . . .

Once you've gotten some practice, connect topics from your interests to your field of work. If you're a parent, don't forget to consider parenting as one of your fields of work, and look for inspiration for creative parenting. You can connect two topics within your field too. I came across an example of a physicist who wrote physics concepts on pieces of paper, put them into a bowl, and pulled pairs to see what he could connect.

Don't expect any magic to happen straightaway. This exercise will feel clunky, as it's not a way we're accustomed to thinking. Your brain might scream, "What are you doing to me?" Remember, you can't equate frictionless work with outstanding productivity. Remarkable work is often awkward. You may not understand where it is headed.

Your creativity will be limited only by the analogies you can draw. You can train yourself to see analogies better. How? By compartmentalizing your thinking into specific subjects less.

Try Applying Methods or Tools Across Fields

Here's a variation on the exercise you just did. Take a method from your interests and connect it to a problem in one of your other interests. For example, how could a method from urban planning help solve the problem of clutter in minimalism? Consider the methods used in urban planning. Go with whatever comes to mind, like zoning. How could zoning help reduce clutter?

To show you how practical examples might emerge from this way of thinking, here's one. I mentioned how useful I find the drop-in childcare at my gym. This is a method to encourage gym attendance. Therapists could do something similar. They could provide childcare at their office at least one day a week. Parents could book that day for their appointments. This would relieve the stress and barrier of needing to find childcare to attend.

Or perhaps excitement or engagement are a problem in your core field. Imagine, in your interests, you've encountered a push toward turning products into experiences to increase engagement. Inspired, you might turn some aspect of your work into an experience. If you're not sure what I mean by experiences, here's an example: An old terminal at JFK Airport has been transformed into a themed hotel that transports guests back to what air travel was like in the 1960s. Another example is how companies hype products so that waiting to buy the product on release day becomes an experience (e.g., midnight releases for video games or movies). A third is how, instead of limiting options for photos, arts organizations are creating experiences optimized for Instagram. You might know both you and your friends love experiences. In your field, how could you incorporate the concept of immersive experiences?

Or let's say machine learning/AI is employed in one of your interests. How might that be used in another of them? In minimalism, could machine learning/AI be used to figure out which are the essential items in your home? What if you do not know how to write machine learning code? Then your next thought might be "How could I use this impractical idea as inspiration for a practical one? What is it about using machine learning that makes it an appealing solution? How could I replicate that in another way?"

Stuck for ideas? Try transplanting these methods between fields.

- Business models from other fields
- Types of partnerships and methods of collaboration
- Ways of attracting and appealing to customers
- Decision-making methods (discussed in the last chapter)

How Do Your Interests Connect with Your Core Work?

Now that you've experimented with thinking across fields, let's get practical. How can you use your interests to get a competitive advantage? How can you leverage your knowledge from outside of your field to innovate?

What Excites You That's Atypical for Your Field?

Do you have skills, interests, or experience that most people in your profession don't? Consider that what is considered average in one field can be extraordinary in another. David Epstein, the author of *Range*, has talked about how he trained as a scientist but became a sportswriter. His science skills might've been average for a scientist (his view) but were extraordinary for a sportswriter.

Do You Have an Interest in a Field Adjacent to Your Field?

As mentioned, knowledge, methods, and norms from subfields tend to be siloed. By venturing outside your bubble, you can pick up knowledge that's ordinary in another field but unusual in yours. I'm a nonfiction writer. Yet I've benefited greatly from basic tips from fiction writing, screenwriting, and speechwriting. When someone spans two worlds, it can contribute to their greatness. For example, Elizabeth Gilbert's works of nonfiction incorporate skills from her fiction writing. When you notice a pattern like this in others, pinpoint what you can glean from it to be more innovative yourself.

Can You Work at the Intersection of Two of Your Interests?

As a kid, I was interested in business, investing, computers, and politics. No one expected me to train in psychology. Now, the intersection between emotional health and business is an easy, appealing crossover for me, but it's not for everyone. If the interests you can connect aren't commonly mashed up, it's tempting to think there's no value in it. But your unusual interests can be what allows you to make a unique contribution.

What Do You Value Highly That Is Downplayed in Your Field?

This point relates back to the example of Steve Jobs's calligraphy class. During the early days of computing, aesthetics were not highly valued in that field. Jobs incorporated that value to amazing effect. Different fields have different prevailing values and tend to downplay other values that are not predominant. Some fields are all about speed (sports, tech, etc.). Others are dominated by conservatism or the principle "first, do no harm" (e.g., medicine, law). Innovation can come from incorporating values minimized in your field. Try this quiz to identify the values prioritized in your field.

Quiz

How much are the following values prioritized in your field?

Rate each of these from 1 to 7, from not at all (1) to extremely (7).

Write a number between 1 and 7 next to the item. If you don't want to write on your book or you're reading an ebook, you'll find a link to this quiz on the book's resource page on AliceBoyes.com.

- Speed
- Exceptional customer experience
- Extreme efficiency and optimization
- Broad positive social impact
- Ethics and the principle of "first, do no harm"
- Empathy
- Thinking big
- Conservatism and following traditions
- Aesthetic beauty
- Fun
- Clear, compelling messaging and communication (as in fields like marketing)
- Rigor and attention to detail

Next, retake the quiz, but this time write the number that reflects how much you value each item. Look at the discrepancies between the numbers. Being both more or less interested in a particular value can provide a point of difference. For instance, I'm somewhat less interested in being detailed and rigorous than a typical scientist would be. In the research world, standards are kept high by nitpicking. I see the value of that and can fall into line when need be. However, plenty of times flawed studies in obscure journals or knowledge from outside the scientific realm pique my interest.

Here's another way to frame this topic. In relation to your core work, try answering this question: "What am I supposed to care about and what am I not supposed to value as much?"

Do Any of Your Interests Strengthen Your Abstract Thinking, Imagination, or Maker Skills?

Earlier, I mentioned research on elite scientists' interests in the arts, crafts, and design. If these fields are of zero interest to you, it's not the end of the world. However, there seem to be particular skills from the arts that help people be innovative.

Warning: This is a long list, but we'll simplify it in a second. To quote from a study,[6] the relevant skills include:

- observing
- imagining
- abstracting
- pattern recognition
- pattern forming
- analogizing
- body or kinesthetic thinking
- empathizing
- dimensional thinking
- modeling
- playing
- transforming—integrating a set of thinking tools in a serial fashion (e.g., using models to yield patterns that can be visually displayed)
- synthesizing—integrating tools to get an overall "feel" for a system or subject so that one knows what one feels and feels what one knows

These are a tough set of ideas to get your head around. Boiled down, many of them relate to imagination, experimentation, and bringing ideas to life. For example, if you enjoy a hobby that involves making, then building prototypes will be a more comfortable activity for you. This is an instance when involvement in a hobby is important beyond having an interest in a topic.

EXPERIMENT

What do you like to do that involves experimenting, creating, or imagining worlds? If you don't have hobbies that nurture these skills, what might you gravitate to?

What Lenses Do You See the World Through?

Particular hobbies train up certain types of thinking. My travel hacking hobby has trained me to hunt for loopholes and work-arounds. Investing has helped me see everything through the lens of compounding returns. Compounding intensifies the results you get from effort. Therefore I try to apply this principle across my life domains. For example, I say to myself, "If I devote the time to teaching my child this skill now, it will make both of our lives easier in a compounding way."

Work influences how I live my life too. Principles for engaging writing make excellent principles for living. There are tips for connecting with readers like "vulnerability invites connection." There are also principles for making writing more interesting. These include "show, don't tell," "specifics are more interesting than generalizations," and "people learn through stories." I think of these in other life domains too, like how "show, don't tell" is a good way to teach my child.

EXPERIMENT

Identify the lenses you see the world through because of your various interests. How can you make more use of these?

Steal Solutions

Imagine long wait times are a problem that plagues your workplace. Look to any other space you're interested in. See how they've solved the problem of customers being annoyed about wait times. Case in point: If you're obsessed with Disney Parks, you might examine how they've eased that problem.

Sometimes when you want to steal a solution from another field, you might need to think abstractly. For instance, how have other groups solved a problem of having too many promising ideas and deciding which of them to allocate resources to? How have other fields created a culture of people freely giving ideas and others supporting those (like the "yes, and . . ." principle from improv)?

EXPERIMENT

If you've got a problem to solve, generate examples of how a similar problem has been solved in other arenas.[7] Think about technologically innovative companies, sports, the arts, the natural world, other cultures, etc.

Move from Consumer to Creator

Formats popular in one domain are unexplored in others.

If there's an activity you love as a consumer, try becoming a creator. Perhaps you love taking audio-guided walking tours when you travel. Could you make these for your job? New hires to your company might like a tour around the neighborhood or even your building!

Perhaps you're a science teacher who takes the board game Guess Who? and replaces all the faces with the faces of famous scientists. In the traditional version of the game, each player chooses a mystery character. Their opponent attempts to identify that character through yes/no questions like "Does your person have a mustache?" You change the rules. Players need to ask questions about the mystery character's discoveries.

Or perhaps you take the concept of a scavenger hunt and use that as a tool. It could be used to teach, for team-building, or to help create a culture of experimentation and resourcefulness. In a scavenger hunt, people normally look for physical objects, but instead you make it web-based. Instead of random objects, the "items" to find are innovative examples of solutions to problems. When you strike a format you enjoy, consider if you could transplant it to your field. You might enjoy the format because it's fun, efficient, or thought-provoking. Or it could be a combination of these.

HOW TO MOVE FROM IDEAS TO INNOVATION

People have fears and misconceptions about innovating that make them think, *That's not me.* Here are ways to think about innovation to make it less daunting.

Although it might sound odd to say it, innovation doesn't have to be particularly innovative. While your ultimate goal won't be to be too closely derivative, when you collect easy wins, you can strengthen your identity as an innovator and do some good in the world. The following are all quick ideas for transforming ideas into innovations.

- In science, studies are often replications with a twist. In any field, you can run an experiment that compares a current best practice to a version with a twist. Your version with the twist may become the new best practice.

- In the world of start-ups, derivative ideas abound: "We're the Peloton of X" or "the Airbnb of X."

- Merely placing an idea in a different context can be innovative. Where I live, several supermarket chains offer a basket of free fruit for children. Parents will shop longer if their child isn't hungry and is occupied by eating. Why not put those in other places (like banks) to keep kids busy with a snack while their parents are getting a task done?

- Simple psychology concepts can have hundreds of unexplored applications. There's a plethora of research on behavioral nudges, like displaying compelling messaging right at a critical decision point or making something drastically easier to increase uptake.[8]

- Here's another example of using a simple psychological principle. We know that people feel less stressed-out when they're waiting if they know how long they'll have to wait. This is why train stations and bus stops display the time until the next bus. My ob-gyn's office started doing something similar. They have a whiteboard behind the reception desk where they write how far behind each doctor is. For example, "Dr. A is 45 minutes behind, Dr. B is 15 minutes behind, Dr. C is 25 minutes behind." I like this example because it illustrates the principle from the work-arounds chapter about changing the problem to be solved. The whiteboard doesn't solve the problem that doctors get behind. It does somewhat ease the stress people feel about the fact that their appointment is running late. Another reason I like this example is that it shows that prototyping can be simple. People sometimes feel intimidated by the concept of prototyping. A whiteboard behind the desk shows how simple and barrier-less prototyping can be. And sometimes the prototype is enough.

- Friction points are easily observed and sometimes simply remediated. I recently read an example of a store that offers customers two different colors of shopping baskets. You pick up a basket of one color if you'd like to browse in peace, and the other color if you'd like attention from the salesperson.

The ordinary course of living your life offers abundant opportunities to observe solutions that work outside your field. Even just at the design level, you can likely come up with several examples: customer service that surprises and delights; instructions that are clear and helpful; simple features of products that make them easier or more enjoyable to use; or anything that makes a confusing or intimidating process easier. You can even observe how playfulness can improve the customer experience. My IVF doctor's office has a free gumball machine filled with pink and blue gumballs.

SHOULD YOU BOTHER INNOVATING IN SMALL WAYS?

Britain's National Health Service has a stated goal of increasing the average lifespan by five years.[9] With ambitious goals like this, a compelling argument can be made that success will come only from sweeping interventions. These could relate to science and technology, such as vaccines, or to social policy, like removing tax from fruits and vegetables. This argument has merit, but small, scrappy interventions can have value too.

Scrappy innovations create a culture of innovation in a workplace. If an organization has a core mission statement or set of values, it can't be simply a plaque on the wall. It needs to be brought to life in the frequent interactions between staff and customers and between teammates. People's frequent actions should reflect the core goals. Small innovations that reflect the core mission statement can help reinforce this. For individuals who come up with innovations, small wins can shift their self-identity to being an innovator rather than merely a consumer of others' innovations. Actions drive thoughts and feelings, so being more innovative will lead to more of those thoughts and feelings. Experience implementing small innovations can help with developing a bias toward action rather than over-thinking. And a culture of innovation driven by all team members is likely to become contagious, leading to more visionary thinking.

The main catch to be aware of with small innovations is to make sure that these don't decrease people's support for and sense of urgency about bolder moves. A quirk of human psychology is that when we make a little effort to support a cause, it can make larger changes feel less urgent.[10]

Your Takeaways

1. What's a simple innovation you could try in your workplace this week? (If your workplace is a home or a nontraditional work-place, this question still applies to you!)
2. What idea from this chapter did you gloss over the fastest? What did you decide was irrelevant? Take a quick look back at that. Come up with a creative way it could be relevant. Stretch your brain beyond your comfort zone.

CHAPTER 14

....

Do Things Other People Aren't
Prepared to Do

To recap, for all these quizzes, scoring mostly As and Bs means you can probably skim the chapter. If you score mostly Cs and Ds, read in more detail. Choose the best answer. If no answer is a perfect fit, choose the closest.

Quiz

....

1. Are there methods or assumptions in your field that make little sense to you? For instance, how people or projects are evaluated, how decisions are made, or what's seen as worthwhile work?

    (A) Yes. I buck assumptions that defy common sense.

    (B) I would like to challenge dubious assumptions and flawed methods, but I'm inhibited by time, resources, specific ideas, or a lack of courage.

(C) I can identify what bothers me about my field, but I haven't thought beyond that.

(D) I've never thought about this topic.

2. Of the methods you use regularly to perform your work, what proportion are standard and routine?

    (A) 80 percent or under.

    (B) 90 percent.

    (C) 95 percent.

    (D) 100 percent.

3. How often do you tap into resources not commonly used in your field? These could include technologies, partnerships, ways of presenting information, etc.

    (A) Frequently.

    (B) I've done it before, but not recently.

    (C) I can think of one example.

    (D) Not at all.

4. Do you avoid pursuing promising ideas because it would require using innovative methods?

    (A) The opposite. I seek opportunities to use innovative methods.

(B) Sometimes. I'd like to use innovative methods more, but it feels unmanageable with my workload.

(C) Subconsciously I probably avoid nonstandard methods.

(D) I'd rather pursue a less interesting idea than figure out an unfamiliar procedure.

5. What's your attitude toward obstacles?

(A) They're often rewarding. I learn more and come up with more creative solutions when I need to navigate an obstacle.

(B) I feel confident about working through obstacles but not exactly positive about them.

(C) I prefer to avoid obstacles than tackle them.

(D) Obstacles make me intimidated and depressed.

This chapter invites you to reflect on any lazy ways work is done in your field. Does the herd mentality prevail? Might there be opportunities to show leadership and vision by challenging conventions?

For example, creativity researchers rely heavily on the Alternative Uses Test. This is a test we discussed previously. It's the one where people are asked to come up with creative uses for common objects like a brick or polystyrene cup. The same test appears in hundreds of studies.

Anyone who does research in this area has a critical choice to make. Either they use the test everyone else does or they can make up their own.

It's not efficient to reinvent the wheel. Conventional ways of doing things become so entrenched, people see them as wheels.

The Alternative Uses Test isn't a bad test. But sometimes norms that a field comes to rely on are far from ideal. Remember the story about the emperor who had no clothes? No one was willing to call out that fact. What's broken in your field that people accept as normal? This doesn't need to be a big point. It could simply be an inefficient element of your typical workflow that everyone tolerates and goes along with because it's only a few minutes here and there, but across time and many people, that adds up. Or perhaps there's a way you could help your customers have a frustration-free experience with a simple switch, but currently you rely on their figuring out a confusing process on their own. Are there flawed assumptions? Flawed methods? Times when what is tolerated and accepted as good enough isn't? Perhaps there's a process that frustrates you because of its inefficiency or inequity.

Which of your strengths allow you to challenge these faults? This chapter will help you see alternatives to doing what everyone else does. You'll learn how you can challenge flawed processes that most others accept as "just how things are done."

If you're a perfectionist, you're in an ideal position to do this. Perfectionists are more bothered by conventions that others accept as good enough. They notice when common assumptions rest on a shaky or an untested foundation. They notice when approaches have limitations. However, they often channel their perfectionism into conforming or doing a high volume of work. They don't risk sticking their neck out to test a dubious assumption or overcome obvious limitations. If this is you, consider rechanneling your perfectionism. (Paradoxically, lazy people can sometimes also be good at challenging conventions, because they're unwilling to tolerate doing low-value work or complying with inefficient processes.)

Small Barriers Put People Off.
This Is Your Opportunity.

People have gotten phenomenal sh*t done. We've extended the human lifespan by decades, gone to the moon, and built electric cars. On the flip side, there's a less admirable facet of human psychology. Small barriers disproportionately put us off.

Research on "nudges" shows this. How likely someone is to adopt a behavior changes when you make it easier or harder. Whether we do important things can often depend on tiny factors. Even whether an option is opt in or opt out will sway some decision-makers. One example is determining whether people will sign up for making automatic contributions to a retirement savings plan. Another example is that having to wait, even for short periods, influences decisions too. For instance, around 5 to 10 percent of people who intend to install solar panels change their minds if getting a permit takes more than a week or so.[1]

When people are in rat-on-a-wheel survival mode in their lives, they'll focus on the path of least resistance. They'll focus on getting through and churning out the volume of work they need to prove their worth. In survival mode, you won't be focused on your long-term contributions because that feels too hard. However, if you're willing to overcome even slight obstacles, you can make your work stand out.

Who Has Time or Energy for That? What
If You Feel Like a Rat on a Wheel?

If you're slammed with work, that might be your hardest creative challenge. Use your creative skills to figure out how to incorporate being innovative into your workflow. Look for ways to innovate in how you do the tasks that are required of you, rather than adding extras to your plate.

If you'd like to separate yourself from the herd, the following are some practical ways of doing that. Again, there are a lot of ideas in this chapter, and it's not a to-do list. Pick one concept you'd like to try out.

Whether you recognize it, there are aspects of who you are, what you know, and whom you know that make you an ideal candidate for challenging any ineffective ways things get done in your field.

Take a Fresh Look at Your Field's Unwritten Rules and Assumptions

Every field has unwritten rules. This can be micro, like what sources are valid to reference in a formal document or presentation. Or they can be bigger. What are valid ways to make predictions? How are people, ideas, and work products evaluated? How are resources allocated to ideas and people? (We've touched on these concepts already in the last two chapters.)

Sometimes a field's unwritten rules are safeguards. For example, norms about what types of sources you can cite help distinguish between reliable and unreliable information. But sometimes unwritten rules are just conventions or the means by which powerful people and institutions stay unchallenged.

EXPERIMENT

Get clear on the ways your field operates that irritate you. If you haven't done it in prior chapters, make a few notes about what the assumptions and conventions typical of your field are. Spend ten minutes on this. Identify any of these that bother you, that seem imperfect. What are some alternatives? If you need help, use these prompts. You don't need to answer all these questions. Pick what sticks out to you.

- What counts as valid knowledge?
- How are decisions made?
- How are people and ideas selected for opportunities and resources?
- What behaviors lead to folks being elevated as highly valued members of teams?
- How do people improve and get pushed toward higher quality work?
- What is considered a good enough situation, even if people recognize it as less than ideal?
- What's considered essential that might not be?
- Complete this sentence: "Conventional wisdom in my field is the best way to do X is Y." For example, the best way to
  - give feedback is . . .
  - help people learn is . . .
  - work efficiently is . . .
  - motivate people is . . .
  - allocate scarce resources is . . .

If you identify an irritation that's within your control, write a few bullets about what challenging the convention might look like.

Let the Obstacles You Face Spark Your Solutions

When you're thwarted, try a "the obstacle is the way" approach.[2] How can the obstacles you face provide direction to you? Let's say that an obstacle you face is regulation. How does identifying the obstacle help you see a path forward? Perhaps you find a way of working that isn't subject to the regulation that's thwarting you. Or perhaps you join with colleagues to start an alternative regulatory body or create a new way for projects to get a stamp of approval, thus removing the need to go a traditional route.

Or say that conservatism and too much caution are problems in your field. You might find a group of people who agree with you about this and form an association of renegades so you're not out there alone in attempting that.

If your field's systems and processes don't provide what you need to do better work, what are your options? How can you set up your own systems to get more of what you need?

Immerse Yourself in Sources of Inspiration

In pop productivity, there is often an undercurrent of opinion that motivation is for wimps. The notion is we should all be ruled by discipline and strong habits, and strong people shouldn't need motivation. Let's challenge that.

I mentioned earlier that how much time you spend trying to be creative will affect how creative you are. If you want to be inspired (and subsequently inspiring to others), connect with your inspirations.

Connecting with your creative inspirations differs from keeping up with trends. It's different from reading blogs or other sources for keeping up with what's trendy in your field now. Immersing yourself in inspirations can help you get back to basics. It can help you not to myopically follow whatever your field's current preoccupations are.

Identify your close and far inspirations. Close inspirations will be within your field or nearby industries. Far inspirations tap into what you're trying to achieve emotionally or tonally, but less directly. For instance, if you want to be braver, your inspirations could be explorers. If you want to discover what's fundamental about the world, perhaps you spend more time observing space, nature, or people. To be visionary, study the thinking of people whom you consider visionaries. To feel less constrained, find examples of freedom, whether in people, nature, science, or whatever.

Spending more time connected to your inspirations will help you solve problems through analogy. You'll struggle to draw on analogies you haven't recently encountered. If you spend more time with your inspirations (in person or through reading), you'll find it easier to think of analogies, provided you put a little effort into this. If nature is an inspiration to you, how does the natural world have a bearing on your work? If a visionary from a long time ago and/or a completely different field inspires you, what challenges they faced are analogous to your current work challenges? We need to be deeply immersed in a subject or situation (at least temporarily) for analogies to our work to come to mind.

Utilize Unconventional Allies

Fields have established norms for how people collaborate.

- Journalists ask experts for interviews.
- Scientists attend weekly research group meetings.
- Improv teams say "yes and . . ."
- Medical teams have handovers and rounds.
- Coders post to GitHub.
- YouTubers who do DIY projects have fans who leave ideas and suggestions in the comments on videos.

What types of collaboration are missing in your profession? What do you see potential in?

Your life experiences have exposed you to diverse examples of how people collaborate. Pay attention to how collaboration happens in spheres that interest you. Is there anything you could transfer to your work field?

Perhaps you're involved in a fan community or you participate heavily in a Reddit forum. What have you observed about how and why people collaborate when it's voluntary? What makes it so fun and rewarding that folks do it in their free time? For instance, in the travel hacking hobby, people run monthly meetups in their area. Deals are often shared there that aren't shared online. Visitors (friends of friends) can show up to these. The community also runs conferences. The content of these is oriented toward beginners, but these events give experienced travel hackers an excuse to hang out together.

When have you observed people collaborating even at the risk of increased competition? When do people potentially lose by sharing, but they do it anyway? What can you learn from those observations?

Who has knowledge that is valuable to you? There's a good chance none of us can call Jeff Bezos or Elon Musk to ask a quick question. So also ask yourself, "Who can I access to ask questions?" What's the overlapping part of that Venn diagram? For instance, journalists who write about productivity have heard it all. They're in a prime position to tell me if my ideas sound fresh. Since I've been interviewed a lot, I have those relationships.

Taking it a step up, how might you get more access to knowledgeable people? It could be by having a podcast or a YouTube channel, being a speaker on a panel, or developing some other platform.

Be Willing to Change Your Attitude

In the book *The Obstacle Is the Way,* author Ryan Holiday points out the benefits of this key thinking switch. Try switching your attitude from "I have to do this" to "I get to do this."

I might swap "I have to write my column, it's due in a couple of days," to "I get to write my column and share my knowledge. It's a privilege that people want to listen to my ideas and suggestions."

Or "I have to go through my editor's comments," to "I get to have someone help me make my work better. What a gift and privilege that is."

You don't need to maintain a sunny attitude all the time. That's not realistic or always helpful. (As I've said before, anger can be helpful for getting things done.) However, it's useful to switch into different attitudes, depending on what seems most productive in a particular moment or scenario. Sometimes I'll say to myself, "Okay, I'm going to put my stoicism suit on."

Go Beyond Filtered Information

In the internet age, algorithms point us to what we might like. As a result, a few ideas gain widespread popularity. Many of us discover the same ideas at the same time. When our thinking is funneled, it's efficient but reduces the diversity of ideas we encounter.

Think about the filters that determine which ideas you're exposed to. For example, Google Scholar is a search platform that allows anyone to search scientific studies. When you search Google Scholar, you can order a scientist's publications by those that have the most citations. A citation is when a study is mentioned in another research paper. The more citations a paper has, the more influential it is.

This is a great shortcut for identifying important work when you don't have time to read everything. However, it creates a positive feedback loop. What's popular gets more so. What's overlooked stays overlooked.

Since the world is set up to filter information for you, you'll need strategies to counter this. If you don't, you'll be exposed to the same ideas everyone else is.

Without specific strategies and habits for encountering novel ideas, you'll find your thinking will be constricted and directed down a narrow path.

EXPERIMENT

How can you ensure you're not being exposed to the same ideas as everyone else in your field? What systems can you create for yourself so you're not being exposed only to what's trendy or in the zeitgeist?

Do Things Other People Find Too Tedious

Paradoxically, creativity and vision can often arise from doing things that other people find too tedious. Earlier I gave the example of a newbie real estate investor making a list of dozens of lenders. Someone willing to do this screams "likely to succeed."

Here are other specific examples of how a willingness to do what others aren't can accelerate your success.

Be Willing to Wait

A friend of mine is gradually building a farm in Northern California. He excitedly told me he had bought a composting toilet from Craigslist for a fraction of the cost to buy it new. He had alerts set up for this item for a year before he hit the jackpot.

See Past Flaws That Don't Matter or Obstacles You Can Navigate

The same friend has told me about other steals he has gotten, like buying a high-end scanner from eBay that had a nonessential broken part. He has also driven substantial distances to pick up Craigslist items (such as an Airstream trailer) instead of restricting himself to his local area.

Consider obstacles that would put off most people. For example, a resource that's in another language and needs translating. What obstacles are you willing to navigate that would lead others to throw up a white flag?

Go Back to Old Ideas

Folks are often reluctant to go back to old material, even when it offers potentially invaluable information to guide decisions. In such a fast-paced world, quoting a book written over ten years ago can make you sound like a philosopher! Revisiting old ideas can add a lot of value. Some argue that creativity is finding an idea from history that you can adapt to current problems and needs.[3]

Consider Prototyping

You might not see how the concept of prototyping applies to you and your work. If you think this way, you're thinking too narrowly about what prototyping is.

Prototyping isn't just for physical products. You could make a prototype if you want to offer a new service, change an element of your workflow or your customers' flow, try a simple idea, collaborate with unconventional allies, offer an online course, or create another resource.

Prototyping can help you if you want to test the market for a product before you have the product or for a service before you've designed the service. It could be as simple as a sample agenda for a meeting between unconventional collaborators.

Be willing to make a prototype of an idea. Most people aren't, and their ideas are still stuck inside their heads.

Work Visually

Humans are visual creatures. Much more of the human brain is devoted to visual processing than any of our other senses. In the corporate world, the written word is the preferred method of communicating. Working in this environment, people can come to see themselves as incapable of creating visually. By learning visual communication skills, you can distinguish yourself from the crowd. This increases the likelihood others will experience your communication as profound.

EXPERIMENT

Collect methods for presenting information visually that stir your interest. Spend an hour googling this to get some ideas.

Communicate with Humor

This is a similar point to the last one. Communication can be much more effective when it's humorous. Humor helps ideas spread and take hold, yet people see barriers to using humor that may not exist. You might doubt your capacity to use humor or other people's openness to it. Consider whether those barriers might be imagined. For example, many people likely considered humor in airline safety videos unimaginable until an innovative company did it.

Create Resources, Such as Tools, Models, Tests, Quizzes, and Flowcharts

Back in chapter 10, I mentioned that sharing useful automations is phenomenal networking. In psychology, some of the most famous researchers are those who have written popular quizzes. Their tools are used by other researchers and clinicians throughout the world. When you create and disseminate resources, you increase the likelihood of your thoughts being spread and having an impact.

EXPERIMENT

What useful information or resources do you have locked in your head or inside your desk drawer? How could you share those?

Your Takeaways

1. Earlier I said you're uniquely positioned to make novel contributions to your field. What are you prepared to do that most people aren't? Even if you're still unwilling to do 90 percent of the suggestions in this chapter, or they don't seem valuable enough to pursue, there will be a few things that you are willing to do that almost everyone else isn't. What these are will come from your specific personality, experience, and skills.

2. How could you collect an easy win by doing something that's only slightly difficult? What's not time-consuming yet potentially enlightening? Nevertheless, most others wouldn't attempt it.

CHAPTER 15

. . . .

How to Think Like an Expert

To recap, for all these quizzes, scoring mostly As and Bs means you can probably skim the chapter. If you score mostly Cs and Ds, read in more detail. Choose the best answer. If no answer is a perfect fit, choose the closest.

Quiz

. . . .

Do you think like an expert?

1. How anxious do you get when you're "in the weeds" with a difficult work problem?

    (A) Mildly or not at all. I'm experienced at getting out and I trust my processes for doing so.

    (B) Moderately. Eventually I'll get the work done, but I don't have a methodical approach.

    (C) When this happens, I have severe doubts about whether I'm up to the task.

(D) If I felt like this with a project, I would immediately give up.

2. How valuable do you see your slow hunches and incomplete ideas? These are ideas you intuit to mean something or have promise but that aren't fully formed.

   (A) Some of my best work comes from these. I often return to incomplete ideas months or even years later.

   (B) Sometimes I recognize that a new idea I have is an off-shoot of a fuzzy idea I had a long time ago. I don't know how that happens, though.

   (C) I mostly get frustrated by my incomplete ideas. I'm confused about whether they have value.

   (D) I'm not aware of having any of these.

3. How confident are you that the perspective you bring to problems is valuable?

   (A) I've got a way of looking at problems that is useful for many conundrums, inside and outside my field.

   (B) I see my expertise as being useful within a narrow area.

   (C) I assume that whatever insights I have are not interesting.

   (D) I don't think I've gained enough experience in my field yet to have this.

4. How much do you think in analogies?

> (A) Frequently. I deliberately use near (within my field) and far (outside my field) analogies to understand problems.

> (B) I guess I do, but it's not a planned strategy.

> (C) I rarely use far analogies. I sometimes use near analogies.

> (D) I rarely use either type.

5. Do new problems remind you of problems you've successfully solved before? For example, do you recognize when you can use a strategy you've used for a prior project on a new one?

> (A) That happens often. New problems always feel like old problems.

> (B) I do this, but I probably miss some connections when projects aren't similar on the surface.

> (C) I realize the connections only halfway through the new project. For example, I get stuck and use a strategy and realize I should've used that strategy from the outset.

> (D) I don't make these connections.

Some readers of this book will already be experts in their particular field. If you're not yet, you can accelerate your path by understanding how experts think. As you'll see, experts think in specific ways that are directly tied to their capacity to be creative and visionary. If you're already an expert, this chapter will help you lean into your strengths that come from your expertise.

As I write this, experts are out of fashion. The recent zeitgeist has focused on how experts can be too narrowly entrenched in their own small arena of expertise. People who offer an outsider's perspective can contribute a lot that insiders overlook. Outsiders sometimes solve problems that expensive teams of experts have been stumped by.[1] These outsiders sometimes have a random piece of knowledge or an unusual analogy. They connect these to the problem at hand in a way that the experts miss.

These are valid points. However, there are valuable characteristics of how experts think too. In this chapter, we'll review these characteristics of expert thinking. Evaluate your strengths and where you have room to grow. By the end of the chapter, you'll think more like an expert and/or better recognize the strengths you have as an expert.

Experts Are Experts in Their Processes

Experts become experts from having done a volume of work. From this, they gain intimate knowledge about their own processes for getting things done. They learn how they break down a daunting project to make it manageable. They know and accept the creatively messy stages they go through. With experience, they've learned to trust the processes they use to get through those clunky stages. They trust that methodically using these processes will lead to polished, insightful work.

You can get to this point through sheer volume of experience. You can get there faster if you pay close attention to how you work and the ways you're refining that. When you have more trust in your capacities to get through the weeds, you'll have more confidence in your ability to take on groundbreaking projects.

When you're not an expert yet, it's hard to trust what you know about yourself. For instance, I know stopping work mid-flow before I'm stuck or exhausted works for me. On one level, it's hard to resist the cultural push to work to exhaustion. But I've gained enough experience with writing now that I can trust my process.

EXPERIMENT

What self-knowledge about how you get things done do you need to trust more? What helps you be a high performer even if it's not your image of how a high performer works?

Experts See the World Through the Lens of Their Expertise

A critique of experts is that they see the world through the lens of their specialization. Imagine you ask experts from different backgrounds what should characterize ideal city planning. An engineer will give you an answer about systems, a psychologist about human behavior, an activist about reversing systemic disadvantage, a trucker about deliveries, and a botanist about trees.[2]

Seeing the world through a particular lens isn't a bad thing. For instance, during the coronavirus pandemic, experts with different backgrounds offered specific perspectives. Some folks offered expertise in contract tracing from working in the fields of STDs and HIV. Others had expertise in the spread of disease from experience with seasonal flu. When you bring a lens of specific experiences to bear on a problem, it can allow you to have insights others won't.

Don't be scared to bring your lens of experience into the teams and problems you work on. As we've previously covered, yours might come from your background or interests. It could also be from the prior projects you've worked on. Sometimes people have an instinct that a new problem reminds them of a problem they've faced before but can't yet artic-ulate why.

A lens is only bad if you don't recognize it as such, or if you're not prepared to remove it sometimes and try to see through one offered by others. Paradoxically, when you're clearer about your own perspective, this can make you more interested in the way others see things. It's more obvious who may have a different but valuable lens. Being interested in others' perspectives is a core element of curiosity, which in turn is a core element of creativity.[3]

EXPERIMENT

What lenses do you see the world through? Do you hold back from of-fering those perspectives?

Experts Don't Necessarily Do What They Recommend to Others

Habits experts recognize when they've outgrown a habit and ditch it.[4] While experienced house flippers might suggest a beginner sit down with a spreadsheet to cost out a rehab, they themselves will judge projects on the fly during a walkthrough with their contractor. I don't get the im-pression that Tim Ferriss has a four-hour workweek (no shade intended here—I love his stuff).

I'm not saying experts are hypocrites. Experts usually base their behavior on the principles behind their advice, but not always the spe-cifics. Experts often use simplified and more intuitive versions of what they recommend to others. For example, I use quick and dirty versions of proven techniques for anxiety. I also use simple strategies, like going for a walk, ahead of more complex techniques most of the time.

If you want to think more like an expert, try simplifying the advice you read. Recognize that models can become bloated. Understand the principles behind a strategy or method and not merely the step-by-step how-to. This will make you a better judge of which parts of the method matter in a given situation and which don't.

Experts Use Structural Analogies and Causal Reasoning

Ideas often come about through observation, analogy, or causal reasoning (like understanding positive feedback loops).

Ordinarily, people find it difficult to use analogies that don't share surface-level elements, at least in formal settings. Experts do an awful lot of reasoning by analogy. For example, it's estimated that expert scientists bring up three to fifteen analogies per hour in team meetings.[5]

Experts group problems by their structural elements and think about causal mechanisms.[6] Here's an example of what I mean.

A Positive Feedback Loop Is a Common Causal Mechanism

The most obvious example of a positive feedback loop is microphone feedback when sounds keep getting reamplified. Global warming is another. Water absorbs more heat from the sun than ice does. When ice melts, the temperature of the earth rises and causes more ice melting.[7] Here's a more off-the-wall example of a positive feedback loop. Influencers get gigs promoting prestigious brands. Their association with that brand further cements their influencer status. Our automatic thinking is: "They must have cachet if the brand chooses them." Associations the public have with the brand are mentally attributed to the influencer. The more powerful the influencer seems, the more followers they get. The more followers they get, the more they get prestigious brand deals.

You could come up with countless similar examples in the "how the rich get richer" vein.

If you want to think more like an expert, try thinking more in structural level analogies.

EXPERIMENT 1

Let's do some quick practice at thinking in analogies and using causal reasoning. What's a positive feedback loop you can think of? Think creatively. What's one in a different sphere from the examples I've given?

For bonus points, think of an example of a negative feedback loop. This is when one process shuts off or slows down another. Example: After a toilet is flushed, water rises in the toilet's tank, which closes a valve that turns off subsequent water flow.

For more practice at thinking structurally, check out the IDEO Nature Cards (free online). I'll include a link to them on the book's resource page on AliceBoyes.com. These cards link processes from the natural world with business problems. I've used analogies from those cards to better understand concepts.

EXPERIMENT 2

Pick a productivity problem you have. Try framing that problem in terms of some of its structural features.

Here are some examples:

- You're expected to overwork.
- You need to be elastic to cope with uneven supply and demand.
- Your competitor has access to unlimited cheap capital.

When you've picked a problem, ask yourself, "How has this problem been solved in different industries, countries, or time periods?"

Come up with an analogy from an unrelated domain in which those same structural elements are also present. Ask yourself if anything about that analogy could help you solve your problem. If not, try another analogy.

Experts Have Confidence in the Value of Their Slow Hunches and Incomplete Ideas

Great ideas don't always come out fully formed. They can arrive as incomplete ideas or slow hunches. To recap, an incomplete idea is what it sounds like. It's an idea with gaps in it. A slow hunch is when you sense that a nugget of an idea is interesting or important. Your understanding of its full implications and relevance, of what the exact mechanisms are, emerges over time.

When you're not an expert, it's hard to trust your incomplete ideas and slow hunches. It's difficult to trust they're valuable. For a start, your hunches will be based on less knowledge and experience than an expert's hunches will be. You will also have less lived experience of your hunches or incomplete ideas turning into something great, such as:

- When you went down a tangent or rabbit hole to learn something that wasn't your immediate priority, and then you used that information six months later.
- When you listened to a talk at a conference outside your narrow area of interest, and it provided a spark that helped you complete an idea.
- When you had a random conversation with someone outside your field, came away feeling oddly excited to have met them, and called them for advice or to work on a project together a year later.

Nurturing incomplete ideas and slow hunches requires psychological skills. You need to tolerate uncertainty about which of your hunches will bear fruit and which will be busts. And you'll need to tolerate the uncertainty of whether you'll ever complete your incomplete ideas.

You'll need to overcome hesitancy you might have about asking others to help you complete your ideas. People sometimes feel embarrassed or anxious to share any idea that isn't fully formed. When you share an incomplete idea, it lets people into your thinking process. They may alert you to a different way of thinking about it you haven't considered. In doing so, they may let you into their thinking processes—that is, how they understand concepts and solve problems.

When folks have written about the value of slow hunches and incomplete ideas, they've generally been focused on how scientists develop new theories. The concept is broader than this, though. To help you get clearer on the concept of incomplete ideas, here are some examples:

- There's something you'd like to do, but there's no obvious way to make it manageable. You don't know practically how you'd achieve it. Aspects of it might be far outside your skill set.
- There's something you'd like to do, but it's not well aligned with your current responsibilities. You're not sure how to justify pursuing it in terms of your strategic goals or the core work you're supposed to be doing.
- You might be drawn to an idea that doesn't seem big enough to pursue. If you keep feeling drawn to it, you might eventually understand a way to make it significant enough to be worthwhile, or why it always was.
- You're not sure how to reconcile two seemingly incompatible goals.
- You've observed a pattern, but you're not sure what the causal mechanisms are. This could be related to the topic of your work or the process of your work. For example, perhaps you have observed that other people seem to easily do what you find difficult, but you're not sure how they do that. It might take you a while to understand their

different thought processes that are resulting in a performance gap between them and you.

You can think of productivity advice that you don't immediately follow but that seems important as an incomplete idea. Instead of being self-critical about how you have no follow-through, revisit the idea periodically. See if an enjoyable path to applying the tip or a way it's relevant to your most pressing problems becomes clearer when you revisit it.

EXPERIMENT

Mull over these questions:

- How can you be tuned in to your slow hunches and incomplete ideas?
- How can you be more willing to periodically revisit them until their relevance or a path becomes clear?
- Who can help you complete some of your incomplete ideas or clarify your slow hunches? It could be people in your network. Or it might be role models you don't personally know but whose thought processes you can access through their writing, interviews, or biographies.

Experts Think About Work Outside Work

I mentioned earlier that some productivity and mental health experts recommend completely switching off from work after hours. Everyone needs time when they're not thinking about work. However, as usual, rigid rules are the enemy of psychological health and of productivity. Research has shown that people who reflect on how to solve problems outside of working hours generate more novel ideas. They're more creative.[8]

You can do this without going crazy by having routines for how you do it. Pair certain activities, like going for a walk or driving from work to the gym, with mulling over your work problems. Pair other activities, like playing with your child, with taking a break from thinking about work. If you're consistent in your pairings, your brain will get the drill. I try to be open to work thoughts right after I finish a deep work session or when I first wake up.

When we slow down, the brain switches into what's called the default mode. You might've heard of it before. The jobs of this mode include autobiographical thinking and moral reasoning.[9] Therefore, it makes sense that when we stop focusing, we will mull over relationships, anxieties, and decisions, past and future. This will sometimes veer off into rumination. If you respond self-compassionately to your thoughts, it'll help make sure self-criticism doesn't dominate and ruin your relaxation time.

You can improve the quality of your relaxed thinking if you distinguish between two awkwardly named concepts: affective rumination and problem-solving pondering. The former is related to emotions. Affective rumination is usually about things that have already happened. When people do it, they feel strong negative emotions. On the other hand, problem-solving pondering tends to be emotionally neutral or associated with positive feelings. It's also more likely to be about current or future plans, not rehashing past events.

Rumination has negative effects on people's capacity to recover from work. It's strongly related to feelings of acute and chronic tiredness. Problem-solving pondering doesn't seem to have the same detrimental effect.[10]

Understanding the effect of problem-solving pondering on mental health is tricky for one particular reason. People who do more affective rumination also tend to do more problem-solving pondering. Problem-solving pondering turns into rumination when people get frustrated. The take-home message is that rumination is mostly negative and problem-solving pondering is mostly positive. If you fall into rumination, switch to other thoughts.

If you resent thinking about work outside of work, question whether you're ruminating, if your work projects feel meaningful enough to you, and whether you have enough recovery time devoted to nonwork thoughts.

Experts Are Good at Picking Out the Most Novel Features of Work

Experts can take in knowledge quickly. Whenever they read something new, the vast majority of it will be familiar to them. If 90 percent of a study I read is familiar to me, I can focus on the parts of it that are novel. This is much less mentally taxing. It means I can quickly read a higher volume of research without getting exhausted. Also, whatever is novel to an expert probably is truly novel.

Since all their mental attention isn't consumed by the content, experts can pay attention to features beyond the content. For example, if you hear someone speak on your expert topics in a way that's incredibly compelling, you can pay attention to what makes their presenting style so enthralling, not just the content.

An expert can pick up unusual features of content. For example, if you're an expert software engineer reading someone else's code, you might pick out any nonstandard but innovative features of it.

Once you reach this stage, you can lean into it. Instead of fleetingly thinking, *That's interesting,* and then promptly forgetting about it, you can file away anything novel you come across in your incomplete ideas dossier.

Experts Hang with Other Experts

I occasionally listen to the BiggerPockets real estate investing podcast. One of the phrases the hosts use is "rock stars know rock stars." They argue that the top 20 percent of people in one subfield will know the top 20 percent of people in other subfields within the industry.

- The top 20 percent of house flippers will know the top 20 percent of plumbers and property managers.
- The top 20 percent of agents will know the top 20 percent of lenders.
- The top 20 percent of plumbers will know the top 20 percent of electricians.

If you want to level up, this is a handy principle to understand. How can you join this virtuous network? Or better utilize it?

Your Takeaways

1. What's one way of thinking like an expert that you're already quite good at? How could you utilize this more?
2. Of all the ways you could think more like an expert, which seems most valuable to you? How could you do this in one simple way?

CHAPTER 16

How to Be Braver

To recap, for all these quizzes, scoring mostly As and Bs means you can probably skim the chapter. If you score mostly Cs and Ds, read in more detail. Choose the best answer. If no answer is a perfect fit, choose the closest.

Quiz

1. Do you see yourself as a brave, creative person?

    (A) Yes.

    (B) It fluctuates—sometimes yes, but sometimes I doubt whether I can be original.

    (C) I'm held back by being a scaredy-cat.

    (D) No, I see myself as timid and conventional. I don't like to rock the boat.

2.   How often do you attempt to be visionary?

  (A) Often.

  (B) Sometimes.

  (C) Rarely.

  (D) I don't even consider trying.

3.   In the work context, what does being brave mean to you?

  (A) Taking on difficult projects and channeling my emotions to help me stay focused.

  (B) I think of bravery as an occasionally needed skill for tasks I don't do often.

  (C) Just surviving my workweek feels like an act of bravery.

  (D) I think of it only as things like public speaking or asking for a raise.

4.   Does the way you do your core tasks reflect your most important values (whatever these are—e.g., curiosity, openness, fun, fairness, exploration)?

  (A) I act on my values—e.g., I approach meetings, emails, conversations, disagreements, and so on all with an attitude of curiosity.

(B) My behavior looks like anyone else's, but subtly I act my values in my everyday tasks.

(C) I occasionally try to do tasks in ways that reflect my values, but most of the time I fall into conventions.

(D) I approach recurring tasks the standard way—e.g., I act in meetings the way everyone else does.

5. How bravely do you handle difficult emotions?

(A) I often use difficult emotions to propel me to innovative solutions.

(B) I occasionally use difficult emotions to fuel my bravery.

(C) I can still get my work done when feeling negative emotions, but I'm focused only on getting it done.

(D) I freeze in response to difficult emotions, or I blame others.

In this final chapter, we'll bring together everything we've covered so far. By the end, you should have a cohesive sense of what you've gotten out of reading this book. You'll have vision for where the skills you've learned could take you, and a sense of excitement about what the future could bring.

Being Brave Isn't What You Think It Is

Being creative and visionary requires bravery. In reality, being brave is not much like the stereotypes. It's mostly not about withstanding anything physically tough. It's not usually about performing in public. It's not always about having difficult conversations. Rather, being brave is mostly about where you allow yourself to go in your own mind. It's when you:

- devote your mental energy to a larger long-term project rather than taking the easier route of crossing familiar items off your daily to-do list.
- bet on yourself and your capacity to master unfamiliar skills.
- pay attention to the flicker of an idea.
- make observations that don't fit with conventional wisdom.
- contemplate when your perspectives could be flawed.

When you break it down, most brave actions aren't difficult. They're often similar to the behaviors you already do every day, like sending emails, making phone calls, googling things, reading information, asking questions, and following directions. What's different is the goal those actions are serving. To change the goals you're focused on, you need to lift yourself above your daily grind. We've focused on that throughout the book, and this is the cherry on top.

Be Braver by Taking on Bigger, Harder-to-Solve Projects

A giant component of being braver is choosing projects where, if you succeed, they will have a significant impact.

A core theme of this book has been that what you choose to do will influence what you accomplish much more than how fast you work. You can expect that important problems will generally be harder to solve. This is especially true if you take on a problem not yet solved by humanity.

Visionary projects will often require that you get out of your bubble. You'll need ideas from outsiders. These are people who have strengths outside your skill set. They could be people outside your team or outside the recognized experts in your field. Reaching out to these people requires bravery.

A related point is that being brave often involves investing some time in not being traditionally efficient. You need self-trust to allow yourself to spend time in touch with your inspirations, nurturing your creativity, or googling and reading about random things you're curious about. You need trust that your investment will end up being more productive than always choosing to crank out one more moderately productive activity.

EXPERIMENT

In practical terms, how can you transition from moderately productive tasks to projects with much greater potential impact? To answer this, bring together what you've learned throughout the book.

Continue to Keep Your Eye Out for Productivity Shame

I often hear people confess that self-help and productivity books leave them with the impression that they're lazy.

To recap what I said earlier, if you feel this way, it's not you, it's us (meaning the self-help industry). It's hard to write about these topics in a way that doesn't make people who are already feeling overwhelmed feel more so.

Remember what I said way back in chapter 4. From an evolutionary perspective, it would make zero sense that big chunks of the populace would have evolved to be lazy. We all have an innate drive to be productive sometimes and lazy sometimes. Being lazy periodically is self-protective. It's not smart to wear yourself out. You don't need to overcome some inner sloth. You already have a healthy drive to be productive.

When you take the pressure off yourself to be productive every minute of every day, you'll have more emotional and cognitive energy to focus on meaningful projects and big wins.

If you're a leader, help the people you're leading overcome productivity shame and social comparison. Shame makes us hide away. When we're feeling it, we're less likely to take brave actions like speaking up about our incomplete ideas or reaching out to unconventional allies.

A Deep Understanding of Your Internal Processes Will Allow You to Take on Hard Projects

While the behaviors and basic skills involved in important and unimportant projects are similar, the emotions are different. Embarking on a long path can be anxiety-provoking. When a project doesn't have a guarantee of success, that requires tolerating anxiety. You'll need self-knowledge, strategies, and habits so that you don't fall into the trap of choosing to work on tasks with short deadlines and predictable outcomes just because those feel more comfortable and familiar.

If you're going to take on hard things, you need to trust in your skills for managing yourself. You need to know:

- how you can make yourself creatively open.
- how you can channel your difficult emotions to help you focus.

- what routines work for you for sustaining deep work over long periods.
- what processes for prioritizing work best for you.
- your go-to methods for approaching problems you're stuck with.

EXPERIMENT

We've worked on all of this. Reread the last paragraph and assess your current strengths and weaknesses. Which of your processes are you confident in? What still needs work? You won't have mastered every single skill set from reading this book once. Where you see weaknesses, be prepared to go back and revisit the relevant chapters. You'll pick up fresh ideas on a second read. This is especially true if months have passed and different concerns are at the top of your mind. You'll pick up more nuance, since the broad ideas will be familiar to you already. On subsequent reads, you'll come back to the material with a semi-expert perspective that allows you to pick up on more subtle points.

Do the same with any other books that have been influential for you. For example, I reread *The 4-Hour Workweek* this year, after having first read it back in 2007.

Know Your Self-Sabotaging Patterns

Some people reading this will still have the sense that they're not destined to do anything significant, visionary, or original.

EXPERIMENT

What are the self-sabotaging patterns that get in the way of you being visionary? Pick the one you think is the biggest problem. I believe mine is overcomplicating. This causes me to overlook simple ways I could get visionary or highly productive things done. Your self-sabotaging pattern might be a thinking style like "I can't reach out to people I don't know." Or it might be a behavioral pattern like not scheduling time to attempt to be visionary.

Link Bravery to Your Core Values

Some people automatically gravitate toward bravery as one of their top values. If you're not immediately drawn to this, you can use a work-around to inspire yourself to be braver. What's the work-around? You can be authentically brave by linking bravery to your other core values.

Experiment

Think about the values you want to infuse into your life. Pick your top three to five. For example, autonomy, adventure, challenge, big ideas, compassion, competency, excellence, conscientiousness, fun, safety, efficiency, fairness, and freedom. If you need help to identify your values, I'll link to a quiz by psychologist Dr. Susan David on the book's resources page on AliceBoyes.com.

Isolate one to three of your most important values, depending on how much energy you've got for the experiment. You don't need to get overly stressed about your picks. Choose what feels right for you now. Some of your top values might change from time to time. This can happen because you've grown as a person or because your focus changes at a different stage of your life.

Identify what bravely enacting each value would look like. Generate ideas until you strike one that feels appealing and immediately practical. For example:

- Enacting autonomy more bravely might be resisting the temptation to "pray to false idols" by choosing not to measure your success using metrics that don't reflect the true real-world impact of your work.
- Enacting excellence more bravely might involve testing assumptions through data. Or it might involve getting feedback you expect will help you grow but is challenging to ask for. For example, you might want to request feedback from someone you're competitive with.
- Enacting the value of "big ideas" more bravely might involve forming a group of renegade thinkers who work at different companies within your field.
- Enacting the value of adventure more bravely might involve exploring new skills or relationships without a rigid expectation of where that might lead. Perhaps you might devote time once a month to give people who normally wouldn't have access to you one-on-one access. You do this to see what ideas they bring and where that leads.
- Enacting the value of challenge more bravely might involve devoting more attention to developing your slow hunches and incomplete ideas.
- Enacting the value of fun more bravely might involve using more art and humor to stimulate your creativity.

Tip: If you're stuck with this exercise, try googling the dictionary definition of the value you picked. You know what it means, but sometimes looking at different definitions can spur ideas.

FUN EXTENSION EXPERIMENT

Pick people whose originality you admire. Think about the projects they choose and how they approach them. Based on this, what would you guess they'd say their three top values are? How do their values help them overcome obstacles with the challenging and original projects they take on?

If you do this experiment, you'll notice that successful and original people don't all share the same values. For example, compare Bill Gates to Elon Musk. This can help give you confidence you can accomplish great things by enacting *your* values.

Be Braver When You're Experiencing Challenging Emotions

Back in chapter 4 when we discussed growth mindsets, we learned that being productive involves using your difficult emotions as fuel to focus. Now that you're coming to the end of the book, what more do you understand about how to do this than when we started? What do you understand about how you personally can use difficult emotions to help you focus?

- You might better understand the specific scenarios in which you don't do the most important work you could be doing. You might've gained this knowledge either through self-observation or from the chapter on how humans prioritize.

- You might better understand your strengths and how you like to approach problems. You can apply your strengths to the problem of how to focus when you're feeling difficult emotions.

- You might have some different ideas about what you need to focus on. You might want to be brave and innovative, not just undistracted.

- You might've come up with your own if-then rules for how you'll habitually behave when you're feeling challenging emotions. (See chapter 4 if you need to recap.)

Use Creativity to Improve Your Focus When You're Feeling Difficult Emotions

Now that you've been specifically thinking about being creative and visionary, revisit how you can use difficult emotions to focus.

For example, if you're feeling bored, you might try to find an idea from your interests that could make a work task more fun and interesting. If you're feeling frustrated, brainstorm new methods, including those not traditionally used in your field. If you're feeling angry, you might creatively apply one of your values to give you inner guidance about how to handle the situation.

In particular, think about how you react to feeling overwhelmed. When people feel swamped, they either freeze (shut down, ignore tasks), flee (self-distract, quit projects), or fight (attempt to be a faster rat on a wheel). How might you creatively apply your values to respond differently, and make that a habit?

When you're overloaded, how to move from scattered to focused will depend on why you get overloaded. Perfectionists need strategies to get better at seeing the big picture. People who get excited about a lot of things need routines to help them stay focused on their most important project. Those who are poor planners need to learn more about how to do tasks in the most logical order. People who get angry easily need skills for better understanding other people's perspectives. Insecure people need to better recognize their strengths and apply these to tasks they find overwhelming.

You can apply any of the tips you've learned for creative thinking to solving the problem of feeling overwhelmed. Do you need to change the problem you're trying to solve? Do you need to challenge your assumptions? Do you need to find an analogy? Do you need to solve the problem by doing something most other people aren't prepared to do?

How to Infuse Your Typical Tasks with Bravery

Here's a thinking trap about being braver. Sometimes people think they will do all their usual work tasks in a typical way, and then do some brave things as an extra. Pivotal moments can come from doing things that are outside the norm for you. They can also come from approaching your common tasks differently. You'll miss opportunities to be brave if you don't think about how to infuse more bravery into your everyday work.

Note that I'm not suggesting being brave 100 percent of the time. We all need balance. We all need to be challenged enough to feel invigorated by it. But challenge can also result in feeling overburdened. You need to not be challenged so much of the time that you don't have breathing space to recover emotionally in between.

Quickly run through your core work tasks. Examples: writing reports, going to meetings, writing emails, conversing with managers, and so forth. Spell out what being braver might look like for each.

Here are some more examples to spark your thinking:

- Being braver in a meeting might be amplifying the perspective of someone who has spoken up but has been ignored. For example, you speak up and say, "Coming back to Ellen's idea that . . ." and add something to that or ask a question about it. Or being braver in meetings might be questioning assumptions other people are implicitly making. Or it might be asking "What if we're wrong in dismissing the criticism we're receiving. What if it's justified?"
- Being braver in emails might be to have a signature line that invites anyone you're emailing to book a fifteen-minute phone call with you during your weekly office hours. You invite people to pick your brain

about anything they'd like your creative input into. You don't need to self-protectively wall yourself off like most people do. I got this idea from Professor B. J. Fogg, who offers interested folks the opportunity to self-book fifteen-minute appointments with him to ask questions about his work area, which is habits and behavioral design.

- Being braver in giving presentations might be utilizing better storytelling rather than sticking to the dry facts.
- Being braver in your collaborations, whether via email or in person, might involve expressing incomplete ideas more.
- Being braver often involves amplifying the call for diverse opinions and voices. What you want is access to diverse thinking, not just a seat at the table for everyone who already has a preformed strong opinion. (People who already hold strong opinions often have a harder time being flexible than a generally diverse group of people.)[1]

EXPERIMENT

Think about the values you identified earlier. How does enacting those bravely relate to how you do your typical tasks?

Being Brave Enough to Express Intriguing Thoughts Requires Having Those Thoughts in the First Place

If you're rockin' around doing little self-reflection or observation of the world, if you're not practicing a craft, if you're not googling and reading widely, the chances that you'll have fascinating thoughts aren't high. There's an extent to which being braver comes from your having put time and energy into noticing and grappling with unusual ideas and observations.

EXPERIMENT

What leads to you having interesting thoughts to share? How can you play to your strengths and interests in this area? For example:

- If you have a strong predisposition toward doubt or anxiety, you might excel at questioning assumptions or thinking about what might go wrong and what your company is unprepared for.
- If you're adept at putting people at ease socially, you might shine at extracting ideas not shared with other people.
- If you're intensely curious and read widely, you might be a star at bringing thinking from other fields into your work.
- If you're good at perspective taking, you might understand what's making your clients happy or unhappy that other people neglect.

What are your particular strengths with acquiring and recognizing uncommon knowledge?

Cultivate Intellectual Humility

Intellectual humility is not being absolutely sure that your ideas and beliefs are more right than other peoples'. If you have this, you'll be willing to update your views based on new data or persuasive arguments.

In complex, high-stakes decision-making environments, being brave is often about being willing to stay in a state of feeling uncertain. When you're willing to stay uncertain longer, it can prevent you from prematurely closing yourself off to particular viewpoints.

If you're a perfectionist, intellectual humility can be tough. Whenever you start to feel persuaded by a different viewpoint, you might criticize yourself for not having the insight earlier.

Becoming more aware of your assumptions can help you cultivate intellectual humility. For example, let's say you've been assuming that diversity hiring is doing people a favor rather than truly believing diverse minds contribute to success. Recognizing a socially undesirable thought like this is the first step to examining it.

EXPERIMENT

Consider how more intellectual humility could make you braver and how this could benefit your work. What's one simple way you could do this more?

Finishing Up

You made it! Thanks for taking this journey of ideas with me. I'll leave you with one final thought experiment to ponder.

How will working more bravely improve your productivity?

Congratulate yourself on the work you've done engaging with this book. Let go of any ways you think you've been imperfect in doing that. Allow yourself to think back on the material in the coming weeks and months. Implement any immediately obvious insights you've gained in the simplest way you can imagine. If you've felt inspired by specific ideas but haven't figured out how they apply to your most pressing problems, allow those incomplete ideas time and breathing space to complete themselves. You can help that process along by sharing ideas from the book with others, since you'll gain greater clarity yourself by doing that. I'm excited about the creative and visionary work you'll do using the self-knowledge you've invested in learning. If you're ever feeling overburdened in creating that work, relieve yourself from unnecessary (and self-sabotaging) pressure to be productive every minute of every day.

ACKNOWLEDGMENTS

It takes a village to write (and sell) a book.

Thanks to my mother, Kate, for equipping me with the crazy notion I can do anything I set my mind to. Thanks to my daughter, Celeste, for working so hard on reading and math in the next room while I was writing. Hearing her persist through learning those brand-new skills inspired me to work hard on this book. Kissing her little face on all my breaks was such an efficient and effective way to fill up my cup when hours of concentrating had emptied it. Thanks to my spouse, Kathryn, for taking care of homeschooling so I could write.

My superb book team made this project possible. My agent, Giles Anderson, was very patient with me during the proposal stage when I was slowly figuring out what I wanted to say about productivity. Thanks to my editor, Lauren Appleton, for believing in me enough to acquire this title, being fun and easy to work with, and providing spot-on feedback. Publicist Casey Maloney is always a valued source of positivity and support.

Thanks to all the folks who have answered my nosy questions about the way they work, their productivity stumbling blocks, their thoughts, emotions, habits, and patterns of prioritizing and procrastination.

Many editors have helped me improve my writing. Special thanks to everyone from the *Harvard Business Review* universe (current and former), especially Alison Beard, Amy Gallo, and Sarah Green Carmichael. Thanks to the Women at Work crew for helping me through my fear of podcasts. Editor Kate Adams provided early feedback on my book proposal well before it was any good. Thanks to the team at *Psychology Today* for giving me a platform and being very generous in promoting my articles.

Writing a book can be solitary. My author colleagues and friends have been constant sources of support. Shout-out to Guy Winch, Barb Markway, Seth Gillihan, Susan Newman, and Toni Bernhard.

Without my early career mentors, Garth Fletcher, Janet Latner and Fran Vertue, I wouldn't be who I am today.

Finally, thanks to all the researchers who've done the hard work of testing their ideas and have shaped mine.

NOTES

CHAPTER 1. YOU ARE THE SOLUTION, NOT THE PROBLEM

1. Daisley, "Don't Let Your Obsession with Productivity Kill Your Creativity."
2. France, "Kim Kardashian West Fangirls over 'Bridgerton's' Featheringtons Being Inspired by Her Family."
3. Read and Sarasvathy, "Knowing What to Do and Doing What You Know"; Sarasvathy, "Causation and Effectuation."
4. Mankins, "Great Companies Obsess over Productivity, Not Efficiency."
5. Wood, *Good Habits, Bad Habits.*
6. Clear, "This Coach Improved Every Tiny Thing by 1 Percent and Here's What Happened."
7. Chess, Thomas, and Birch, *Your Child Is a Person.*
8. Wood, *Good Habits, Bad Habits.*
9. Martin, "The High Price of Efficiency."
10. Kashdan et al., "Understanding Psychological Flexibility."
11. Lu, Akinola, and Mason, "Switching on Creativity."
12. Healy, "The Surprising Thing the Marshmallow Test Reveals About Kids in an Instant-Gratification World."
13. Sio and Ormerod, "Does Incubation Enhance Problem Solving?"
14. Dijksterhuis and Meurs, "Where Creativity Resides."

CHAPTER 2. YOUR SUCCESS STORY SO FAR

1. O'Keefe, Dweck, and Walton, "Implicit Theories of Interest."
2. McGonigal, "How to Make Stress Your Friend."
3. Epstein, *Range.*

CHAPTER 3. HOW TO LIFT YOURSELF ABOVE YOUR DAILY GRIND

1. Dyer, Gregersen, and Christensen, "The Innovator's DNA."
2. Stavrova, Pronk, and Kokkoris, "Choosing Goals That Express the True Self."

3. Hayes, Strosahl, and Wilson, *Acceptance and Commitment Therapy.*
4. Johnson, *Where Good Ideas Come From.*
5. Epstein, "Piano Tuners and the News in Beirut."
6. Horton, "Is Creativity the Enemy of Productivity?"
7. Markman and Jack, "Why Losing a Job Deserves Its Own Grieving Process."

CHAPTER 4. HOW TO SUSTAIN GROWTH-ORIENTED THINKING

1. Dweck, "What Having a Growth Mindset Actually Means."
2. Galla and Duckworth, "More Than Resisting Temptation."
3. Wright et al., "Time of Day Effects on the Incidence of Anesthetic Adverse Events."
4. Danziger, Levav, and Avnaim-Pesso, "Extraneous Factors in Judicial Decisions."
5. Bariso, "Jeff Bezos Schedules His Most Important Meetings at 10 a.m. Here's Why You Should Too."
6. Glei, "Productivity Shame."
7. Harris, "Making and Breaking Habits, Sanely | Kelly McGonigal."
8. Boyes, "5 Ways Smart People Sabotage Their Success."
9. Gortner, Rude, and Pennebaker, "Benefits of Expressive Writing in Lowering Rumination and Depressive Symptoms"; Spera, Buhrfeind, and Pennebaker, "Expressive Writing and Coping with Job Loss."
10. Germer and Neff, "Self-Compassion in Clinical Practice."
11. Boyes, "Be Kinder to Yourself."
12. Carmichael, "Why 'Network More' Is Bad Advice for Women."
13. Kleon, "Doing the Work That's in Front of You."
14. Rubin, "11 Happiness Paradoxes to Contemplate as You Think About Your Happiness Project."
15. Kashdan et al., "Personalized Psychological Flexibility Index."
16. Kashdan et al., "Curiosity Has Comprehensive Benefits in the Workplace."
17. Kashdan et al., "Understanding Psychological Flexibility."
18. Tamir, "Don't Worry, Be Happy?"; Tamir and Ford, "Choosing to Be Afraid."
19. Kaufman, "The Emotions That Make Us More Creative."
20. Ceci and Kumar, "A Correlational Study of Creativity, Happiness, Motivation, and Stress from Creative Pursuits."
21. Fong, "The Effects of Emotional Ambivalence on Creativity."
22. Kaufman, "Opening Up Openness to Experience."
23. Boyes, "Don't Let Perfection Be the Enemy of Productivity."

CHAPTER 5. HOW TO BECOME A SELF-SCIENTIST

1. Clark, "Why So Many Users of Fitness Trackers Give Up After a Few Months."
2. Newport, *Deep Work.*
3. Rock, Grant, and Grey, "Diverse Teams Feel Less Comfortable—and That's Why They Perform Better."
4. Oaten and Cheng, "Longitudinal Gains in Self-Regulation from Regular Physical Exercise."
5. Fogg, "Start Tiny."
6. Larcom, Rauch, and Willems, "The Benefits of Forced Experimentation."
7. Atchley, Strayer, and Atchley, "Creativity in the Wild."
8. Seppälä, "How Senior Executives Find Time to Be Creative."

PART 2. IMPROVING YOUR REPEATABLE SYSTEMS

1. Burkeman, "Why Time Management Is Ruining Our Lives"; Glei, "Oliver Burkeman."
2. Boyes, "5 Tips to Encourage Independent Play."
3. Epstein, *Range.*
4. Gibson, "Quiet, Please."

CHAPTER 6. CREATE EFFECTIVE PROCESSES YOU CAN REPEATEDLY EXPLOIT

1. American Psychological Association, "Stress in America 2019."
2. Wikipedia, "Halo Effect."
3. Spann, "Are Your Money Beliefs Holding You Back?"
4. Hill and Jackson, "The Invest-and-Accrue Model of Conscientiousness."
5. Clear, "Forget About Setting Goals. Focus on This Instead."
6. Grenny, "5 Tips for Safely Reopening Your Office."
7. Rubin and Craft, "Podcast 276."
8. *McKinsey Quarterly*, "Making Great Decisions."

CHAPTER 7. PRIORITIZING—THE HIDDEN PSYCHOLOGY THAT DRIVES YOUR DECISION-MAKING

1. Zhu, Bagchi, and Hock, "The Mere Deadline Effect."
2. Hargrove and Nietfeld, "The Impact of Metacognitive Instruction on Creative Problem Solving."
3. Boyes, "Don't Let Perfection Be the Enemy of Productivity."
4. Allen, *Getting Things Done.*
5. Gillihan, *The CBT Deck*; Winch, *Emotional First Aid.*
6. Kashdan, "5 Tips to Becoming a Killer Scientist Who Changes the World."
7. Kaufman and Gregoire, *Wired to Create.*
8. Christian and Griffiths, *Algorithms to Live By.*

CHAPTER 8. PROCRASTINATION

1. Shin and Grant, "When Putting Work Off Pays Off."
2. Jarrett, "Why Procrastination Is About Managing Emotions, Not Time"; Lieberman, "Why You Procrastinate (It Has Nothing to Do with Self-Control)."
3. Boyes, "6 Common Causes of Procrastination."
4. Ramsay, "Procrastivity (a.k.a. Sneaky Avoidance) and Adult ADHD Coping."
5. Boyes, "How to Recognize Anxiety-Induced Procrastination."
6. David, *Emotional Agility.*
7. Zandan, "How to Stop Saying 'Um,' 'Ah,' and 'You Know.'"
8. Wikipedia, "Minimum Viable Product."
9. Vadrevu, "What the Hell Does 'Minimum Viable Product' Actually Mean Anyway?"
10. Boyes, "5 Things to Do When You Feel Overwhelmed by Your Workload."
11. Harris, *The Happiness Trap.*
12. Boyes, "How to Get Through an Extremely Busy Time at Work."
13. Boyes, "7 Strategies for Conquering Procrastination and Avoidance."

CHAPTER 9. HOW TO CUSTOMIZE YOUR PRODUCTIVITY SOLUTIONS AND BREAK THROUGH PSYCHOLOGICAL RESISTANCE TO CHANGE

1. Winch, "How to Turn Off Work Thoughts During Your Free Time."
2. Horton, "Is Creativity the Enemy of Productivity?"
3. Ritter et al., "Diversifying Experiences Enhance Cognitive Flexibility."
4. Gilbert, Anderson, and Walters, "It's OK to Feel Overwhelmed."
5. Brownlee, "Tesla Factory Tour with Elon Musk."
6. Michalko,"Turn Your Assumptions Upside Down."
7. Ferriss, "17 Questions That Changed My Life."
8. Kelley and Kelley, *Creative Confidence*.
9. Prochaska, DiClemente, and Norcross, "In Search of How People Change."

CHAPTER 10. FREE YOURSELF FROM REPETITIVE COMPUTER TASKS THROUGH AUTOMATION

1. Boyes, "Don't Let Perfection Be the Enemy of Productivity."
2. Cain and Rogers, "A Look at the Demanding Schedule of Elon Musk, Who Plans His Day in 5-Minute Slots, Constantly Multitasks, and Avoids Phone Calls."
3. Newport, "Here's a No Gimmicks, No Nonsense, No-BS Approach to Producing Elite Work"

PART 3. HOW TO BE MORE CREATIVE AND VISIONARY

1. Carson, *Your Creative Brain*.
2. Dyer and Gregersen, "Learn How to Think Different(ly)."
3. Dyer and Gregersen, "Learn How to Think Different(ly)."
4. Lucus and Nordgren, "People Underestimate the Value of Persistence for Creative Performance."
5. Gino and Ariely, "The Dark Side of Creativity."

CHAPTER 11. LOOPHOLES AND WORK-AROUNDS

1. Gino and Ariely, "The Dark Side of Creativity."
2. Kestenbaum and Benincasa, "How Frequent Fliers Exploit a Government Program to Get Free Trips."
3. Art of Play, "History of the Nine Dot Problem."
4. Boyes, "5 Mindsets That Get in the Way of Creating Wealth."

CHAPTER 12. NOVELTY

1. The BiggerPockets Podcast, "BiggerPockets Podcast 368."
2. Yi, *100 Easy STEAM Activities*.
3. Boyes, "How to Stop Obsessing over Your Mistakes."
4. Authors@Google, "Emotional First Aid."
5. Lamott, *Bird by Bird*.
6. Vegan Bodegacat, "Eating What @Sweet Simple Vegan Tells Me to for a Day."

7. Humphries, "How Not to Choose Which Science Is Worth Funding."
8. Urban, "How to Name a Baby."
9. Kaufman and Gregoire, *Wired to Create.*

CHAPTER 13. HOW DIVERSE INTERESTS BENEFIT YOUR CAPACITY TO BE CREATIVE AND VISIONARY

1. Rubin and Craft, "Podcast 75."
2. Schellenberg and Bailis, "Can Passion Be Polyamorous?"
3. Root-Bernstein, Bernstein, and Garnier, "Correlations Between Avocations, Scientific Style, Work Habits, and Professional Impact of Scientists."
4. Kashdan et al., "Curiosity Has Comprehensive Benefits in the Workplace"; Von Stumm, Hell, and Chamorro-Premuzic, "The Hungry Mind."
5. Nutt, "Can't Focus?"
6. Root-Bernstein et al., "Correlation Between Tools for Thinking."
7. Kelley and Kelley, *Creative Confidence.*
8. The Behavioural Insights Team, "Publications."
9. Hancock, "Adding Years to Life and Life to Years."
10. Hagmann, Ho, and Loewenstein, "Nudging Out Support for a Carbon Tax."

CHAPTER 14. DO THINGS OTHER PEOPLE AREN'T PREPARED TO DO

1. Schkloven, "How North Las Vegas Is Streamlining Solar Projects."
2. Holiday, *The Obstacle Is the Way.*
3. Duggan, "How Aha! Really Happens."

CHAPTER 15. HOW TO THINK LIKE AN EXPERT

1. Epstein, *Range.*
2. fs, "Mental Models."
3. Kashdan et al., "Multidimensional Workplace Curiosity Scale."
4. Clear, "I'm No Longer Writing Twice per Week. Here's Why."
5. Dunbar and Blanchette, "The In Vivo/In Vitro Approach to Cognition."
6. Rottman, Gentner, and Goldwater, "Causal Systems Categories."
7. Jamrozik and Gentner, "Relational Labeling Unlocks Inert Knowledge."
8. Weinberger et al., "Having a Creative Day."
9. Zomorodi, *Bored and Brilliant.*
10. Querstret and Cropley, "Exploring the Relationship Between Work-Related Rumination, Sleep Quality, and Work-Related Fatigue."

CHAPTER 16. HOW TO BE BRAVER

1. Kashdan, "Is Diverse Thought Being Suppressed in the COVID-19 Crisis?"; Milliken, Bartel, and Kurtzberg, "Diversity and Creativity in Work Groups."

REFERENCES

Allen, David. *Getting Things Done: The Art of Stress-Free Productivity*. Penguin, 2003.

American Psychological Association. "Stress in America 2019." https://www.apa.org/news/press/releases/stress/2019/stress-america-2019.pdf.

Art of Play. "History of the Nine Dot Problem." August 2, 2016. https://www.artofplay.com/blogs/articles/history-of-the-nine-dot-problem.

Atchley, Ruth Ann, David L. Strayer, and Paul Atchley. "Creativity in the Wild: Improving Creative Reasoning Through Immersion in Natural Settings." *PLoS One* 7, no. 12 (2012): e51474.

Authors@Google. "Emotional First Aid: Guy Winch." YouTube video, 43:08. August 16, 2013. https://www.youtube.com/watch?v=vBqoA1V6Fgg.

Bariso, Justin. "Jeff Bezos Schedules His Most Important Meetings at 10 a.m. Here's Why You Should Too." *Inc.* https://www.inc.com/justin-bariso/jeff-bezos-schedules-his-most-important-meetings-before-lunch-heres-why-you-should-too.html.

Behavioural Insights Team, The. "Publications." https://www.bi.team/our-work/publications/.

BiggerPockets Podcast, The. "*BiggerPockets Podcast* 368: $3,500 Per Month from One BRRRR Deal with Palak Shah." Podcast audio, February 6, 2020. https://www.biggerpockets.com/blog/biggerpockets-podcast-368-palak-shah.

Boyes, Alice. *The Anxiety Toolkit: Strategies for Fine-Tuning Your Mind and Moving Past Your Stuck Points*. TarcherPerigee, 2015.

———. "Be Kinder to Yourself." *Harvard Business Review*, January 12, 2021. https://hbr.org/2021/01/be-kinder-to-yourself.

———. "Don't Let Perfection Be the Enemy of Productivity." *Harvard Business Review*, March 3, 2020. https://hbr.org/2020/03/dont-let-perfection-be-the-enemy-of-productivity.

———. "5 Mindsets That Get in the Way of Creating Wealth." *Psychology Today*, November 27, 2019. https://www.psychologytoday.com/us/blog/in-practice/201911/5-mindsets-get-in-the-way-creating-wealth.

———. "5 Things to Do When You Feel Overwhelmed by Your Workload." *Harvard Business Review*, August 6, 2018. https://hbr.org/2018/08/5-things-to-do-when-you-feel-overwhelmed-by-your-workload.

———. "5 Tips to Encourage Independent Play." *Psychology Today*, July 28, 2020. https://www
.psychologytoday.com/us/blog/in-practice/202007/5-tips-encourage-independent
-play.

———. "5 Ways Smart People Sabotage Their Success." *Harvard Business Review*, November 13,
2018. https://hbr.org/2018/11/5-ways-smart-people-sabotage-their-success.

———. *The Healthy Mind Toolkit: Simple Strategies to Get Out of Your Own Way and Enjoy Your
Life*. TarcherPerigee, 2018.

———. "How to Get Through an Extremely Busy Time at Work." *Harvard Business Review*, March
26, 2019. https://hbr.org/2019/03/how-to-get-through-an-extremely-busy-time-at-work.

———. "How to Recognize Anxiety-Induced Procrastination." *Psychology Today*, August 13,
2019. https://www.psychologytoday.com/us/blog/in-practice/201908/how-recognize
-anxiety-induced-procrastination.

———. "How to Stop Obsessing Over Your Mistakes." *Harvard Business Review*, February 25,
2019. https://hbr.org/2019/02/how-to-stop-obsessing-over-your-mistakes.

———. "7 Strategies for Conquering Procrastination and Avoidance." *Fast Company*, May 2, 2018.
https://www.fastcompany.com/40564662/7-strategies-for-conquering-procrastination
-and-avoidance.

———. "6 Common Causes of Procrastination." *Psychology Today*, October 15, 2019.
https://www.psychologytoday.com/us/blog/in-practice/201910/6-common-causes
-procrastination.

Brownlee, Marques. "Tesla Factory Tour with Elon Musk!" YouTube video, 15:19. August 20,
2018. https://www.youtube.com/watch?v=mr9kK0_7x08.

Burkeman, Oliver. "Why Time Management Is Ruining Our Lives." *The Guardian*, December
22, 2016. https://www.theguardian.com/technology/2016/dec/22/why-time-management-is
-ruining-our-lives.

Cain, Áine, and Taylor Nicole Rogers. "A Look at the Demanding Schedule of Elon Musk,
Who Plans His Day in 5-Minute Slots, Constantly Multitasks, and Avoids Phone Calls."
Business Insider, February 24, 2020. https://www.businessinsider.com/elon-musk-daily
-schedule-2017-6.

Carmichael, Sarah Green. "Why 'Network More' Is Bad Advice for Women." *Harvard Business
Review*, February 26, 2015. https://hbr.org/2015/02/why-network-more-is-bad-advice
-for-women.

Carson, Shelley. *Your Creative Brain: Seven Steps to Maximize Imagination, Productivity, and
Innovation in Your Life*. Jossey-Bass, 2010.

Ceci, Michael W., and V. K. Kumar. "A Correlational Study of Creativity, Happiness, Motivation,
and Stress from Creative Pursuits." *Journal of Happiness Studies* 17, no. 2 (2016): 609–626.

Chess, Stella, Aubrey Thomas, and Herbert G. Birch. *Your Child Is a Person: A Psychological
Approach to Childhood Without Guilt*. Viking Press, 1965.

Christian, Brian, and Tom Griffiths. *Algorithms to Live By: The Computer Science of Human
Decisions*. Henry Holt, 2016.

Clark, Alice. "Why So Many Users of Fitness Trackers Give Up After a Few Months." *Sydney
Morning Herald*, October 15, 2018. https://www.smh.com.au/technology/why-so-many
-users-of-fitness-trackers-give-up-after-a-few-months-20181015-p509ou.html.

Clear, James. "Forget About Setting Goals. Focus on This Instead." https://jamesclear.com
/goals-systems.

———. "I'm No Longer Writing Twice per Week. Here's Why." https://jamesclear.com/once
-per-week.

———. "This Coach Improved Every Tiny Thing by 1 Percent and Here's What Happened." https://jamesclear.com/marginal-gains.

Daisley, Bruce. "Don't Let Your Obsession with Productivity Kill Your Creativity." *Harvard Business Review*, March 10, 2020. https://hbr.org/2020/03/dont-let-your-obsession-with -productivity-kill-your-creativity.

Danziger, Shai, Jonathan Levav, and Liora Avnaim-Pesso. "Extraneous Factors in Judicial Decisions." *Proceedings of the National Academy of Sciences of the USA* 108, no. 17 (2011): 6889–92.

David, Susan. *Emotional Agility: Get Unstuck, Embrace Change, and Thrive in Work and Life.* Avery, 2016.

Dijksterhuis, Ap, and Teun Meurs. "Where Creativity Resides: The Generative Power of Unconscious Thought." *Consciousness and Cognition* 15, no. 1 (2006): 135–46.

Duggan, William. "How Aha! Really Happens." *Strategy+Business*, November 23, 2010. https://www.strategy-business.com/article/10405?gko=06d13.

Dunbar, Kevin, and Isabelle Blanchette. "The In Vivo/In Vitro Approach to Cognition: The Case of Analogy." *Trends in Cognitive Sciences* 5, no. 8 (2001): 334–39.

Dweck, Carol. "What Having a Growth Mindset Actually Means." *Harvard Business Review*, January 13, 2016. https://hbr.org/2016/01/what-having-a-growth-mindset-actually-means.

Dyer, Jeffrey H., Hal Gregersen, and Clayton M. Christensen. "The Innovator's DNA." *Harvard Business Review*, December 2009. https://hbr.org/2009/12/the-innovators-dna.

Dyer, Jeff, and Hal Gregersen. "Learn How to Think Different(ly)." *Harvard Business Review*, September 27, 2011. https://hbr.org/2011/09/begin-to-think-differently.

Epstein, David. *Range: Why Generalists Triumph in a Specialized World.* Riverhead Books, 2021.

———. "Piano Tuners and the News in Beirut." *The Range Report* (blog), August 11, 2020. https:// davidepstein.com/piano-tuners-and-the-news-in-beirut/.

Ferriss, Tim. "17 Questions That Changed My Life." *Tim Ferris* (blog). https://tim.blog/wp -content/uploads/2020/01/17-Questions-That-Changed-My-Life.pdf.

Fogg, B. J. "Start Tiny." Tiny Habits. https://tinyhabits.com/start-tiny/.

Fong, Christina Ting. "The Effects of Emotional Ambivalence on Creativity." *Academy of Management Journal* 49, no. 5 (2006): 1016–30.

France, Lisa Respers. "Kim Kardashian West Fangirls Over 'Bridgerton's' Featheringtons Being Inspired by Her Family." CNN Entertainment, April 21, 2021. https://www.cnn.com/2021 /04/21/entertainment/kim-kardashian-bridgerton-featheringtons-trnd/index.html.

fs. "Mental Models: The Best Way to Make Intelligent Decisions (~100 Models Explained)." https://fs.blog/mental-models/.

Galla, Brian M., and Angela L. Duckworth. "More Than Resisting Temptation: Beneficial Habits Mediate the Relationship Between Self-Control and Positive Life Outcomes." *Journal of Personality and Social Psychology* 109, no. 3 (2015): 508–525.

Germer, Christopher K., and Kristin D. Neff. "Self-Compassion in Clinical Practice." *Journal of Clinical Psychology* 69, no. 8 (2013): 856–67.

Gibson, Lydialyle. "Quiet, Please: Susan Cain Foments the 'Quiet Revolution.'" *Harvard Magazine*, March–April 2017.

Gilbert, Elizabeth, Chris Anderson, and Helen Walters. "It's OK to Feel Overwhelmed. Here's What to Do Next." TED Connects video, 101:43. April 2, 2020. https://www.ted.com/talks /elizabeth_gilbert_it_s_ok_to_feel_overwhelmed_here_s_what_to_do_next/.

Gillihan, Seth J. *The CBT Deck: 101 Practices to Improve Thoughts, Be in the Moment, & Take Action in Your Life.* PESI Publishing, 2019.

Gino, Francesca, and Dan Ariely. "The Dark Side of Creativity: Original Thinkers Can Be More Dishonest." *Journal of Personality and Social Psychology* 102, no. 3 (2012): 445–59.

Glei, Jocelyn K. "Oliver Burkeman: Against Time Management." *Hurry Slowly*. Podcast audio, January 30, 2018. https://hurryslowly.co/015-oliver-burkeman/.

———. "Productivity Shame." *Hurry Slowly*. Podcast audio, May 14, 2019. https://hurryslowly.co/216-jocelyn-k-glei.

Gortner, Eva-Maria, Stephanie S. Rude, and James W. Pennebaker. "Benefits of Expressive Writing in Lowering Rumination and Depressive Symptoms." *Behavior Therapy* 37, no. 3 (2006): 292–303.

Grenny, Joseph. "5 Tips for Safely Reopening Your Office." *Harvard Business Review*, May 20, 2020. https://hbr.org/2020/05/5-tips-for-safely-reopening-your-office.

Hagmann, David, Emily H. Ho, and George Loewenstein. "Nudging Out Support for a Carbon Tax." *Nature Climate Change* 9, no. 6 (2019): 484–89.

Hancock, Matt. "Adding Years to Life and Life to Years: Our Plan to Increase Healthy Longevity." Speech, London, UK, February 12, 2020. GOV.UK. https://www.gov.uk/government/speeches/adding-years-to-life-and-life-to-years-our-plan-to-increase-healthy-longevity.

Hargrove, Ryan A., and John L. Nietfeld. "The Impact of Metacognitive Instruction on Creative Problem Solving." *Journal of Experimental Education* 83, no. 3 (2015): 291–318.

Harris, Dan. "Making and Breaking Habits, Sanely | Kelly McGonigal." *Ten Percent Happier with Dan Harris*. Podcast audio, December 26, 2019. https://podcasts.apple.com/us/podcast/219-making-and-breaking-habits-sanely-kelly-mcgonigal/id1087147821?i=1000460795293.

Harris, Russ. *The Happiness Trap: How to Stop Struggling and Start Living*. Trumpeter, 2008.

Hayes, Steven C., Kirk D. Strosahl, and Kelly G. Wilson. *Acceptance and Commitment Therapy: The Process and Practice of Mindful Change*. Guilford Press, 2011.

Healy, Melissa. "The Surprising Thing the Marshmallow Test Reveals About Kids in an Instant-Gratification World." *Los Angeles Times*, June 26, 2018.

Hill, Patrick L., and Joshua J. Jackson. "The Invest-and-Accrue Model of Conscientiousness." *Review of General Psychology* 20, no. 2 (2016): 141–54.

Holiday, Ryan. *The Obstacle Is the Way: The Timeless Art of Turning Trials into Triumph*. Portfolio, 2014.

Horton, Anisa Purbasari. "Is Creativity the Enemy of Productivity?" Secrets of the Most Productive People, Fast Company. Podcast audio, March 27, 2019. https://www.fastcompany.com/90325414/ithe-relationship-between-creativity-and-productivity.

Humphries, Mark. "How Not to Choose Which Science Is Worth Funding." *The Spike* (blog), May 9, 2017. https://medium.com/the-spike/how-not-to-choose-which-science-is-worth-funding-c6b4605ce8f1.

Jamrozik, Anja, and Dedre Gentner. "Relational Labeling Unlocks Inert Knowledge." *Cognition* 196 (2020): 104146.

Jarrett, Christian. "Why Procrastination Is About Managing Emotions, Not Time." BBC Worklife, January 23, 2020. https://www.bbc.com/worklife/article/20200121-why-procrastination-is-about-managing-emotions-not-time.

Johnson, Steven. *Where Good Ideas Come From: The Natural History of Innovation*. Riverhead, 2011.

Kashdan, Todd B. "5 Tips to Becoming a Killer Scientist Who Changes the World." *Psychology Today*, December 5, 2012. https://www.psychologytoday.com/us/blog/curious/201212/5-tips-becoming-killer-scientist-who-changes-the-world.

———. "Is Diverse Thought Being Suppressed in the COVID-19 Crisis?" *Psychology Today*, March 22, 2020. https://www.psychologytoday.com/us/blog/curious/202003/is-diverse -thought-being-suppressed-in-the-covid-19-crisis.

———. "Multidimensional Workplace Curiosity Scale." https://toddkashdan.com/wp-content /uploads/2021/02/Workplace-Curiosity-M-WCS-measure-Kashdan-et-al.docx.

———. "Personalized Psychological Flexibility Index." https://toddkashdan.com/wp-content /uploads/2020/07/Personalized-PF-Index.docx.

Kashdan, Todd B., David J. Disabato, Fallon R. Goodman, James D. Doorley, and Patrick E. McKnight. "Understanding Psychological Flexibility: A Multimethod Exploration of Pursuing Valued Goals Despite the Presence of Distress." *Psychological Assessment* 32, no. 9 (2020): 829–50.

Kashdan, Todd B., Fallon R. Goodman, David J. Disabato, Patrick E. McKnight, Kerry Kelso, and Carl Naughton. "Curiosity Has Comprehensive Benefits in the Workplace: Developing and Validating a Multidimensional Workplace Curiosity Scale in United States and German Employees." *Personality and Individual Differences* 155 (2020): 109717.

Kaufman, Scott B. "Opening Up Openness to Experience: A Four-Factor Model and Relations to Creative Achievement in the Arts and Sciences." *Journal of Creative Behavior* 47, no. 4 (2013): 233–55.

———. "The Emotions That Make Us More Creative." *Harvard Business Review*, August 12, 2015. https://hbr.org/2015/08/the-emotions-that-make-us-more-creative.

Kaufman, Scott B., and Carolyn Gregoire. *Wired to Create: Unraveling the Mysteries of the Creative Mind*. TarcherPerigee, 2015.

Kelley, Tom, and David Kelley. *Creative Confidence: Unleashing the Creative Potential Within Us All*. Currency, 2013.

Kestenbaum, David, and Robert Benincasa. "How Frequent Fliers Exploit a Government Program to Get Free Trips." NPR, July 13, 2011. https://www.npr.org/sections/money/2011/07/13 /137795995/how-frequent-fliers-exploit-a-government-program-to-get-free-trips.

Kleon, Austin. "Doing the Work That's in Front of You." *Austin Kleon* (blog), June 16, 2020. https://austinkleon.com/2020/06/16/doing-the-work-thats-in-front-of-you/.

Lamott, Anne. *Bird by Bird: Some Instructions on Writing and Life*. Anchor, 1995.

Larcom, Shaun, Ferdinand Rauch, and Tim Willems. "The Benefits of Forced Experimentation: Striking Evidence from the London Underground Network." *Quarterly Journal of Economics* 132, no. 4 (2017): 2019–55.

Lieberman, Charlotte. "Why You Procrastinate (It Has Nothing to Do with Self-Control)." Smarter Living, *New York Times*, March 25, 2019. https://www.nytimes.com/2019/03/25 /smarter-living/why-you-procrastinate-it-has-nothing-to-do-with-self-control.html.

Lu, Jackson G., Modupe Akinola, and Malia F. Mason. "Switching on Creativity: Task Switching Can Increase Creativity by Reducing Cognitive Fixation." *Organizational Behavior and Human Decision Processes* 139 (2017): 63–75.

Lucas, Brian J., and Loran F. Nordgren. "People Underestimate the Value of Persistence for Creative Performance." *Journal of Personality and Social Psychology* 109, no. 2 (2015): 232–43.

Mankins, Michael. "Great Companies Obsess over Productivity, Not Efficiency." *Harvard Business Review*, March 1, 2017. https://hbr.org/2017/03/great-companies-obsess-over -productivity-not-efficiency.

Markman, Art, and Michelle Jack. "Why Losing a Job Deserves Its Own Grieving Process." Fast Company, April 8, 2020. https://www.fastcompany.com/90487012/why-a-losing-a-job -deserves-its-own-grieving-process.

Martin, Roger L. "The High Price of Efficiency." *Harvard Business Review* (January–February 2019). https://hbr.org/2019/01/the-high-price-of-efficiency.

McGonigal, Kelly. "How to Make Stress Your Friend." Filmed June 2013 in Edinburgh, Scotland. TED video, 14:16. https://www.ted.com/talks/kelly_mcgonigal_how_to_make_stress_your_friend.

McKinsey Quarterly. "Making Great Decisions." April 1, 2013. https://www.mckinsey.com/business-functions/strategy-and-corporate-finance/our-insights/making-great-decisions.

Michalko, Michael. "Turn Your Assumptions Upside Down." The Creativity Post, September 16, 2012. https://www.creativitypost.com/article/turn_your_assumptions_upside_down.

Milliken, Frances J., Caroline A. Bartel, and Terri R. Kurtzberg. "Diversity and Creativity in Work Groups: A Dynamic Perspective on the Affective and Cognitive Processes That Link Diversity and Performance." In *Group Creativity: Innovation Through Collaboration*, eds. Paul B. Paulus and Bernard A. Nijstad. Oxford University Press, 2003, 32–62.

Newport, Cal. *Deep Work: Rules for Focused Success in a Distracted World.* Grand Central Publishing, 2016.

———. "Here's a No Gimmicks, No Nonsense, No-BS Approach to Producing Elite Work." *Observer*, January 7, 2016. https://observer.com/2016/01/heres-a-no-gimmicks-no-nonsense-no-bs-approach-to-producing-elite-work/.

Nutt, Amy Ellis. "Can't Focus? Maybe You're a Creative Genius." *Washington Post*, March 4, 2015. https://www.washingtonpost.com/news/speaking-of-science/wp/2015/03/04/cant-focus-maybe-youre-a-creative-genius/.

Oaten, Megan, and Ken Cheng. "Longitudinal Gains in Self-Regulation from Regular Physical Exercise." *British Journal of Health Psychology* 11, no. 4 (2006): 717–33.

O'Keefe, Paul A., Carol S. Dweck, and Gregory M. Walton. "Implicit Theories of Interest: Finding Your Passion or Developing It?" *Psychological Science* 29, no. 10 (2018): 1653–64.

Prochaska, James O., Carlo C. DiClemente, and John C. Norcross. "In Search of How People Change: Applications to Addictive Behaviors." *American Psychologist* 47, no. 9 (1992): 1102–114.

Querstret, Dawn, and Mark Cropley. "Exploring the Relationship Between Work-Related Rumination, Sleep Quality, and Work-Related Fatigue." *Journal of Occupational Health Psychology* 17, no. 3 (2012): 341–53.

Ramsay, Russell. "Procrastivity (a.k.a. Sneaky Avoidance) and Adult ADHD Coping." *Psychology Today*, July 16, 2020. https://www.psychologytoday.com/us/blog/rethinking-adult-adhd/202007/procrastivity-aka-sneaky-avoidance-and-adult-adhd-coping.

Read, Stuart, and Saras D. Sarasvathy. "Knowing What to Do and Doing What You Know: Effectuation as a Form of Entrepreneurial Expertise." *Journal of Private Equity* 9, no. 1 (2005): 45–62.

Ritter, Simone M., et al. "Diversifying Experiences Enhance Cognitive Flexibility." *Journal of Experimental Social Psychology* 48, no. 4 (2012): 961–64.

Rock, David, Heidi Grant, and Jacqui Grey. "Diverse Teams Feel Less Comfortable—and That's Why They Perform Better." *Harvard Business Review*, September 22, 2016. https://hbr.org/2016/09/diverse-teams-feel-less-comfortable-and-thats-why-they-perform-better.

Root-Bernstein, Robert S., Maurine Bernstein, and Helen Garnier. "Correlations Between Avocations, Scientific Style, Work Habits, and Professional Impact of Scientists." *Creativity Research Journal* 8, no. 2 (1995): 115–37.

Root-Bernstein, Robert, Megan Van Dyke, Amber Peruski, and Michele Root-Bernstein. "Correlation Between Tools for Thinking; Arts, Crafts, and Design Avocations; and Scientific Achievement Among STEMM Professionals." *Proceedings of the National Academy of Sciences of the USA* 116, no. 6 (2019): 1910–17.

Rottman, Benjamin M., Dedre Gentner, and Micah B. Goldwater. "Causal Systems Categories: Differences in Novice and Expert Categorization of Causal Phenomena." *Cognitive Science* 36, no. 5 (2012): 919–32

Rubin, Gretchen. "11 Happiness Paradoxes to Contemplate as You Think About Your Happiness Project." *Happier* (blog), March 23, 2011. https://gretchenrubin.com/2011/03/11-happiness -paradoxes-to-contemplate-as-you-think-about-your-happiness-project/.

Rubin, Gretchen, and Elizabeth Craft. "Podcast 75: Develop a Minor Expertise, a Deep Dive into Signature Color, and How Do You Help a Rebel Sweetheart to Get a New Job?" *Happier.* Podcast audio, July 27, 2016. https://gretchenrubin.com/podcast-episode/podcast-75.

———. "Podcast 276: Design Your Summer, Solutions to Create Sibling Harmony, and How Cornstarch Can Enliven a Boring Afternoon." *Happier.* Podcast audio, June 3, 2020. https:// gretchenrubin.com/podcast-episode/276-design-your-summer-2020.

Sarasvathy, Saras D. "Causation and Effectuation: Toward a Theoretical Shift from Economic Inevitability to Entrepreneurial Contingency." *Academy of Management Review* 26, no. 2 (2001): 243–63.

Schellenberg, Benjamin J. I., and Daniel S. Bailis. "Can Passion Be Polyamorous? The Impact of Having Multiple Passions on Subjective Well-Being and Momentary Emotions." *Journal of Happiness Studies* 16, no. 6 (2015): 1365–81.

Schkloven, Emma. "How North Las Vegas Is Streamlining Solar Projects." *Las Vegas Sun*, December 27, 2018. https://lasvegassun.com/news/2018/dec/27/program-speeds-solar -projects-in-north-las-vegas/.

Seppälä, Emma. "How Senior Executives Find Time to Be Creative." *Harvard Business Review*, September 14, 2016. https://hbr.org/2016/09/how-senior-executives-find-time-to-be -creative.

Shin, Jihae, and Adam M. Grant. "When Putting Work Off Pays Off: The Curvilinear Relationship Between Procrastination and Creativity." *Academy of Management Journal*, April 23, 2020. doi: 10.5465/amj/2018.1471.

Sio, Ut Na, and Thomas C. Ormerod. "Does Incubation Enhance Problem Solving? A Meta-Analytic Review." *Psychological Bulletin* 135, no. 1 (2009): 94–120.

Spann, Scott. "Are Your Money Beliefs Holding You Back?" *Forbes*, January 14, 2018. https://www.forbes.com/sites/financialfinesse/2018/01/14/are-your-money-beliefs-holding -you-back/#4a831cef79bd.

Spera, Stefanie P., Eric D. Buhrfeind, and James W. Pennebaker. "Expressive Writing and Coping with Job Loss." *Academy of Management Journal* 37, no. 3 (1994): 722–33.

Stavrova, Olga, Tila Pronk, and Michail D. Kokkoris. "Choosing Goals That Express the True Self: A Novel Mechanism of the Effect of Self-Control on Goal Attainment." *European Journal of Social Psychology* 49, no. 6 (2019): 1329–36.

Tamir, Maya. "Don't Worry, Be Happy? Neuroticism, Trait-Consistent Affect Regulation, and Performance." *Journal of Personality and Social Psychology* 89, no. 3 (2005): 449–61.

Tamir, Maya, and Brett Q. Ford. "Choosing to Be Afraid: Preferences for Fear as a Function of Goal Pursuit." *Emotion* 9, no. 4 (2009): 488–97.

Urban, Tim. "How to Name a Baby." Wait But Why, December 11, 2013. https://waitbutwhy .com/2013/12/how-to-name-a-baby.html.

Vadrevu, Ravi. "What the Hell Does 'Minimum Viable Product' Actually Mean Anyway?" *freeCodeCamp* (blog), April 14, 2017. https://www.freecodecamp.org/news/what-the -hell-does-minimum-viable-product-actually-mean-anyway-7d8f6a110f38/.

Vegan Bodegacat. "Eating What @Sweet Simple Vegan Tells Me to for a Day." YouTube video, 16:16. September 14, 2020. https://www.youtube.com/watch?v=3Ty6WWI-pX8.

Von Stumm, Sophie, Benedikt Hell, and Tomas Chamorro-Premuzic. "The Hungry Mind: Intellectual Curiosity Is the Third Pillar of Academic Performance." *Perspectives on Psychological Science* 6, no. 6 (2011): 574–88.

Weinberger, Eva, Dominika Wach, Ute Stephan, and Jürgen Wegge. "Having a Creative Day: Understanding Entrepreneurs' Daily Idea Generation Through a Recovery Lens." *Journal of Business Venturing* 33, no. 1 (2018): 1-19.

Wikipedia. "Halo Effect." Last modified April 19, 2021. https://en.wikipedia.org/wiki/Halo _effect.

———. "Minimum Viable Product." Last modified April 4, 2021. https://en.wikipedia.org /wiki/Minimum_viable_product.

Winch, Guy. *Emotional First Aid: Healing Rejection, Guilt, Failure, and Other Everyday Hurts.* Avery, 2013.

———. "How to Turn Off Work Thoughts During Your Free Time." TED Salon: Brightline Initiative video, 12:17. https://www.ted.com/talks/guy_winch_how_to_turn_off_work _thoughts_during_your_free_time/transcript.

Wood, Wendy. *Good Habits, Bad Habits: The Science of Making Positive Changes That Stick.* Pan Macmillan, 2019.

Wright, Melanie Clay, et al. "Time of Day Effects on the Incidence of Anesthetic Adverse Events." *Quality & Safety in Health Care* 15, no. 4 (2006): 258–63.

Yi, Andrea Scalzo. *100 Easy STEAM Activities: Awesome Hands-on Projects for Aspiring Artists and Engineers.* Page Street Publishing, 2019.

Zandan, Noah. "How to Stop Saying 'Um,' 'Ah,' and 'You Know.'" *Harvard Business Review*, August 1, 2018. https://hbr.org/2018/08/how-to-stop-saying-um-ah-and-you-know.

Zhu, Meng, Rajesh Bagchi, and Stefan J. Hock. "The Mere Deadline Effect: Why More Time Might Sabotage Goal Pursuit." *Journal of Consumer Research* 45, no. 5 (2019): 1068–84.

Zomorodi, Manoush. *Bored and Brilliant: How Spacing Out Can Unlock Your Most Productive and Creative Self.* St. Martin's Press, 2017.

INDEX

About the Author

Alice Boyes holds a PhD in psychology. Her doctoral research was about relationships and was published in the prestigious *Journal of Personality and Social Psychology*. She worked as a clinical psychologist in her native New Zealand from 2008 to 2013, while also blogging and writing for magazines. When opportunity knocked, she made a career switch to writing. She is the author of two prior books, *The Anxiety Toolkit*, a *Wall Street Journal* bestseller, and *The Healthy Mind Toolkit*. Alice is a frequent contributor to the *Harvard Business Review* and *Psychology Today*, and her articles have received more than twenty-two million views. She's mom to one daughter, born in 2016.